YEN
BLOC

YEN BLOC

BLOC Toward Economic Integration in Asia

C. H. Kwan

BROOKINGS INSTITUTION PRESS
Washington, D.C.

Library of Congress Cataloging-in-Publication data

Kwan, C. H. 1957–
  Yen Bloc : toward economic integration in Asia / C. H. Kwan
    p.   cm.
  Includes bibliographical references and index.
    ISBN 0-8157-0083-0
  1. Asia—Economic integration.   2. Monetary policy—Asia.   I. Title.
HC412.K895 2001   2001001712
337.1'5—dc21   CIP

9 8 7 6 5 4 3 2 1

The paper used in this publication meets minimum requirements of the American National Standard for Information Sciences—Permanence of Paper for Printed Library Materials: ANSI Z39.48-1984.

Typeset in Minion

Composition by R. Lynn Rivenbark
Macon, Georgia

Printed by R. R. Donnelley and Sons
Harrisonburg, Virginia

To
Yuko and Megumi

Contents

PART TWO

FORMING A YEN BLOC IN ASIA

Figures

Tables

Boxes

Preface

Interest in the formation of a yen bloc has increased in recent years against a background of a deepening economic interdependence between Japan and its Asian neighbors and a growing recognition of the need to reform the prevailing international financial architecture. The onset of the Asian currency crisis, the introduction of the euro in Europe, and the implementation of Japan's financial reform program dubbed the Big Bang, in particular, have aroused active discussions on the issue among policymakers in both Japan and Asia's developing countries.[1]

The term *yen bloc* is used here to refer to a grouping of countries that use the yen as an international currency and that maintain stable exchange rates against the yen. A yen bloc does not at present exist beyond Japan's national borders. Rather, with most of their international transactions denominated in U.S. dollars and their currencies pegged loosely to the dollar, Asia's developing countries, it is fair to say, belong to a de facto dollar bloc. A question

1. This book focuses on Japan and the developing countries of Asia. The latter include the newly industrializing economies (NIEs) of Asia, members of the Association of Southeast Asian Nations (ASEAN), and China, which together are here called the Asian countries. The Asian NIEs are Hong Kong, Singapore, South Korea, and Taiwan. (They are also known as *newly industrializing countries,* but for the sake of consistency, the term *newly industrialized economies* is used throughout this book.) The members of ASEAN are Brunei, Cambodia, Indonesia, Laos, Malaysia, Myanmar, the Philippines, Singapore, Thailand, and Vietnam. When referring to statistics, however, Singapore is excluded to avoid double counting, while Brunei, Cambodia, Laos, Myanmar, and Vietnam are ignored because of lack of data.

naturally arises as to whether the yen can, or will, replace the dollar as the key currency in Asia.

My first attempt to answer this question dates back to 1992, when I argued that, given a widely fluctuating yen-dollar rate, pegging to the dollar was no longer consistent with macroeconomic stability in Asian countries and that they should peg closer to the yen by targeting a basket of currencies in which the yen carries a substantial weight.[2] By reducing the exchange rate risk associated with yen-denominated transactions, such a major shift in their foreign exchange rate regime should promote wider use of the yen as a regional currency, paving the way for the formation of a yen bloc.

In a book published in Japanese in 1995, I elaborated this theme further, looking at the issue from four complementary perspectives: a Japanese perspective along the lines of the internationalization of the yen; an Asian perspective based on the theory of optimal currency peg; a regional perspective applying the theory of optimum currency areas; and a global perspective focusing on a tripolar international monetary system centering on the dollar, the deutsche mark, and the yen.[3] While retaining this general framework, in this volume I focus more on subsequent developments.

I have arrived at my current stance on the four approaches that form the core of this book through different routes.

In formulating my view of the yen bloc from a Japanese perspective, I benefited from my participation in the Council on Foreign Exchange and Other Transactions, which advises the Japanese minister of finance. As a specialist member of the council between 1997 and 1999 I witnessed the government's stance on the internationalization of the yen change from passive to active at a time when the Asian crisis was deepening day by day. Some of my analyses and recommendations were incorporated into the council's official report, *Internationalization of the Yen for the Twenty-First Century: Japan's Response to Changes in Global Economic and Financial Environments*, submitted to Finance Minister Kiichi Miyazawa in April 1999.

The Asian perspective grew out of my dissatisfaction with the traditional approach of predicting Asian growth using the U.S. economic growth rate, when I was covering the Asian economies as a business economist at the Nomura Research Institute in Tokyo in the late 1980s. In my search for an alternative leading indicator, I noted a very robust relation between the yen-dollar rate and Asian economic growth, which obviously hinged crucially on the fact that Asian currencies were to one extent or another pegged to the

2. Kwan (1992).
3. Kwan (1995a).

dollar. I then asked, What would be the implications for the stability of Asian countries should they peg to the yen instead?

The theory of optimum currency areas, which forms the basis of the regional approach, is a standard tool of economic analysis and has been widely used to study the desirability of forming a monetary union in Europe. The growing emphasis on certain convergent criteria as preconditions for monetary integration in Europe is particularly relevant to the case of Asia.

Finally, my view of the yen bloc from a global perspective was shaped by my participation in research projects sponsored by the Tokyo Club Foundation for Global Studies. In addition, thanks to the courtesy of Michael Armacost, president of the Brookings Institution in Washington, I was given the opportunity to spend almost a year at the Brookings Center for Northeast Asian Policy Studies between September 1999 and June 2000 to complete the manuscript for this book.

In the course of preparing the manuscript I received useful comments from researchers on both sides of the Pacific, to whom I would like to express my gratitude. On the American side, I learned much from Ronald McKinnon of Stanford University, Max Corden of Johns Hopkins University, and Robert Litan, Barry Bosworth, and Bates Gill of the Brookings Institution. At the Brookings Institution Press, thanks go to Diane Hammond, Carlotta Ribar, and Julia Petrakis, who, respectively, edited, proofread, and indexed the pages. On the Asian side, I benefited from discussion with Takatoshi Ito of Japan's Ministry of Finance, Akira Kohsaka of Osaka University, Kenichi Ohno of the National Graduate Institute for Policy Studies, and Ngiam Kee Jin of the National University of Singapore.

Finally, this book would not have been possible without the support and encouragement of Shozo Hashimoto, president of the Nomura Research Institute, and other colleagues at NRI, to whom I owe a great debt. Last but not least, I would like to thank Kimiko Ishihara for providing excellent research assistance in preparing the figures and tables.

Glossary

acu	Asian currency unit
ADB	Asian Development Bank
ADBI	Asian Development Bank Institute
AFTA	ASEAN Free Trade Area
AMF	Asian Monetary Fund
APEC	Asia Pacific Economic Cooperation
ASEAN	Association of Southeast Asian Nations (Indonesia, Malaysia, the Philippines, Singapore, Thailand, Brunei, Vietnam, Laos, Myanmar, and Cambodia)
ASEM	Asia-Europe Meeting
BIBF	Bangkok International Banking Facilities
BIS	Bank for International Settlements
CEPII	Centre d'Études Prospectives et d'Informations Internationales
CPI	consumer price index
EAEC	East Asian Economic Caucus
ecu	European currency unit
EMU	Economic and Monetary Union (Europe); also used loosely to mean European Monetary Union
EPA	Economic Planning Agency (Japan)
EU	European Union
FEER	fundamental equilibrium exchange rate
G5	United States, Japan, Germany, France, and United Kingdom

G7	G5 plus Italy and Canada
GATT	General Agreement on Tariffs and Trade
GDP	gross domestic product
GNP	gross national product
ICOR	incremental capital-output ratio
IMF	International Monetary Fund
M&As	mergers and acquisitions
MITI	Ministry of International Trade and Industry (Japan)
MOF	Ministry of Finance (Japan)
NIE	newly industrializing (or industrialized) economy (the Asian NIEs are South Korea, Taiwan, Hong Kong, and Singapore)*
OECD	Organization for Economic Cooperation and Development
OPEC	Organization of Petroleum Exporting Countries
REER	real effective exchange rate
SDR	special drawing right
SITC	standard international trade classification (UN)

* International organizations such as the IMF and OECD use "newly industrializing economy," although "newly industrialized economy" is also used elsewhere.

1

Overview

Interest in a yen bloc in Asia has been on the rise. This is happening against a background of growing recognition of the limitation of the Asian countries' traditional exchange rate policy of pegging to the dollar, as revealed by the recent currency crisis in Asia; the implementation of Japan's ambitious financial reform program dubbed the Big Bang; and the emergence of the euro as a challenge to the dominant role played by the U.S. dollar in the international monetary system. As noted in the preface, the term *yen bloc* refers to a group of countries that use the yen as an international currency and that maintain stable exchange rates against the yen.[1] It is analogous to such currency blocs as the former sterling area and the Economic and Monetary Union (EMU) now taking shape in Europe.

1. As pointed out by Holloway (1990), the term *yen bloc* can mean two different things. According to the broad definition, "Japan becomes the center of gravity of the West Pacific economy by virtue of its size—it comprises two-thirds of the region's annual output—and technological lead. As the region becomes increasingly integrated, more business activity enters the gravitational pull of Japan and its corporations. Trade and investment with the rest of the world continue to grow, but at a slower pace than within the region." According to the narrower, monetary definition, "the Japanese currency is used increasingly for regional trade and financial transactions, to the point where countries find it convenient to peg their currencies to the yen. The eventual result may be some form of monetary union, as is evolving in the EC, in which a common currency emerges." In this volume the definition of *yen bloc* is close to the narrower version.

The traditional approach to studying the use of the yen as an international currency, more widely known as the internationalization of the yen (the two expressions are used interchangeably), is framed in terms of Japan versus the rest of the world. In comparison, a yen bloc would be more limited in geographic scope but would involve closer policy coordination and economic ties among member countries.

With most of their international transactions denominated in U.S. dollars and with their currencies pegged loosely to the dollar, Asia's developing countries, it is fair to say, belong to a de facto dollar bloc. Taking this conclusion as my starting point, I try to find the answer to a further question: Is the formation of a yen bloc desirable, and if so, is it possible? The answer hinges on the implications of forming a yen bloc for both Japan and its Asian neighbors, some of which have become more apparent as a result of the crisis in Asia that started in the summer of 1997.

Four Analytical Approaches to a Yen Bloc

The possibility of forming a yen bloc in Asia can be studied from four complementary approaches: a Japanese perspective, an Asian perspective, a regional perspective, and a global perspective. These four approaches share the common understanding that the possibility of forming a yen bloc would be higher if major players perceive that its benefits outweigh its costs.

A Japanese Perspective

My study of the yen bloc from a Japanese perspective focuses on the implications for Japan of forming a monetary union with Asia. If the benefits exceed the costs, then Japan would be likely to pursue it as a policy objective and try to remove barriers hindering its realization. Until the early 1980s, the Japanese government was reluctant to promote the yen as an international currency, fearing that large fluctuations in the demand for the currency would destabilize the Japanese economy and make it difficult to conduct monetary policy. The changing international environment since the mid-1980s, however, has prompted Japan to reverse its stance. At the same time, the official approach to promoting the yen as an international currency has focused on its increasing role in Asia.

With Asia now replacing the United States as Japan's largest trading partner, stabilizing the yen's effective exchange rate through the formation of a yen bloc should help reduce the vulnerability of the Japanese economy to fluctuations in the yen-dollar rate. No country today is attempting to stabilize its currency against the yen as part of its exchange rate policy, thus rendering the yen more volatile than either the U.S. dollar or the deutsche mark in effective terms. A yen bloc would give the yen a built-in stability against other Asian currencies, since countries participating in it would seek to maintain stable exchange rates against the yen. As a group the countries of Asia are now Japan's single largest export market and source of imports; if the yen were to remain stable against other Asian currencies, then its effective exchange rate against the currencies of major trading partners would fluctuate less. In fact a yen bloc in Asia would eliminate exposure to fluctuations in the yen-dollar rate for nearly 40 percent of Japan's exports and imports.

There has been some concern that promoting the yen as an international currency, by increasing the demand for yen-denominated assets (in the form of foreign exchange reserves, for example), might lead to an appreciation of the yen and hurt Japanese exports. This, however, should be balanced against the possibility of a growing supply of yen assets, as more bonds come to be issued in yen. The net effect on the yen-dollar rate can be either positive or negative, depending on the balance between these two forces.

At the microeconomic level, forming a yen bloc with other Asian countries implies that Japan would bear less exchange rate risk in both current account and capital account transactions. More of Japan's trade would be denominated in yen instead of dollars, thereby reducing the foreign exchange risk involved in international trade. Japan's expanding role as a net creditor nation also makes wider use of the yen desirable, as it would help Japan stabilize the value of its overseas assets. Japan has suffered immense capital losses in yen terms since the early 1980s by investing heavily in dollar-denominated assets, as the dollar has followed a downward trend against the yen. To stabilize the value of Japan's overseas assets, the formation of a yen bloc would be desirable, as most of Japan's capital transactions with Asian countries would become yen denominated.

The flow of capital and goods should accelerate among countries participating in the yen bloc because of the diminished foreign exchange risk. This would bring Japanese financial institutions new business opportunities in financing yen-denominated trade transactions, developing their brokerage business in Asian securities, underwriting yen bonds issued by companies in other Asian countries, and listing Japanese companies on Asian stock exchanges.

Promoting the use of the yen as an international currency should also reduce the vulnerability of Japan's banking sector to fluctuations in the yen-dollar rate, as the Bank for International Settlements (BIS) capital adequacy ratios of Japanese banks would no longer be influenced by fluctuations in the yen-dollar rate if their overseas lending were denominated in yen instead of in dollars.

An Asian Perspective

For a small open economy, choosing a currency to use in international transactions can be considered conceptually a two-stage process: the government's choice of an exchange rate regime followed by other economic agents' decisions of which currency to use in denominating trade and capital transactions under the chosen exchange rate regime. Since exchange rate volatility is no doubt one major factor determining risk and return in the second stage, this analysis of a yen bloc should naturally focus upon the attractiveness of the yen as an anchor for other Asian currencies.

With their currencies pegged loosely to the dollar, Asia's developing countries are highly vulnerable to fluctuations in the yen-dollar rate. An appreciation of the yen usually leads to stronger economic growth and rising asset prices in these countries as it promotes exports and capital inflow. Symmetrically, a depreciation of the yen is usually accompanied by a slowdown in economic growth and lower asset prices.

The onset of the economic crisis in 1997, which happened against a background of a sharp depreciation of the yen against the dollar, led developing countries in Asia to reexamine the traditional policy of pegging closely to the U.S. dollar. To insulate themselves from the adverse effect on macroeconomic stability of a widely fluctuating yen-dollar rate, these countries should peg their currencies closer to the Japanese yen by targeting a basket of currencies in which the yen carries a substantial weight.

The optimal weight assigned to the yen in a currency basket that seeks to stabilize economic growth should be high for countries competing with Japan in international markets and low for countries with trade structures complementary to that of Japan. Other things being equal, the Asian newly industrializing economies (NIEs) are more appropriate candidates for joining a yen bloc than are members of the Association of Southeast Asian Nations (ASEAN) and China.

The volatility of Asian currencies against the yen seems to be a major factor restraining the use of the yen as a regional currency. Should Asian countries shift from their traditional regime (of pegging loosely to the dollar) to one of pegging closer to the yen (or of raising substantially the weight of the yen in their currency baskets), the reduction in foreign exchange risk would favor more extensive use of the yen as a regional currency at the microeconomic level. Increasing numbers of Asian importers and exporters would prefer to invoice in yen instead of dollars. Borrowers and investors—including governments and central banks—would have more incentive to hold a larger proportion of their portfolios in yen-denominated financial instruments. At the same time, trade and investment between Asia and Japan should increase. A shift from pegging to the dollar to pegging to the yen (albeit loosely) should therefore represent a major step toward the formation of a yen bloc.

A Regional Perspective

By studying which areas or countries should adopt (genuinely) fixed exchange rates among themselves while allowing flexible rates in relation to the rest of the world, the theory of optimum currency areas can be extended to provide a regional perspective (and a more direct approach) to a yen bloc. The traditional approach to the theory of optimum currency areas tries to single out a crucial economic characteristic that presumably indicates where the borders between blocs should be drawn. Here I focus on three criteria cited in related literature as major determinants of the domain of an optimum currency area, namely, the extent of economic integration, the similarity in economic structures, and the similarity in policy objectives (notably the preference between price stability and employment).

From a microeconomic perspective, the major benefit of forming a monetary union is to reduce the costs and uncertainty involved in transactions among member countries by stabilizing exchange rates. With intraregional trade in Asia (including Japan) surging since the 1985 Plaza Accord, the potential benefit of monetary integration in Asia has increased.

The major cost associated with monetary integration arises from the abandonment of an independent monetary policy. By fixing its exchange rate to that of other members of the union, a country joining a union automatically gives up control over its own monetary policy. When its economy is subject to an external shock, it has no choice but to follow the common monetary policy of the monetary union. Countries with similar economic structures can respond to a common shock with a common monetary policy, and the costs of giving up an independent monetary policy are relatively small. In contrast, countries with heterogeneous economic structures require different policy responses to common shocks, and the costs of sharing a common monetary policy are relatively large. For example, Japan and Korea, both oil importers, can respond to a surge in oil prices with the same monetary policy. This, however, does not apply to Japan and Indonesia, where the latter is an oil exporter. Likewise, the very high cost for Hong Kong to maintain its dollar peg system became apparent during the economic crisis in Asia.

At the same time, the larger the differential in inflation rates among members, the more difficult it is to maintain fixed exchange rates. Other things being equal, countries with similar inflation rates are more likely candidates for a monetary union.

In Asian countries, economic structure and level of inflation are closely related to their level of economic development. Higher income countries such as the Asian NIEs have trade structures similar to that of Japan, while China and the lower income members of ASEAN have trade structures very different from that of Japan. Likewise, countries with higher per capita income tend to have lower inflation rates than those with low per capita income.

In view of the diversity among these countries, it is unlikely that Japan, the Asian NIEs, members of ASEAN, and China together and at once form an optimum currency area. A yen bloc centering on Japan should probably start with the participation of the Asian NIEs, to be followed by Malaysia and Thailand as they reach a higher level of economic development. Countries still at an early stage of economic development such as China, Indonesia, and the Philippines fail to meet the conditions for forming an optimum currency area with Japan.

A Global Perspective

This analysis of a yen bloc from a global perspective focuses on the implications of a more important role for the yen in Asia for the international monetary system. Together with the euro, the emergence of the yen as an international currency that competes with the dollar, by imposing discipline on U.S. economic policy, should enhance the stability of the system.

The performance of the floating rate system, which has been in place since the mid-1970s, has been disappointing. Exchange rates have been highly volatile, and long-term deviations from equilibrium rates have been common. Currency crises recur not only in emerging countries but also in some developed ones. The instability of the international monetary system can partly be attributed to the asymmetry between the United States and other countries under the system. The mere size of the U.S. economy means that, although changes in U.S. policies have immense effect on other countries, the domestic economy is relatively insulated from repercussions through international trade and capital flows. Furthermore, as the key-currency country, the United States enjoys more autonomy in pursuing its own economic objectives.

The United States can take advantage of this asymmetry in the international monetary system in three ways. First, it can pursue a benign neglect policy and concentrate on achieving domestic objectives without caring about its balance of payments and exchange rate, exposing the rest of the world to the adverse consequences of U.S. policy mistakes. Second, even when the balance of payments deficit and exchange rate misalignment are judged to be excessive, the United States has the leverage to force its trading partners to bear most of the burden of adjustment. To reduce its trade deficit, for example, it can pressure Europe and Japan to expand domestic demand instead of tightening its own monetary and fiscal policies, taking advantage of its strong bargaining power at both the bilateral or multilateral levels. Third, the United States may be tempted to abuse the monopoly power enjoyed by the dollar as a medium of exchange in international transactions. The persistently higher rate of inflation in the United States than in its major trading partners and the secular depreciation of the dollar against major currencies that accompanies it may reflect an attempt by the United States to maximize seigniorage.

Thanks to the need to finance its chronic current account deficit by borrowing overseas, the United States has turned into the world's largest debtor country, with external liabilities totaling $1,474 billion (as of the end of 1999). The mirror image is the emergence of Japan as the world's largest creditor country and by far the largest foreign holder of U.S. treasury bonds. Never before has the world's leading creditor country had most of its overseas assets denominated in the currency of the world's largest debtor country. This unprecedented situation has become a major source of instability in the international financial system, as symbolized by the gyration of the yen-dollar rate.

The emergence of international currencies that compete with the dollar may help impose discipline on the economic policy of the United States by rendering the international environment less forgiving of its mistakes. In that case, U.S. policy errors could cause massive portfolio diversification out of dollar assets, and sustaining a large current account deficit may become very costly. The United States may have to reduce imports sharply by fiscal and monetary tightening or maintain very high interest rates to attract capital inflow. Likewise, if the United States allows the dollar to depreciate too far in pursuit of seigniorage, its role as an international currency may be displaced by other competing currencies. Furthermore, in a more symmetrical world, the United States may prefer to take a more cooperative stance in international policy coordination. Monetary integration in Europe has become a reality. If Asian countries come together to form a yen bloc, competition among the three blocs in a tripolar world should therefore contribute to a more stable international monetary system.

Toward a Yen Bloc in Asia

Even if the formation of a yen bloc is desirable for Asia (including Japan), a question remains as to whether it is possible. Although there are barriers to be overcome, the chance of a yen bloc becoming a reality has improved with both the shift in the Japanese government's stance on the issue from a passive one to an active one and the growing recognition of the vulnerability of the dollar peg system adopted by Asia's developing countries.

The Changing International Environment

Asian countries have a long history of pegging their exchange rates to the dollar and using it as the major currency for international transactions. However, the onset of the Asian currency crisis, the introduction of the euro, and progress in Japan's financial Big Bang have prompted both Japan and Asia's developing countries to consider seriously the alternative of assigning a more important role to the yen in the region.

The Asian currency crisis, which began in the summer of 1997, exposed at a stroke the critical risk for an Asian economy to peg its currency to the dollar without considering the regional composition of its international trade and investment. In the course of the currency crisis, many Asian countries were forced to delink their currencies from the dollar and adopt a floating system. As their economic situation stabilizes, these countries are searching for a new exchange rate system that better reflects international economic ties, including trade and capital transactions. More stable exchange rates against the yen should contribute to stable economic growth in these countries. Stability in Asia is, in turn, a vital concern for Japan, as it has close economic, political, and social ties with this region.

The euro is the first currency to challenge the dollar as the key currency. The economic scale of "euroland" is comparable to that of the United States, and it accounts for a high share in global capital markets. In addition, euroland enjoys strong economic ties with such regions as central and eastern Europe and Africa. Given these strengths, it is possible that the euro will in the near future become a key currency, on par with the dollar. The emergence of the euro may lead to the end of the age of the dollar's dominance and promote the search for a new international monetary system. The challenge of the euro may also provide an impetus for a review of past choices concerning currencies used in international transactions. In Japan concern is growing that the role of the euro as an international currency could increase at the expense of the yen.

Meanwhile, Japan's Big Bang is under way and making progress. The revised Foreign Exchange and Foreign Trade Control Law came into effect in April 1998. This was followed in December 1998 with the implementation of principal measures for the reform of the financial system. The Big Bang aims at revitalizing the Japanese financial market to make Tokyo an international financial center on par with New York and London by the year 2001. It has come to be realized that unless the yen is assigned a key role the financial Big Bang could at best turn Tokyo into Japan's Wimbledon, where most of the champions are foreign players.

Policy Changes in Asia and Japan

In contrast to Europe and America, economic integration in Asia has been achieved mainly through the initiative of the private sector, without formal treaties. Likewise, a yen bloc is unlikely to be established under a Japanese initiative; rather it will be the result of the increasing preference for the yen over the dollar by Asian governments and other economic agents, based on their own cost-benefit calculations. Japan can, however, facilitate this process by reducing the costs and risks of using the yen in international transactions for both residents and nonresidents.

As a first step toward the formation of a yen bloc, Asian countries would be expected to peg their currencies to a basket of currencies in which the weight assigned to the yen would be gradually increased. Indeed, since the onset of the Asian currency crisis some Asian currencies have strengthened their synchronization with the yen against the dollar. In view of the diversity among Asian countries, however, it is unlikely that the shift will proceed at the same pace for all. The process is likely to be led by the Asian NIEs, followed by the more advanced members of ASEAN, such as Malaysia and Thailand.

In addition, recognizing the need to promote the use of the yen as an international currency, Japan is likely to take further steps to deregulate and upgrade the Tokyo market as an international financial center to make it attractive to nonresidents. Japan will also further open its markets to Asian products, thus deepening the interdependence between Japan and these countries. This in turn should give the yen a more prominent international role, and encourage Asian countries to shift from a foreign exchange policy based on the U.S. dollar to one based on the yen. As a yen bloc takes shape, the yen will gain stature as an international currency and start to be used more, not just in Asia but also in other parts of the world.

Whether the global monetary system will be characterized by a bipolar system centering on the dollar and the euro or a tripolar one in which the yen also plays an important role will depend very much on how Japan responds to the changing international environment. It is no exaggeration to say that Japan is facing the choice between now or never in its attempt to promote the yen as an international currency. It is this sense of urgency that prompted former prime minister Keizo Obuchi to proclaim to the world Japan's intention to play a more important role in the international monetary system during his visit to Europe in January 1999.

Barriers to Be Overcome

The traditional approach to studying the internationalization of the yen identifies barriers restraining wider use of the yen in international transactions. For example, the strategy of Japanese companies of invoicing in the currencies of export destinations (pricing to market) to maintain market share, together with the fact that Japanese imports mainly consist of primary commodities (usually invoiced in dollars), has limited the use of the yen in denominating trade. At the same time, shallow money markets, distorted by a complex system of withholding tax, have made it difficult for residents and nonresidents to park liquid working balances in yen-denominated short-term instruments.

To enhance the attractiveness of the yen as an international currency, the Japanese Ministry of Finance announced in December 1998 a policy package that included competitive price auctions of financing bills, abolition of withholding tax on interest income for nonresidents and the securities transaction tax, and introduction of thirty-year government bonds and one-year treasury bills. In addition, in its final report on the internationalization of the yen, published in April 1999, the Council on Foreign Exchange and Other Transactions (an advisory group to the minister of finance) called for further measures to improve the repo market (by promoting transactions based on repurchase agreements instead of cash-collateralized lending and borrowing), the government bond market (by introducing five-year government bonds), the settlement system (by moving to a real-time gross settlement system), and services offered by the Bank of Japan to its overseas counterparts. These proposed measures have been implemented step by step.

For Asian countries, pegging their currencies to the yen implies that their macroeconomic performance would depend very much on that of Japan. The Japanese economy suffered its longest recession in the postwar period following the bursting of the asset price bubble in the early 1990s. It goes without saying that, if the yen is to play the role of Asia's key currency, Japan needs first to revitalize its economy. Thanks to the bold measures implemented by the government since October 1998, the stability of the financial system has been restored, and the Japanese economy has shown clear signs of recovery.

Finally, the political aspect of the issue cannot be ignored. So far, the idea of a yen bloc in Asia has been widely dismissed as premature, if not irrelevant, because most Asian countries, remembering their harsh experiences under Japanese occupation during World War II, are reluctant to give Japan a more prominent role in the region than it already has. The Japanese government also hesitates to take a higher profile in Asia or in the world at large. However, the recent experience of monetary integration between Germany and France, and the formation of a de facto deutsche mark bloc in large parts of eastern Europe, much of which suffered at Germany's hands in both world wars, suggest that such political barriers are surmountable.

The real political opposition may come from the United States, if the formation of a yen bloc is interpreted as posing a challenge to the status of the dollar as the key currency. Judging from the fact that the United States has welcomed the emergence of the European Monetary Union as a win-win game between the two sides of the Atlantic, however, there is no reason why it should not take a similar receptive stance toward the formation of a yen bloc in Asia.

So the political costs of a yen bloc in Asia seem to be falling, while the potential economic benefits are rising. The idea of a yen bloc will mature when the economic benefits surpass the political costs. Malaysia's proposal to form an East Asian Economic Caucus, with Japan playing a leading role and the United States being excluded, suggests that this time may not be too far away.

One

The Economic Fundamentals Supporting a Yen Bloc

2

The Rise of Regionalism in Asia

The pattern of economic development in Asia during the postwar era has been likened to a flock of wild geese flying in formation. The development process began in Japan, with the Asian NIEs and, later, the ASEAN economies and China catching up from behind. Traditionally, these economies depended heavily on the United States for trade and investment, but the trend toward intraregional economic interdependence has accelerated since the Plaza Accord in 1985. The end of the cold war also promoted the integration of the socialist countries into the regional economy. The virtuous circle between growing interdependence and rapid economic growth, however, turned into a vicious circle in mid-1997, when a currency crisis started in Thailand and spread to the rest of the region. The new reality of interdependence has called for closer cooperation among Asian governments.

A Virtuous Circle between Interdependence and Economic Growth

Intraregional interdependence among Asian economies has deepened and widened during the postwar period. Through trade and investment, the wave of industrialization that spread from Japan to the Asian NIEs in the 1960s subsequently spread to ASEAN and China.

The Flying Geese Pattern of Economic Development

In the flying geese pattern of economic expansion, countries specialize in the export of products in which they enjoy comparative advantage commensurate with their levels of development and at the same time seek to upgrade their industrial structures through augmenting their capital and technology. Foreign direct investment from the more advanced economies to the less developed ones, through relocating industries from the former to the latter, plays a dominant role in this process.

The flying geese model was first used to describe the life cycles of industries in the course of economic development, with the focus on specific industries in specific countries.[1] Subsequently, it has been extended to study the dynamic changes in the industrial structure (that is, the rise and fall of different industries) in specific countries and, further, to the shift of industries from one country to another.[2]

The life cycle of a specific industry can be traced by following the time path of an indicator of comparative advantage, such as the ratio between production and consumption. This usually takes the form of an inverted V-shaped curve, showing that competitiveness first improves and then deteriorates over time (figure 2-1). Capital accumulation (including the inflow of foreign direct investment) and forward and backward linkages with other industries, by changing the comparative advantage of the country concerned, usually lead to an upgrading of industrial structure. This can be represented by repeating the inverted V-shaped curve showing the production-consumption ratio for emerging industries, which are usually more capital- and technology-intensive than the preceding ones. A typical sequence seen among Asian countries is the shift from the textile industry to the chemical industry, the steel industry, the automobile industry, and the electronics-electrical industry.

When extended to the context of an open economy, the flying geese model is used to describe the shifting of industries from more advanced countries to countries catching up from behind. This is shown in figure 2-2, with the inverted V-shaped curves representing the same industry in different countries. A typical example is the shifting of textile production from Japan to the Asian NIEs and further to members of ASEAN and China. Following the flying geese pattern, a sophisticated division of labor among Asian countries has also taken shape in the electrical and electronic industry.

1. Akamatsu (1962).
2. Chen (1989); Yamazawa (1990).

Figure 2-1. *Asia's Flying Geese Pattern of Economic Development, by Industry*[a]

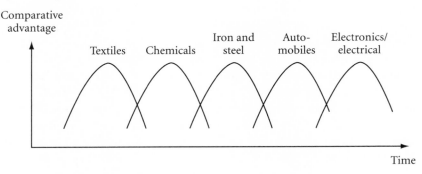

Source: Nomura Research Institute.
a. For a particular country.

Foreign direct investment has played an important role in sustaining the flying geese pattern of economic development in Asia. In the investing countries (usually countries at higher levels of economic development), the relocation of declining industries releases resources (labor and capital) for emerging industries, making it possible to upgrade the industrial structure. In the receiving countries (usually countries at lower levels of economic development), the inflow of foreign direct investment helps to introduce

Figure 2-2. *Asia's Flying Geese Pattern of Economic Development, by Region*[a]

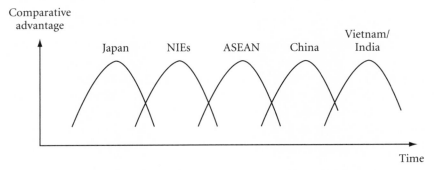

Source: Nomura Research Institute.
a. For a particular industry.

the funds, management know-how, and technology needed for catching up with the industrial countries.[3] This is particularly true for outsourcing-type projects that seek to reduce the cost of production by investing in areas in which the host country enjoys comparative advantage.

Factors promoting foreign direct investment of the outsourcing type include rising costs in the investing countries (push factors) and an improving investment environment in the receiving countries (pull factors). Specifically, currency appreciation in Japan and the Asian NIEs, the economic catching-up process of developing countries, and a general liberalization of host country policies toward foreign direct investment seem to have been the most important factors sustaining such investment flows in Asia since the mid-1980s. At the same time, liberalization of foreign direct investment policy, as exemplified by China's open-door policy, provided immense and unexploited opportunities for investors. The economic catching up of developing countries, particularly members of ASEAN and China, has also made possible a division of labor within the manufacturing sector among Asian countries, including Japan.

Outsourcing has been by far the most important objective of Japanese companies investing in Asia's developing countries. This type of investment commonly involves the relocation of labor-intensive production processes, such as textile manufacturing and electronic products assembly, in search of lower production costs. In most cases, output from Asian production bases is exported, either back to Japan or to third countries. The pattern of investment flow associated with outsourcing objectives, as demonstrated in Asia, is consistent with the flying geese pattern discussed earlier. Successive phases of industries moving out of Japan could be observed: from textiles to chemicals in the 1970s; to metal products and general and transportation machinery in the 1980s; and to electrical machinery in the 1990s (figure 2-3).

The Deepening and Widening of Intraregional Interdependence

Through the removal of the political barriers separating socialist countries and market economies, the global trend toward détente has helped make cooperation across national borders possible in Asia also. The collapse of communist regimes in eastern Europe and the Soviet Union, in particular, had an immense impact on the socialist countries in Asia. The failure of Soviet-style socialism as a model for economic development contrasts

---

3. The flying geese model should be distinguished from the product cycle theory of Vernon (1966), which emphasizes changes over time in the production process (particularly the combination of factors of production), taking factor endowment as given.

Figure 2-3. *Japanese Foreign Direct Investment,*
by Manufacturing Industry, 1970–99[a]

Percent of total

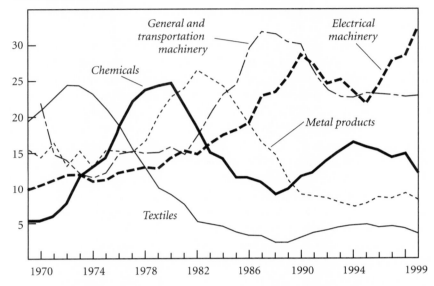

Source: Compiled by Nomura Research Institute based on *Ministry of Finance Statistics Monthly* (Japan).

a. Years are fiscal years; data are five-year moving averages.

sharply with the success of the Asian NIEs and members of ASEAN, which have fundamentally relied on the market in their organization of economic activity. The waning of ideology and the termination of aid from the former Soviet Union have prompted the socialist countries in Asia to reconsider their development strategy. An obvious alternative is to open their doors further to the outside world to take advantage of the dynamism in neighboring countries. During the 1960s, at the height of the cold war, the famous domino theory predicted that if Vietnam were to fall to communism the rest of Southeast Asia would follow. Ironically, the reverse is now taking place, with China and Vietnam fast emerging as the new economic frontiers of Asia.

The expansion of Asia's new frontiers is creating economic zones encompassing countries with different economic and political systems and at various stages of economic development. In addition to the South China economic zone centered in Hong Kong, concepts of regional cooperation at more embryonic stages have emerged. They include the Northeast Asia economic zone (comprising Japan, the Korean peninsula, northern China, and the Russian Far East) and other various growth triangles to be formed among members of ASEAN. These interlocking economic zones form a corridor linking fast-growing economies from the north to the south along the western Pacific Rim.

China has become Asia's largest new frontier. With one-fifth of the world's population and its economy growing at nearly 10 percent a year since converting to an open-door policy in the late 1970s, it is emerging as a regional, if not a global, economic power. China's transformation to a market economy and its opening to the world are having a major effect on neighboring countries. First, China presents itself as a model for other socialist countries in the region, thereby helping to accelerate the reverse domino phenomenon. Vietnam's open-door policy is a good example. Second, the Asian NIEs, which are more developed than China, have benefited from expanding investment and trade ties with China. This is particularly true for Hong Kong and Taiwan, which have been using China actively as an offshore production base. Third, the smooth transition of Hong Kong to Chinese sovereignty was facilitated by the virtual economic integration of China and Hong Kong. Indeed, Hong Kong is expected to play an even larger role as the gateway to China. Fourth, China is competing vigorously with members of ASEAN not only for export markets but also for foreign direct investment.

The impact of the emergence of China as a regional economic power can be analyzed by focusing on the implications for the terms of trade (the ratio of export prices to import prices) of its neighbors.[4] China's industrialization, which can be characterized by export-led growth based on the country's vast labor resources, increases the supply of labor-intensive goods to global markets while at the same time raising demand for capital-intensive goods at home. This leads to a decline in the price of labor-intensive goods relative to capital-intensive goods. The overall impact on world trade is a worsening of China's own terms of trade and an improvement in the terms of trade for the rest of the world.

Through this mechanism, the rest of the world can share the fruit of the growth of the Chinese economy, although for China itself the deterioration in its terms of trade implies a decline in real income, partly offsetting the benefits of higher economic growth. In the rest of the world, distinction should be drawn between countries with trade structures complementary to that of China and those with trade structures competitive with that of China. Higher income countries such as Japan and the Asian NIEs that

4. See Kwan (1995b).

belong to the former group should enjoy an improvement in their terms of trade as the Chinese economy expands. In contrast, lower income countries such as members of ASEAN that belong to the latter group may actually suffer a deterioration in their terms of trade as expanding Chinese exports also drive down their export prices.

The widening of economic interdependence in Asia has been paralleled by a deepening of interdependence through rising intraregional trade and investment. Until the mid-1980s, trade in Asia was dominated by exports across the Pacific, a pattern of trade flow that has changed dramatically since the Plaza Accord among the G5 countries in 1985, which was followed by a sharp appreciation of the yen against the dollar.[5] With Asia growing much faster than the United States and trade friction between the two sides of the Pacific escalating, intraregional trade among Asian countries has increased sharply, while the relative importance of the United States as an export market for these countries has declined (figure 2-4). Although this trend was reversed during the Asian crisis, it has been restored since 1999, when the regional economy started to recover. Reflecting the rising level of intraregional trade, the Asian NIEs, ASEAN, and China together now hold a larger share of world trade than the United States. The four busiest container ports in the world are in the Asian NIEs.[6]

In addition to market size, rising intraregional investment has also contributed to the surge in intraregional trade. Currency appreciation in Japan and the Asian NIEs since the 1985 Plaza Accord prompted their companies to move production facilities overseas. Japan has replaced the United States as the largest source of foreign direct investment in Asia, while the Asian NIEs have also become major investors in China and ASEAN. Led by Japanese electronic and electrical companies, the expansion of a production network across national borders by multinationals has led to buoyant intraregional trade in intermediate products.

Strengthening Multilateral Cooperation at the Government Level

While economic integration in Asia so far has been achieved mainly through the initiative of the private sector, multilateral economic cooperation at the government level, with a focus on ASEAN and the Asia Pacific Economic Cooperation (APEC) forum, has also gathered momentum.

---

5. The G5 countries are the United States, Japan, Germany, France, and the United Kingdom.

6. They are Hong Kong, Singapore, Kaohsiung in Taiwan, and Pusan in South Korea. The ranking is for 1999; see *Containerization International* (March 2000).

Figure 2-4. *Asian Exports, by Region, 1986–99*[a]

Percent of Asian exports

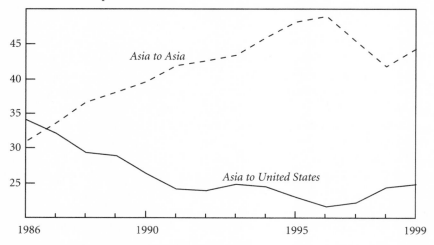

Source: Compiled by Nomura Research Institute based on International Monetary Fund, *Direction of Trade Statistics.*

a. Asia = Japan + NIEs + ASEAN + China.

ASEAN was established in 1967 by Indonesia, Malaysia, the Philippines, Singapore, and Thailand to foster regional economic and political cooperation. Brunei became the sixth member in 1984, followed by Vietnam (1995), Laos and Myanmar (1997), and Cambodia (1999). Up to now ASEAN has played an important role in political cooperation but has yet to achieve significant results in the sphere of economic cooperation. To cope with the rising tide of regionalism and to halt the shift of direct investment to the new competitors such as China, Latin America, and eastern European countries, ASEAN has decided to establish an ASEAN Free Trade Area (AFTA) by 2002. By liberalizing trade in the region, AFTA should encourage a more horizontal division of labor in manufactured goods by making it more attractive for multinationals to build production networks across national borders.

A major barrier to economic cooperation among ASEAN members has been the relatively low degree of complementarity in their economic structures, which can be overcome by extending membership to countries at different stages of economic development. With the socialist countries of Indochina as new members, there should be more diversity in economic structures within ASEAN. Other schemes along this line include promoting economic cooperation among all countries in East Asia. Malaysia's prime minister Mahathir Mohamad, for example, has proposed forming an East Asian Economic Caucus (EAEC), which also would aim to increase Asian countries' bargaining power in international negotiations. Although the EAEC has so far failed to materialize, largely because of opposition by the United States, the annual ASEAN + 3 Informal Summit, which started in 1997 with the participation of leaders from ASEAN members plus China, Japan, and South Korea, represents a first step in this direction.

Meanwhile, APEC has emerged as a major force of economic cooperation among major players on both sides of the Pacific. Since the first ministerial meeting in 1989, APEC's role has centered on the promotion of dialogue and cooperative sectoral projects to deal with the major problems affecting the region's economy. Subsequently, trade and investment liberalization has also become an important item on its agenda. At the 1994 APEC summit, held in Jakarta, participating countries reached a consensus on a two-speed schedule, stipulating that the liberalization of trade and investment be completed by 2010 for the advanced member countries and by 2020 for developing member countries.[7] Following the APEC example, the Asia-Europe Meeting (ASEM) has convened every two years since its leaders met for the first time in London in 1996 to strengthen the political, economic, and cultural ties between the two continents.

From Flying Geese to Falling Geese

The financial crisis that infected most Asian countries in mid-1997 showed how the virtuous circle between increasing interdependence and high economic growth could turn into a vicious circle. Growing competition with Japan and China are identified as major factors triggering the crisis in Asia centering on ASEAN members, which have come to be sandwiched between a leader that has stopped moving ahead and a follower that is catching up fast. In addition, the premature opening up of capital account transactions and distortions in trade and investment have led to misallocation of resources.

Competition with Japan and China

The sharp deterioration in the trade performance of ASEAN countries in the period immediately preceding the 1997 Asian crisis can be largely attributed to the weakness of the yen and high productivity growth in China.

---

7. For an in-depth analysis of APEC, see Funabashi (1995).

While the former reflects Japan's economic plight, the latter reflects China's growing economic might.

After hitting a historical high of 80 yen to the dollar in the spring of 1995, the yen followed a downward trend, falling to 115 yen to the dollar immediately before the Asian crisis in mid-1997. This took place against a background of deteriorating economic fundamentals in Japan (falling asset prices, massive accumulation of bad debt in the banking sector, rising deflationary pressure) and a widening differential between U.S. and domestic interest rates (reflecting the gap in the pace of economic growth). The yen's sharp depreciation against the dollar (and thus the Asian currencies under the dollar peg system) since mid-1995 led to a sharp deterioration in the Asian countries' export performance and current account balances in 1996, paving the way to the subsequent currency crisis.

In addition to the weakening yen, the failure of Thailand and other ASEAN members to cope with growing competition with China by upgrading their industrial structures might have been a major factor contributing to the latest crisis in the region. In line with its level of economic development, Thailand, like other ASEAN countries, has a trade structure similar to, and thus competitive with, that of China (figure 2-5). Competitive relations between nations can be characterized as a zero-sum game, in which one's gain is the other's loss.

Although China only accounts for about 3 percent of Thailand's total trade, it has become an important factor determining economic performance in Thailand largely because the two countries compete with one another for export markets and inflow of foreign direct investment. Growth in labor productivity in China's industrial sector reached nearly 20 percent a year between 1992 and 1997, far outpacing that in ASEAN countries. The devaluation of the yuan at the beginning of 1994 has also helped China offset the negative effect of three consecutive years of double-digit inflation between 1993 and 1995 on export competitiveness.[8] Indeed, between 1992

8. The impact of the yuan's devaluation on Chinese exports should be quite limited. Until late 1993 China had a dual exchange rate system, comprising an official rate and a market-based swap center rate. In January 1994, the two rates were unified by adjusting the official rate to the market rate, leading to a devaluation of the official rate by about 35 percent (from $1 = 5.76 yuan to $1 = 8.7 yuan). Since the swap center rate already applied to about 80 percent of China's external trade before the devaluation, the effective impact of the devaluation on China's export competitiveness (and thus the competitiveness of ASEAN countries) should be much smaller (35 percent × 20 percent = 7 percent) than the simple 35 percent magnitude that the devaluation suggests. Indeed, since the slowdown in ASEAN exports had become apparent only since 1996, it was more likely to be caused by the weakening yen.

Figure 2-5. *Competitiveness and Complementarity between China and Other Asian Countries, 1999*[a]

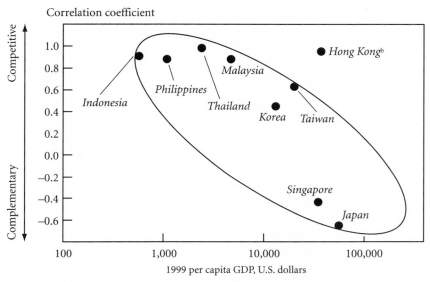

Correlation coefficient

1999 per capita GDP, U.S. dollars

Source: Compiled by Nomura Research Institute based on ADB, *Key Indicators of Developing Asia and Pacific Countries,* supplemented by trade statistics of individual countries.

a. The degree of competition between an Asian country and China is calculated as the correlation coefficient between their respective vectors showing the specialization indexes ([exports − imports] / [exports + imports]) of major categories of manufactured goods. To focus on competition in the manufacturing sector, a four-category classification comprising chemicals and related products (SITC section 5), manufactured goods classified chiefly by material (SITC section 6), machinery and transport equipment (SITC section 7), and miscellaneous manufactured articles (SITC section 8) is used.

b. The specialization indexes for Hong Kong, and thus its degree of competition with China, have been distorted by the presence of reexport trade.

and 1997, more multinationals favored China over ASEAN as a destination to locate direct investment, while ASEAN countries lagged behind China in gaining shares in international markets (particularly in labor-intensive products).

Premature Liberalization of Capital Account Transactions

Increasing inflow of foreign funds has helped Asian countries achieve high economic growth by allowing them to invest more than they save, but at the same time it has created new problems. Volatile capital movement may create macroeconomic instability, and massive inflows may push up real exchange rates, with adverse effects on exports. Making the best use of the inflow of funds for economic development while checking its possible side effects has become an important policy issue for these countries.

Capital inflow promotes economic growth only if it is channeled into productive instead of speculative activities, and developing countries should rely more on foreign direct investment than on short-term capital flows as a source of external finance. Capital inflow could weaken the export competitiveness of the host country by pushing up its real exchange rate through either an appreciation of the nominal exchange rate (under a floating exchange rate system) or higher inflation (under a fixed exchange rate system). This is analogous to the so-called Dutch disease, in which the discovery of some natural resource, such as oil, tends to drive up the real exchange rate and shrink the domestic manufacturing sector. Likewise, inflow of short-term funds, by lowering interest rates and boosting the money supply, usually leads to rising stock and property prices, which in turn raise consumption at the expense of domestic savings. In this case, by crowding out domestic savings, inflow of short-term funds may not contribute to higher total investment and thus to economic growth. In contrast, inflow of foreign direct investment, by increasing production capacity and productivity, reduces inflationary pressure and helps maintain export competitiveness. In addition, foreign direct investment is usually undertaken with a long time horizon and is therefore less volatile than portfolio flows, which respond sensitively to changes in interest rate differentials and exchange rate expectations. No wonder countries suffering most during the latest currency crisis in Asia (Thailand, Indonesia, and Korea) were those with very high ratios of short-term debt.

In the case of Thailand, the liberalization of capital account transactions in general, and in particular the establishment of the Bangkok International Banking Facilities (BIBF) in March 1993 as an offshore banking center, attracted massive inflows of capital. Short-term debt surpassed foreign direct investment as a source of net capital inflow in 1991, and by 1996 the former had risen to six times the latter ($12 billion versus $2 billion).[9] On the one hand, this made it possible to sustain the country's immense current account deficit; on the other hand, it made macroeconomic control difficult.[10] Indeed, both the banking sector and the monetary authorities failed

---

9. World Bank, *Global Development Finance 1999*.

10. Thai companies can borrow from overseas through the BIBF at a lower cost than through traditional channels. For BIBF banks, transactions are exempted from the reserve requirements, interest rate regulations, and foreign exchange controls that apply to onshore

to pursue appropriate measures to keep the expanding asset price bubble in check. The inflow of funds was more than enough to finance the current account deficit and led to rapid monetary growth, which fueled speculative activities in Thailand's stock and property markets. When the asset price bubble finally burst in 1996, the financial system was left with massive bad debts. The situation was aggravated by investors' withdrawal of their funds from Thailand and by speculators' short-selling activities in anticipation of a major devaluation of the baht.

The Failure of the Import Substitution Strategy

Until the 1980s, the flow of foreign direct investment into Asia was aimed mainly at outsourcing, to take advantage of the lower cost of production there, but recently investment aiming at circumventing trade barriers has also been on the rise. As part of their import substitution strategy, many developing countries in Asia have combined high tariffs with policies granting preferences to foreign direct investment in specific industries. While the outsourcing type of investment is export oriented and consistent with an international division of labor according to comparative advantage, investment that circumvents trade barriers may actually distort the optimal allocation of resources, leading to a hollowing out of industry in the investing country and a reduction in investment efficiency in the receiving country. Japanese automakers, for example, are investing in Asia not to reduce the cost of production but to circumvent the very high tariffs imposed on imported cars in the host countries.[11] Indeed, companies aiming to develop local markets were adversely affected by the latest currency crisis in Asia. Producers of transportation machinery, chemicals, and iron and steel, for example, were forced to curtail production to cope with falling domestic demand. Among them, those heavily dependent on imported inputs (whose prices had risen sharply in local currency terms) suffered most.

In contrast, foreign companies exporting from the region weathered the latest crisis far better than those targeting local markets. Companies exporting from ASEAN countries benefited from lower production costs (in terms

---

transactions, while the corporate tax rate is reduced to 10 percent from the standard rate of 30 percent. Before the crisis, many foreign banks without branches in Thailand had also made use of these advantages by extending loans to Thai companies through the BIBF, while at the same time hoping to use it as a stepping-stone toward obtaining full banking licenses in Thailand.

11. The location of such projects therefore may not be consistent with the level of economic development of the receiving countries, and the flying geese pattern of transfer of industry from more advanced countries to less developed ones does not apply.

of foreign currencies) and improved export competitiveness. This was particularly true for those relying mainly on local sources for supply of primary and intermediate inputs (labor, raw materials, and parts and components, for example), including companies in food processing, mining, and precision machinery.

The Asian Financial Crisis

The devaluation of the Thai baht on July 2, 1997, had repercussions on most Asian currencies, with the baht crisis quickly turning into an ASEAN currency crisis and later an Asian currency crisis when in October the Hong Kong dollar and the Korean won also became targets for speculators. The contagion effect reflected the belief among market participants either that other Asian countries had close ties with one another or that they shared similar problems. The regional nature of the crisis has called for collaborative actions among Asian countries in the form of a regional monetary fund. While the crisis has cast doubt over the sustainability of the "East Asian miracle," supply-side considerations continue to favor the region as the fastest growing region in the world in the years to come.[12]

The Contagion Effect: Domino or Competitive Devaluation

Although all Asian currencies experienced downward pressure following the baht's devaluation, three groups of countries can be distinguished according to the constraints facing policy authorities. The first group consists of ASEAN countries and South Korea, which suffered from a vicious circle of currency depreciation and accumulating bad debt. The second group is made up of Singapore and Taiwan, which allowed exchange rates to depreciate to stimulate exports. The third group includes China and Hong Kong, which, supported by immense foreign exchange reserves, resisted currency devaluation largely on political grounds.

Among ASEAN members and South Korea, the sharp depreciation of their currencies had adverse effects on their economies. Companies with liabilities denominated in foreign currencies found the repayment burden in terms of the local currency rising in proportion to the scale of devaluation. Local banks that raised funds overseas and lent in local currencies also suffered immense capital losses. While banks that both borrowed and lent in

---

12. Following a World Bank publication of this title, the term *East Asian Miracle* has been widely used to praise the successful development of the region. See World Bank (1993).

foreign currencies avoided direct capital losses resulting from the devaluation, they accumulated bad loans as more and more of their borrowers were forced to default. Many banks became themselves insolvent as a result. The deterioration in the balance sheets of the banking sector led to a serious credit crunch problem, which adversely affected all borrowers, including exporters receiving rising orders as their products became cheaper in international markets. In this way, what started as a currency crisis turned into a financial crisis and, further, into an economic crisis afflicting all sectors.

Given the negative impact of currency depreciation on the bad debt problem, allowing exchange rates to fall in order to stimulate exports was simply not a viable option for ASEAN members and South Korea. Rather, they struggled very hard to stop their currencies from depreciating further, some more successfully than others. In an effort to sever the vicious circle between currency depreciation and deteriorating economic performance, Thailand, Indonesia, and South Korea sought help from the International Monetary Fund (IMF) under very strict conditionality, including monetary and fiscal tightening, restructuring of financial institutions, better exposure of companies, and market opening. All three countries suffered sharp declines in output in 1998. The Indonesian economy shrank 13.2 percent in 1998, amid political turmoil that led to the resignation of President Suharto, who had ruled the country for more than thirty years. Malaysia did not turn to the IMF for a financial bailout but undertook IMF-sanctioned austerity measures such as the deferral of proposed megaprojects and reduced government spending. This virtual IMF program, however, failed to restore market confidence or revive economic growth, prompting the government to introduce a new approach in September 1998, centering on drastic capital controls. The Philippines weathered the crisis relatively smoothly, with only marginal decline in output, thanks to market confidence inspired by the IMF funding and programs that were still in force when the crisis hit its neighbors.

Singapore and Taiwan compose the group that allowed exchange rates to depreciate to stimulate exports. The pace of depreciation of their currencies was relatively moderate and under control. Both are net creditor countries and have maintained surpluses in their current accounts. In Taiwan, for example, currency depreciation during the Asian crisis can be interpreted as an attempt by the government to retain export competitiveness in the face of currency depreciation in its troubled neighbors. Taiwan has little foreign debt and immense foreign assets. Depreciation of the local currency therefore had little impact on the soundness of the country's financial system. In

Figure 2-6. *China and Japan as Sources of the U.S. Trade Deficit, 1988–99*

Billions of U.S. dollars

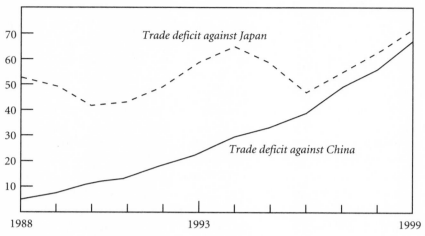

Source: U.S. Department of Commerce.

addition, Taiwan still maintained strict controls on capital flows, and the central bank had foreign exchange reserves amounting to nearly $90 billion (ten-months' import coverage) available to defend the NT dollar.

Throughout the Asian crisis, the Chinese yuan had stayed firm despite sharp depreciation in other Asian currencies. In addition to very tight controls on capital flows, which sheltered the Chinese currency from speculation, China avoided a devaluation for the following reasons. First, China's external balance was in good shape. Although exports slowed, so did imports, so that China's trade surplus stayed high. China's foreign exchange reserves had risen at a rapid pace since 1994, reaching $140 billion (equivalent to twelve months of imports) at the end of 1997, thanks to robust trade performance and massive inflow of foreign capital in the form of foreign direct investment. In contrast, China's foreign debt was at a low level compared with other Asian countries. Second, China ran a trade surplus with the United States ($49.7 billion in 1997, according to U.S. statistics), almost as large as that of Japan ($55.7 billion) for the same year (figure 2-6). A devaluation of the yuan would aggravate trade friction with the United States and delay China's entry into the World Trade Organization. Third, a devaluation of the yuan might spark another round of speculation on the Asian currencies that were still under pressure, including the Hong Kong dollar. This certainly would further delay the recovery of the regional economy, with negative effects on China itself. Politically, China would also have to take the blame for any adverse consequences on global financial markets. In contrast, by maintaining the value of its currency, China could strengthen its leadership in the region.

Thailand's shift to a managed floating system that triggered the currency crisis in Asia happened to take place one day after the return of Hong Kong to Chinese rule. Financial markets in Hong Kong at first were immune from the crisis, and the boom in the stock market continued. But speculation in the Hong Kong dollar escalated in late October: interest rates surged (with the overnight rate in the interbank market reaching 300 percent on October 23), and stock prices plummeted. But the Hong Kong dollar remained firm against the U.S. dollar. This episode confirmed the authorities' determination and ability to defend the dollar peg. To cope with possible attacks on the Hong Kong dollar, the authorities had accumulated foreign exchange reserves reaching $92.8 billion at the end of 1997, equivalent to 7.5 times the amount of Hong Kong dollars outstanding. Whether Hong Kong could maintain the dollar peg was widely viewed as a litmus test of whether the transition to Chinese sovereignty was a success. Leaders in both Hong Kong and China were thus extremely keen to avoid a devaluation. Sporadic attacks on the Hong Kong dollar continued into the summer of 1998, when the government was forced to support stock prices to fend off speculators using foreign exchange reserves.[13]

The Need for Regional Monetary Cooperation

The latest crisis clearly shows that Asian countries have a common interest in the financial stability of the region. Following the Mexican debt crisis in late 1994, there was growing recognition of the need to reinforce cooperation among monetary authorities in Asia.[14] Subsequent efforts, including com-

---

13. A widely used strategy of speculators during the crisis was to sell the Hong Kong dollar and stock futures simultaneously. To defend the Hong Kong dollar, the authorities had to raise interest rates, causing stock prices to decline. Speculators thus could profit from the stock futures market even when the Hong Kong dollar stayed firm.

14. The proposal by Governor Bernie Fraser of the Reserve Bank of Australia in September 1995 to establish an Asian version of the Bank for International Settlements was a good example. The proposed new institution was supposed to exchange information and experiences regarding international finance and monetary policies and to develop contingency plans to deal with international financial crises. It was also expected to offer a venue for sharing information and experience regarding supervision and surveillance of financial systems, as well as to provide central banking services (such as reserve management) to member central banks. Subsequently, some bilateral and multilateral agreements were reached among Asian central banks on mutual emergency financing with U.S. treasury bonds as collateral (so-called repo

mitments made to lend to each other using U.S. treasury bonds as collateral (repo agreements), proved helpless in coping with, let alone preventing, the latest Asian crisis. Additional coordinated efforts, preferably in the form of establishing a regional monetary fund, will be needed to prepare for a similar crisis in the region in the future.

In the wake of the Asian crisis, Japan proposed the establishment of an Asian Monetary Fund (AMF) to supplement the role of the IMF, with firmer commitments and more flexible rules. The AMF proposal is based on the recognition of the regional nature of currency crises, which calls for a regional response. Indeed, in recent years emergency financial support schemes for Mexico, Thailand, Indonesia, and South Korea were arranged on a regional basis. Instead of coping with financial crises on an ad hoc basis, it is more efficient to institutionalize such efforts in a formal framework, which may also play a positive role in crisis prevention.

Although the details of an AMF have yet to be worked out, the basic idea is to pool part of the foreign exchange reserves of Asian countries so they can provide each other with credit lines to cope with currency crises. By exploiting economies of scale, such a facility has the additional advantage of reducing the need for individual Asian countries to hold large foreign exchange reserves. Policy coordination among Asian authorities, including joint intervention in foreign exchange markets by Asian central banks, should also help alleviate the contagion effect of currency devaluation.[15]

The Asian countries have learned from the latest crisis that the amount of speculative capital is much larger than an individual country's foreign reserves for defending against a currency attack and that the IMF alone can no longer act as a lender of last resort for countries in trouble. Thailand, Indonesia, and South Korean had no choice but to seek help from the IMF when they were on the verge of running out of foreign exchange reserves. The response of the IMF in turn has been criticized as too little and too late. In addition, there has been rising doubt as to whether the conditionality

---

agreements). Japan also took steps to establish closer links with the monetary authorities of the Asian countries, including signing intervention agreements with Hong Kong and Singapore in February 1996 and repo agreements with seven Asian Pacific countries (Australia, Hong Kong, Indonesia, Malaysia, Philippines, Singapore, and Thailand) in April 1996. In addition, the first meeting among central bank governors from major countries in the Asia-Pacific region was held in July 1996.

15. Shinohara (1999) suggests that the mechanism for emergency support should include borrowing from member countries (similar to the IMF's General Agreement to Borrow), fund-raising through capital markets, and extending guarantees to member countries.

imposed by the IMF on borrowing countries based on fiscal and monetary austerity as well as financial liberalization and structural reform were appropriate for Asia's circumstances.[16]

On the other hand, critics—led by the U.S. government—are concerned that an AMF could undermine the role of the IMF and aggravate the moral hazard problems of countries seeking help.[17] The importance of moral hazard, however, has probably been exaggerated, as no country chooses to embarrass itself and suffer the indignity and pain of an IMF program voluntarily.[18] The relations between the Asian Development Bank and the World Bank also show that regional and global institutions can coexist and even complement one another. Indeed, a regional monetary fund can do a better job than the IMF, as it has a more focused mandate as well as greater regional expertise. Competition between the IMF and an AMF would likely result in more appropriate rather than more lenient conditionality attached to emergency loans, because if they lend recklessly they will soon run out of resources as borrowers default.

At first Japan was forced to withdraw the AMF initiative because of U.S. opposition and to accept the less ambitious Manila Framework (November 1997) as a compromise. The Manila Framework contains initiatives for regional surveillance, to complement global surveillance by the IMF, and enhancement of economic and technical cooperation, particularly to strengthen domestic financial systems and regulatory capacities. It also includes measures to strengthen the IMF's capacity to respond to financial crises (quota increase and the New Arrangement to Borrow) and a cooperative financial arrangement that would supplement IMF resources.

Efforts to further regional financial cooperation regained momentum in the summer of 1998, when the negative repercussions of the Asian crisis came to be felt in Wall Street, forcing the United States to change its stance. With U.S. sanction, Japan announced the New Miyazawa Initiative in

---

16. For critical reviews of the IMF's response to the Asian crisis, see Feldstein (1998); Jeffrey Sachs, "The Wrong Medicine for Asia," *New York Times,* November 3, 1997; Joseph Stiglitz, "The Insider: What I Learned at the World Economic Crisis," *New Republic,* April 17, 2000. Jomo (2001) reports on the issue from the perspective of the Asian countries hit by the crisis.

17. The United States is also concerned that it may not be invited to join. For example, Bergsten (1998) suggests that the idea for an AMF should be expanded to include the United States as a key member. Some Asian countries, however, worry that the United States may have much more influence in such an institution than the money it contributes, as in the case of the IMF.

18. Rose (1999). Ito (1999) notes that governments receiving financial support from the IMF usually fall, as in the case of Mexico, Thailand, Indonesia, and South Korea.

October 1998, committing $30 billion to help Asian countries weather the crisis. Furthermore, finance ministers of Japan, China, South Korea, and the ten members of ASEAN agreed in May 2000 to work toward a regional financing mechanism that involves bilateral agreements to swap official reserves with local currencies during times of crisis (the Chiang Mai Initiative). These swap arrangements represent looser terms for borrowers compared with the repo agreements signed before the crisis, as they need offer only local currencies (which their central banks can print in unlimited amount) instead of U.S. treasury bonds as collateral.

In the longer term an AMF should also aim at improving the efficiency of financial intermediation among Asian countries. Even excluding Japan, Asia's domestic savings exceed domestic investment. By running an aggregate current account surplus, the region acts as a net supplier of funds in international financial markets, although some of them (notably ASEAN members) remain net borrowers. Immense capital inflows, which have given the wrong impression that the region is heavily dependent on foreign savings, have actually been more than offset by the accumulation of foreign exchange reserves and private outflows. Since the bulk of the Asian countries' foreign exchange reserves is invested in dollar assets, U.S. treasury bonds in particular, "an unkind observer may say that the Asian central banks provided part of the liquidity to New York or London, which the hedge funds borrowed at cheap rates to play in the Asian markets."[19] Avoiding destabilizing round-tripping through financial markets in the West requires improving financial intermediation within the region. This in turn calls for both stabilizing exchange rates among Asian countries and strengthening such market infrastructures as regional credit rating agencies and currency settlement systems.

At a more general level, a chief lesson of the Asian crisis is that Asia was excessively dependent on financial institutions based in Washington, on the authorities of the United States, and on private (predominantly Anglo-Saxon) markets, which took their cues from both.[20] The "Washington consensus" guided the responses of all those crucial actors and therefore dictated policy requirements to the crisis countries.[21] Existing international

19. Yam (1997, p. 47). This observation—made by Joseph Yam, chief executive of the Hong Kong Monetary Authority, in a speech delivered in December 1995—seems to have been vindicated by the experience of the Asian crisis.

20. Bergsten (2000).

21. The term *Washington consensus* was first used by Williamson (1990) to refer to policy reforms he believed "Washington" would agree were needed in Latin America. These reforms include fiscal discipline; a redirection of public expenditure priorities toward fields offering

economic organizations such as the IMF and the World Bank have also failed to provide Asia with a role consistent with its economic progress. Viewed from this perspective, an AMF can be interpreted as an attempt by Asian countries to escape domination by Washington and to achieve financial independence.

The End of the East Asian Miracle?

Some commentators argue that the latest currency crisis in Asia may mark the end of the East Asian miracle, as "predicted" by Paul Krugman, but there are good reasons to remain optimistic about the future of the Asian economies.[22] While short-term economic growth largely depends on demand-side factors, long-term growth is determined mainly by supply-side considerations. Although the Asian countries suffered a deep recession following the crisis, high economic growth can still be achieved in the longer term. This is because the basic factors contributing to the East Asian miracle—high savings rates, heavy investment in human resources, and market-friendly stance of economic policy—have not changed with the latest shock.

Asian countries can achieve high growth rates even in the absence of net capital inflow (table 2-1). For example, Thailand's savings rate averaged 34.9 percent of gross domestic product (GDP) between 1991 and 1996, twice as high as that of Mexico. An additional net inflow of funds equivalent to 7.7 percent of GDP boosted gross capital formation (investment) to 42.6 percent of GDP and allowed Thailand to achieve a growth rate of 8.2 percent a year in the same period. If the relation between the investment ratio and GDP growth (that is, incremental capital-output ratio, or ICOR) remains unchanged at 5.2 (42.6 / 8.2), domestic savings alone should still be able to sustain economic growth at about 6.7 percent.

Relaxing some of the assumptions underlying this simulation favors higher growth rates in Asia. First, it is unlikely that net inflow of foreign capital will stop altogether. Direct investment that aims at utilizing the region as an offshore production base may actually increase to take advantage of

---

both high economic returns and the potential to improve income distribution, such as primary health care, primary education, and infrastructure; tax reform (to lower marginal rates and broaden the tax base); interest rate liberalization; a competitive exchange rate; trade liberalization; liberalization of foreign direct investment inflows; privatization; deregulation (in the sense of abolishing barriers to entry and exit); and secure property rights. However, in a sharp deviation from its original meaning, Washington consensus has been used more and more as a synonym for market fundamentalism.

22. Krugman (1994).

Table 2-1. Simulated GDP Growth in the Absence of Capital Inflow, Six Asian Countries, 1991–96

Country	Savings (S) (as a percent of GDP)	Capital inflow (F) (as a percent of GDP)	Investment (I = S + F) (as a percent of GDP)	GDP growth (G) (percent)	Incremental capital-output ratio (ICOR = I/G)	GDP growth in the absence of capital inflow (G' = S/ICOR) (percent)
Thailand	34.9	7.7	42.6	8.2	5.2	6.7
Malaysia	35.0	6.5	41.5	9.0	4.6	7.5
Indonesia	32.1	2.6	34.7	7.8	4.4	7.2
Philippines	19.0	3.2	22.2	2.8	8.1	2.4
South Korea	35.4	1.5	36.9	7.4	5.0	7.1
China	40.1	-1.0	39.2	11.5	3.4	11.7

Source: Compiled by Nomura Research Institute based on ADB, Asian Development Outlook, 1997 and 1998.

weaker currencies (and thus lower production costs in dollar terms). Second, investment efficiency should improve (and the ICOR should fall), as white elephant projects financed by foreign capital come to a halt. Finally, savings rates may actually increase as lower asset prices suppress consumption, reversing the negative effect of rising asset prices on the savings rates during the bubble period.

3

Deepening Japan-Asia Interdependence

The trend toward deepening economic interdependence in Asia has accelerated since the global realignment of exchange rates in the latter half of the 1980s. The increase in foreign direct investment among Asian countries and the integration of China into the regional economy have boosted intraregional trade at the expense of exports to the United States. At the same time, Asian countries' pace of industrialization has gathered momentum, with manufactured goods now accounting for the bulk of their exports. Taking advantage of Asia's dynamism, the axis of Japan's foreign economic relations is shifting from the United States to Asia. Although this trend was interrupted by the crisis in Asia, it has resumed since 1999.

These recent changes in the direction of trade and investment have strong implications for the pattern of macroeconomic interdependence between Japan and its Asian neighbors. First, the yen-dollar rate has replaced economic growth in the United States as the major factor determining short-term economic growth in Asia, which tends to increase as the yen appreciates and decrease as the yen depreciates. Second, reflecting this income effect, Japanese exports to the region tend to increase with a stronger yen and decrease with a weaker yen. Finally, in the long term Japan has benefited from the rise of Asia in the form of an improvement in Japan's terms of trade. The relocation of declining industries to Asia through foreign direct investment also helps upgrade Japan's industrial structure. This process should be distinguished from the hollowing-out problem resulting from domestic distortions that impede productivity growth.

The Yen-Dollar Rate and Asian Economic Growth

With their currencies loosely pegged to the U.S. dollar, fluctuations in the yen-dollar rate have led to macroeconomic instability in Asia's developing countries. When the yen appreciates against the dollar, for example, it also appreciates against Asian currencies. By altering the relative prices between Japan and other Asian countries, the changing yen-dollar rate has immense impact on international trade and investment flows as well as on the burden of debt repayment in the countries concerned. In general, higher income countries with trade structures competitive with that of Japan are more likely to benefit from a stronger yen (and to be hurt by a weaker yen) than lower income countries with trade structures complementary to that of Japan.

Correlation and Causality

Fluctuations in the yen-dollar rate have replaced the U.S. economic growth rate as the major factor determining short-term macroeconomic performance in Asian countries since the Plaza Accord in 1985. Every time the yen appreciates against the dollar, the economic growth rate in Asia (outside Japan) picks up, as happened between 1986 and 1988 and again between 1991 and 1995 (figure 3-1).[1] These periods were also accompanied by an expansion of the bubble economy, with asset prices rising sharply. The reverse is true when economic growth in Asia decelerated and the asset price bubble burst on the back of a weaker yen between 1989 and 1990 and again between 1996 and 1998. The slowdown in Asian economic growth during the latter episode, which had become apparent even before the currency crisis, actually took place against a background of robust growth in the United States. Symmetrically, the rebound of the yen since the autumn of 1998 (from a bottom of 147 yen to a dollar) was followed by rising stock prices, falling interest rates, stabilizing exchange rates, and a resumption of economic growth in Asia's developing countries.

The relation between the yen-dollar rate and Asian economic growth can be confirmed by the method of simple regression (table 3-1). A 1 percent appreciation (depreciation) of the yen against the dollar tends to raise

1. The exchange rates of Asian currencies can be ignored here because under the dollar peg system they follow closely the yen-dollar rate.

Figure 3-1. *The Yen-Dollar Rate and Short-Term Asian Economic Growth, 1982–99*[a]

Percent change from previous year

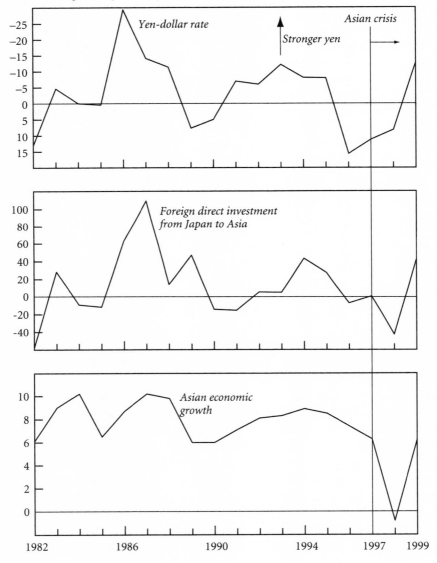

Source: Compiled by Nomura Research Institute based on official statistics of countries concerned.

a. Asia = NIEs + ASEAN + China. Figures for foreign direct investment from Japan to Asia correspond to fiscal year.

Table 3-1. *Major Determinants of Asian GDP Growth, 1982–97*[a]

U.S. GDP growth	Yen-dollar rate		*Adjusted R²*	*Durbin-Watson statistic*
	Current	*Lagged one year*		
0.39 (2.42)	...	...	0.245	1.576
...	−0.077 (−3.00)	...	0.347	1.799
...	−0.066 (−2.61)	−0.043 (−1.60)	0.413	1.668
0.33 (2.60)	−0.069 (−3.15)	...	0.539	1.822
0.32 (2.71)	−0.059 (−2.82)	−0.040 (−1.80)	0.606	1.691

Source: Kwan (1998a).

a. Dependent (Asian GDP growth) and independent variables (U.S. GDP growth and yen-dollar rate) are measured in terms of rate of change so that the coefficients correspond to elasticities. Since a larger number for the yen-dollar rate denotes a weaker yen, the negative coefficients show the negative impact of a weaker yen (or the positive impact of a stronger yen) on Asian economic growth. Figures in parentheses denote *t*-values.

(reduce) GDP in Asia by 0.109 percent (0.066 percent in the current year, and 0.043 percent in the following year). The yen-dollar rate alone explains 41.3 percent of Asian economic growth in terms of adjusted R^2. When the U.S. economic growth rate is also included as an independent variable, the explanatory power increases to 60.6 percent in terms of adjusted R^2, although the elasticity drops marginally to 0.099 percent (0.059 percent in the current year and 0.040 percent in the following year).

A weaker yen affects economic growth in Asian economies mainly through the following five channels: a slowdown in foreign direct investment from Japan, a decline in the lending capability of Japanese banks, a decline in export competitiveness against Japanese products, a decline in the cost of imports from Japan, and a decline in the cost of financing yen-denominated external debt. While the effects of the first three factors on Asian economies are negative, they are partly offset (and in some cases more than-offset) by the positive effects of the last two factors. (By symmetry, the impact of a stronger yen can be easily derived as the opposite of a weaker yen.)

First, a weaker yen lowers investment from Japan to Asia. With the cost of production in Japan relative to that in Asian countries falling, the incentive for Japanese companies to relocate production facilities overseas is reduced.

The resulting slowdown of foreign direct investment has the effect of depressing the Asian economies not only on the demand side but also on the supply side.

Second, the capital adequacy ratios of Japanese banks decline as the yen depreciates, so that they have less room to expand overseas lending. The capital adequacy ratio (also known as the BIS ratio) is defined as the ratio between capital and risk assets, and international banks are required to maintain this ratio at a minimum level of 8 percent. For Japanese banks, although their capital is denominated in yen, 80 percent of their overseas lending (which forms about 30 percent of their risk assets, the rest being domestic lending) is denominated in dollars. A weaker yen reduces the capital adequacy ratio by increasing the value of risk assets (the denominator) in yen terms. Other things being equal, Japanese banks need to reduce lending either at home or abroad in order to meet the capital adequacy requirement. A depreciation of the yen by one yen against the dollar is estimated to reduce the capability of Japanese banks to lend by one trillion yen (about $10 billion).[2]

Third, a depreciation of the yen against the dollar, by reducing Japanese export prices in dollar terms, makes Japanese exports less expensive relative to those of Asian countries. As a result, the competitiveness of Asian exports against Japanese products in international markets deteriorates. This is particularly true for higher income countries that have trade structures similar to that of Japan.

Fourth, on the positive side, a weaker yen reduces import prices in Asian countries, as they are heavily dependent on Japan as a source of capital and intermediate goods. Lower import prices, which usually mean lower input prices, in turn boost profits and output for Asian countries.

Fifth, a depreciation of the yen reduces the burden of debt repayment of the Asian countries. The positive impact on economic growth is proportional to the size of external debt denominated in yen. Since the bulk of Asian countries' yen-denominated debt is in the form of official development assistance from the Japanese government, poorer countries are more likely to benefit. By symmetry, the same countries suffer a higher burden of repayment in dollar terms when the yen appreciates.

Among these five transmission channels, the shift in export competitiveness is probably the most important in the short run. Korean export growth, for example, accelerates every time the yen strengthens and slows down

2. Koo (1998).

Figure 3-2. *Korean Export Performance and the Yen-Dollar Rate, 1981–99*

Percent change from previous year

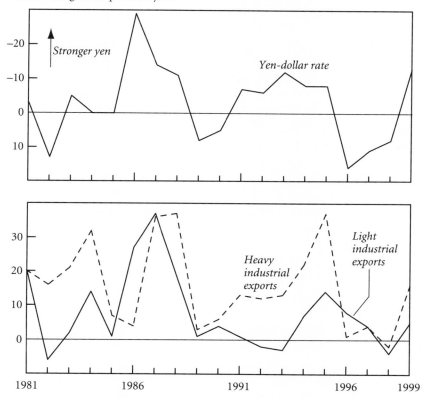

Source: Compiled by Nomura Research Institute based on Korean trade statistics.

every time the yen weakens (figure 3-2). This pattern is particularly apparent for heavy industrial products, not so much because they are dependent on the Japanese market as because of their keen competition with Japanese products in international markets. The emergence of a global market implies that the commodity composition of trade (and thus the degree of competition with Japan) is more important than the regional composition of trade (dependence on Japan as a market) in determining the impact of the yen-dollar rate on Asian exports. Although it is very difficult to find Korean cars in Tokyo, the short-term performance of Korea's automobile industry correlates strongly with the yen-dollar rate.

Competitive versus Complementary Trade Relations with Japan

A weaker yen is more likely to dampen economic growth in countries with trade structures competitive with Japan's as the negative effect of a decline in export competitiveness tends to dominate the positive effect of lower import prices (box 3-1). The reverse may be true for countries with trade structures complementary to that of Japan. With Japan importing labor-intensive products and exporting capital-intensive ones, countries with similar trade structures (South Korea, for example) have competitive relations with Japan. On the other hand, countries importing capital-intensive products while exporting labor-intensive ones (such as China) have complementary relations with Japan.

The degree of competition or complementarity between two countries can be calculated as the correlation coefficient between the vectors showing the trade structures (broken down by industry) of import-export trade of the two countries concerned. The result confirms that higher income countries, such as the Asian NIEs, have trade structures in competition with that of Japan, while lower income countries, such as members of ASEAN and China, have trade structures complementary to that of Japan (figure 3-3).

In the case of South Korea, whose exports have come to be dominated by capital- and technology-intensive products, economic relations with Japan can be characterized as competitive rather than complementary. When the yen depreciates, imports from Japan (parts and components, capital goods, and so on) become cheaper in dollar terms. Since export prices of Japanese competitors also decrease as a result of a weaker yen, however, Korean exporters are forced to reduce export prices even more so that the country's terms of trade tend to deteriorate as the yen depreciates (figure 3-4). For a very open economy like South Korea, export prices come close to output prices while import prices make up a large portion of the cost of input. A deterioration in the terms of trade thus usually implies a decrease in corporate earnings (or profitability) at the microeconomic level, with negative impact on economic growth.[3]

In contrast, in the case of Indonesia, which imports machinery from Japan to drill oil, the trade relations with Japan can be characterized as complementary rather than competitive. Although a depreciation of the yen

---

3. Symmetrically, Korean exporters can easily translate higher import prices into even higher export prices as the yen appreciates. As a result, the country's terms of trade improve, with positive effect on corporate profits and economic growth.

means cheaper imports from Japan and thus lower cost of production, it does not necessarily mean lower prices of oil (both in dollar terms). As a result, at the macroeconomic level its terms of trade improve, while at the microeconomic level corporate earnings increase with a weaker yen.

Like Indonesia, China also has complementary trade relations with Japan and thus is likely to be hurt by a stronger yen rather than by a weaker yen. Depreciation of the yen does not necessarily reduce China's export competitiveness, because the commodity mix of its exports (dominated by labor-intensive products) is very much different from that of Japan's exports (dominated by high-technology products). China may suffer some decline in the inflow of foreign direct investment from Japan as the yen depreciates, but even this will be minimal because Japanese companies have come to look at China more as a market than as an offshore production base. Rather, with a weaker yen, China enjoys lower prices of imports from Japan and a lower burden of financing its yen-denominated debt. Thus a weakening yen is more likely to benefit than to hurt China's balance of payments and, by extension, should act as a factor supporting rather than depressing the Chinese currency. This conclusion is in sharp contrast to the claim by Chinese officials during the Asian crisis that the yen's sharp depreciation put downward pressure on the yuan.

The degree of competition and complementarity between an Asian country and Japan can change sharply over time, as the experience of Malaysia vividly illustrates. Thanks to a large inflow of foreign direct investment since the late 1980s, Malaysia transformed itself from a developing country heavily dependent on exports of primary commodities to a newly industrializing economy highly competitive in manufacturing. Primary commodities as a share of total Malaysian exports dropped from about 70 percent in the mid-1980s to about 30 percent by the mid-1990s, while that of manufactured goods rose from 30 percent to 70 percent. Malaysia became better positioned to benefit in terms of stronger exports when the yen appreciated sharply during the first half of the 1990s. Indeed, led by electronics products, Malaysia's exports surged between 1993 and 1995, pushing economic growth to an annual rate of 9 percent. This contrasted sharply with the situation during the previous strong yen period, when Malaysia suffered two consecutive years of zero growth in 1985 and 1986.

Asia as a Major Determinant of Japanese Economic Performance

With its ties to Asia strengthening, Japan's economic fortune increasingly hinges on the future of the region. In the short run, exports to Asia act as a

Box 3-1. *Trade Repercussions of a Weaker Yen*

As the yen depreciates, Japanese export prices decline in dollar terms. For an Asian country that pegs its currency to the dollar, this implies a deterioration in their export competitiveness against Japanese products on the demand side and falling cost of production on the supply side.

This situation can be analyzed using the standard supply-demand diagram, with domestic prices (measured in local currency terms; or equivalently, in dollar terms under the dollar peg system) on the vertical axis and output on the horizontal axis.

Loss in export competitiveness is represented by a leftward shift in the downward-sloping demand curve, as overseas demand is diverted to cheaper Japanese products, reducing both output and the domestic price level. Fall in import prices (of intermediate inputs) is represented by a rightward shift in the upward-sloping supply curve (the marginal cost curve), resulting in an increase in output but a decrease in the domestic price level. Since the shifts in the demand and supply curves have opposite implications for output, the final outcome depends on the relative magnitude of these two forces.

For a country that competes directly with Japan but imports little from it, the shift in the demand curve is more significant than that in the supply curve, and output shrinks as the yen depreciates. In contrast, for a country that competes little with Japan but is heavily dependent on imports from it, the positive supply-side effect dominates and output increases. In both cases, a depreciation of the yen drags down the domestic price level.

built-in stabilizer for total Japanese exports. In the long run, the catching-up of Asia affects Japan's real income and comparative advantage by altering its terms of trade.

Japan's Strengthening Ties with Asia

Japan's international trade and investment have become increasingly oriented toward Asia since the mid-1980s. This has taken place against a background of rising trade friction with the United States (push factor) and the rapid pace of economic growth in the Asian economies (pull factor).

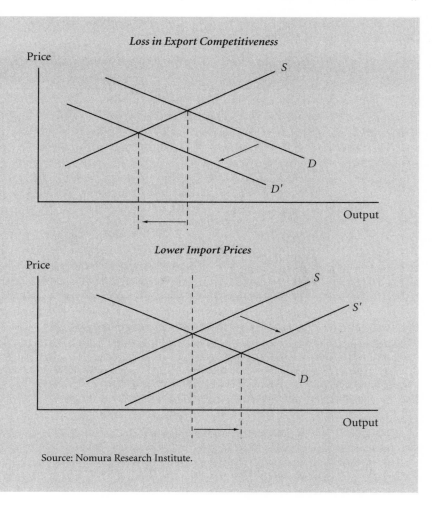

Source: Nomura Research Institute.

Despite a tactical retreat during the Asian crisis, the Asianization of the Japanese economy is likely to continue.

The appreciation of the yen since the 1985 Plaza Accord has prompted Japanese companies to move production facilities to Asia to take advantage of lower production cost. Led by electronics companies, headquarters of Japanese manufacturers specialize in high value-added products and research and development, while subsidiaries in Asian countries are taking over the manufacturing of standardized products. In the first half of the 1990s, with the income level in Asia rising, Japanese companies tended to

Figure 3-3. *Competitiveness and Complementarity between Japan and Other Asian Countries, 1999*[a]

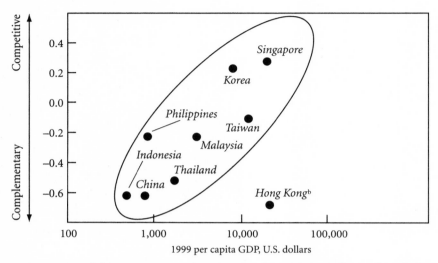

Source: Compiled by Nomura Research Institute based on ADB, *Key Indicators of Developing Asia and Pacific Countries,* supplemented by trade statistics of individual countries.

a. The degree of competition between an Asian country and Japan is calculated as the correlation coefficient between their respective vectors showing the specialization indexes ([exports − imports] / [exports + imports]) of major categories of manufactured goods. To focus on competition in the manufacturing sector, a four-category classification comprising chemicals and related products (SITC section 5), manufactured goods classified chiefly by material (SITC section 6), machinery and transport equipment (SITC section 7), and miscellaneous manufactured articles (SITC section 8) is used.

b. The specialization indexes for Hong Kong, and thus its degree of competition with Japan, have been distorted by the presence of reexport trade.

emphasize the region more as a market in itself than as an export platform. This was particularly true for Japanese investment in China, which surged more than ten times between 1990 and 1995.

Japanese subsidiaries in Asia suffered a major setback during the Asian crisis when most Asian currencies tumbled against the dollar and demand declined throughout the region, forcing them to curtail production and investment. Among them, those aiming to develop local markets were hurt worse than those using the region as an export platform, which benefited from an improvement in their competitiveness in international markets as the Asian currencies depreciated. Those with large borrowing

Figure 3-4. *The Yen-Dollar Rate and Korea's Terms of Trade, 1980–99*[a]

Percent change from previous year

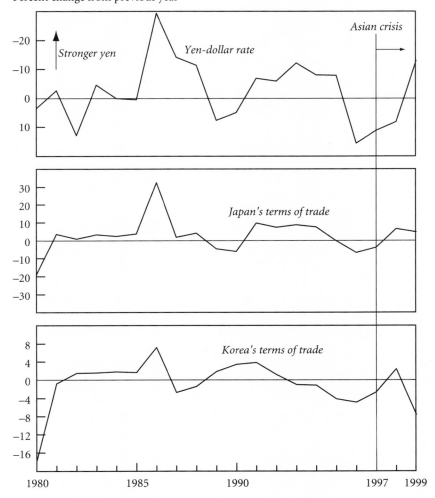

Source: Compiled by Nomura Research Institute based on official statistics.
a. Terms of trade = export prices/import prices.

in foreign currencies and heavily dependent on imported intermediate goods also had to face a higher debt burden and rising input costs in local currency terms.

With most Asian countries recovering strongly from the crisis since 1999, however, Japanese investment in the region is expected to pick up again.

China's entry into the World Trade Organization will also offer Japanese companies new investment opportunities.[4] Indeed, led by China, major ASEAN countries (Thailand, Indonesia, Malaysia, Vietnam, the Philippines), Taiwan, South Korea, and India continue to rank among the top ten most promising destinations for Japanese investment.[5]

Asia has also grown in importance as Japan's trading partner. The Asian NIEs, the ASEAN countries, and China together now account for about 40 percent of Japanese trade on both the export side and the import side, far exceeding the corresponding shares of the United States (figures 3-5 and 3-6). Rising Japanese investment in Asia since the mid-1980s has led to a rapid increase in two-way trade. At first, the investment boom was accompanied by a sharp rise in Japanese exports of capital goods and intermediate goods to, and a widening of Japan's trade surplus with, Asia. Subsequently, Japanese subsidiaries in Asia have expanded their exports back to Japan, while Japanese manufacturers of parts and components have set up more production facilities in Asia, substituting exports from Japan with local production. As a result, the bilateral trade imbalance started to fall in the mid-1990s, a trend that was aggravated by the sharp slowdown in Asian economic growth during the 1997–98 crisis.

Meanwhile, manufactured goods have come to make up a larger share of Japanese imports from the region. This, in addition to the increase in imports of both intermediate and finished goods from Japanese subsidiaries, also reflects the progress in industrialization in the Asian countries. In particular, manufactured goods as a percentage of Japanese imports from China have risen from less than 30 percent in the mid-1980s to more than 80 percent now (figure 3-7). The traditional trade relation between Japan and Asia characterized by a vertical division of labor, with Asia specializing in primary commodities and Japan specializing in manufactured goods, has given way to one dominated by intra-industry trade.

---

4. Other things being equal, China's entry into the World Trade Organization should encourage a division of labor in the manufacturing sector between China and the rest of the world according to comparative advantage and favor investment in its export sector. Foreign investment in China may actually decline in areas that can be substituted for by trade as import tariffs are sharply reduced. To penetrate the Chinese market, Japanese automakers, for example, would from now on prefer to ship from their headquarters instead of producing locally.

5. Japan Bank for International Cooperation, "JBIC FY2000 Survey: The Outlook of Japanese Investment."

Figure 3-5. *Japanese Exports, by Region, 1985–2000*

Percent

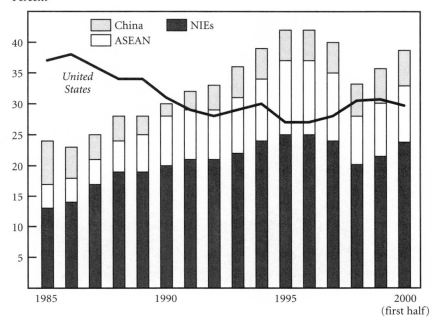

Source: Compiled by Nomura Research Institute based on Japanese trade statistics.

Asia as a Stabilizer for Japanese Exports

With Asia replacing the United States as Japan's largest overseas market, exports to the region now hold the key to overall performance of Japanese exports. It has been observed that Japanese exports to Asia tend to accelerate as the yen appreciates and to decelerate as the yen depreciates, in contrast to standard economic theory that predicts the opposite pattern. This paradoxical relation between the yen-dollar rate and Japanese exports to Asia can be explained by examining first the link between the yen-dollar rate and Asian exports and then the link between Asian exports and Japanese exports to the Asia. As discussed above, to one extent or another the Asian countries are competitors of Japan in international markets, and their currencies are loosely pegged to the dollar. An appreciation of the yen, by driving up Japanese export prices in dollar terms, boosts Asian exports not only to Japan but also to other countries. On the other hand, to expand

Figure 3-6. *Japanese Imports, by Region, 1985–2000*

Percent

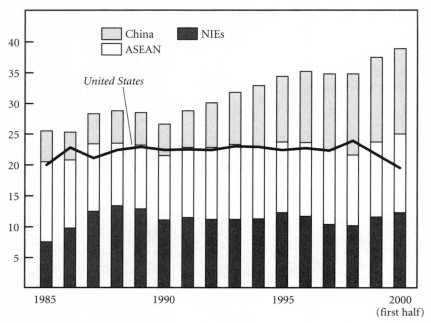

Source: Compiled by Nomura Research Institute based on Japanese trade statistics.

exports, these countries have to import more capital and intermediate goods (including parts and components) from Japan. This reflects the high degree of complementarity between Japanese exports and Asian imports. An appreciation of the yen therefore boosts Japanese exports to Asia indirectly through this income effect. Symmetrically, a weaker yen reduces Japanese exports to Asia by dragging down economic growth in the importing countries.

Theoretically, an appreciation of the yen should curb Japanese exports to Asia by driving up their prices in dollar terms, but the negative price effect here is very small. This is because the Asian countries' imports from Japan are composed mainly of intermediate goods that are difficult to replace by alternative sources. Thus the (indirect) income effect through stronger economic growth in Asia dominates the negative price effect.

This logic can be illustrated by looking at the competitive-complementary relations between Japanese and Korean automakers. When the yen

Figure 3-7. *Share of Japanese Imports of Manufactured Goods,*
by Importing Region, 1985–99[a]

Percent

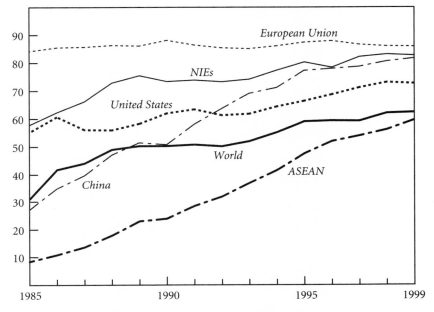

Source: Japanese Ministry of International Trade and Industry.
a. Manufactured imports as a percentage of total imports from the region concerned.

appreciates, Japan's Toyota loses its market share in the global market to
Korea's Hyundai. But since Hyundai uses engines made by Japan's Mitsubishi, expansion of Hyundai's car exports leads to more exports of Mitsubishi's engines to Korea. This pattern applies not only to the automobile
industry but to other assembling industries as well.

As a reflection of this relation, Japanese exports tend to shift from the
United States and Europe to Asia when the yen is strong and to shift back to
the United States and Europe when the yen is weak.[6] This explains why Asia's
share of Japanese exports shows strong positive correlation with the strength

6. When the yen is strong (weak), the reduction (increase) in Japanese exports to Europe
and the United States is mainly in finished products, while the increase (reduction) in exports
to Asia is largely in intermediate products.

Figure 3-8. *The Yen-Dollar Rate and Asia's Share of Japanese Exports, 1982–2000*

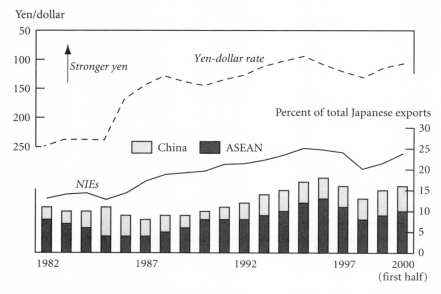

Source: Compiled by Nomura Research Institute based on Japanese trade statistics and IMF, *International Financial Statistics*.

of the yen against the dollar (figure 3-8).[7] When applied to the situation since the autumn of 1998, it is no exaggeration to say that Japanese exports to Asia have been increasing not despite but because of the yen's rebound. In this way, exports to Asia serve as a built-in stabilizer for Japan's total exports, partly offsetting the decline (increase) in exports to the United States and Europe when the yen is strong (weak).

The Rise of Asia and Japan's Terms of Trade

Over the long term, the catching-up of Asia is changing Japan's comparative advantage in international trade. Should the market mechanism function efficiently, full employment in Japan can be maintained as the wage rate adjusts and resources (labor and capital) shift from one sector to another. In

7. This correlation, which applied only to the Asian NIEs in the 1980s, has become apparent since the early 1990s for the ASEAN countries and China, reflecting rising Japanese investment and progress in industrialization in these countries.

this case, the impact on real income acts mainly through changes in the terms of trade. Other things being equal, an improvement in the terms of trade raises real income. Whether Japan's terms of trade will improve or deteriorate depends on whether the countries concerned have trade structures that are complementary to, or competitive with, that of Japan.[8]

Economic growth in countries with trade structures that complement Japan's is likely to improve the terms of trade for Japan. China's industrialization, for example, increases the supply of labor-intensive goods (Japan's importable goods) while raising the demand for capital-intensive goods (Japan's exportable goods) in global markets. This leads to a decline in the prices of labor-intensive goods relative to capital-intensive goods, which implies an improvement in Japan's terms of trade.

In contrast, economic growth in countries with trade structures that compete with Japan's is likely to worsen Japan's terms of trade. Thus South Korea's rising exports of capital-intensive goods (Japan's exportable goods) and imports of labor-intensive products (Japan's importable goods) should lead to a decline in the price of the former relative to the latter, resulting in a deterioration in both Korea's and Japan's terms of trade.

Indeed, Japan's terms of trade have improved sharply since the 1980s on the back of the yen's appreciation, suggesting that on the whole the catching-up of the Asian countries has had a positive rather than negative effect on Japan's real income (figure 3-9).[9] Within this framework, the yen's appreciation can be interpreted as a process in which the improvement in Japan's terms of trade is realized while maintaining domestic price stability. At the same time, the improvement in the terms of trade also provides Japanese companies an incentive to relocate resources (capital and labor) from the importable sector to the exportable sector, where Japan's comparative advantage lies.

---

8. The analysis here is based on the recognition that Asia's developing countries as a group are big enough to have an impact on international prices, although the small-country assumption may apply to most of them individually.

9. The concept of complementarity versus competition with Japan has been used to analyze both the impact of a stronger (weaker) yen on Asia and the impact of the emergence of Asia on Japan's terms of trade. I argue that in the former case the competitive aspect dominates, so that the overall effect of a stronger (weaker) yen on Asia is a positive (negative) one, and that in the latter case the complementary aspect dominates, so that the overall impact of rising output in Asia on Japan's terms of trade is positive. These two conclusions do not contradict one another as long as countries with trade structures competing with Japan have a higher share of Asia as a group in terms of trade volume (to be consistent with the former case), while countries with trade structures complementary to that of Japan are growing much faster (to be consistent with the latter case).

Figure 3-9. *The Yen-Dollar Rate and Japan's Terms of Trade, 1978–99*

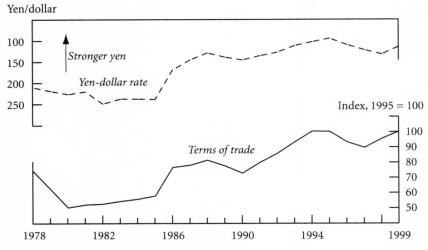

Source: Compiled by Nomura Research Institute based on Japanese trade statistics.

In the long run, the catching-up of the Asian countries may come to have a negative effect on Japan's terms of trade as they achieve a higher level of industrialization and their trade structures become more competitive with that of Japan. As the experience of Japan itself suggests, however, productivity growth in a developing country usually slows as its technology gap with the industrial countries narrows. Indeed, economic growth in the Asian NIEs has moderated since the early 1990s, and growth of manufactured imports into Japan has come to be led by China and the ASEAN countries.

Japan's Hollowing-Out Problem

Until the onset of the latest economic crisis in Asia, there had been much concern that growing competition with Asia might lead to a hollowing out of Japan's industry. Subsequent developments, however, clearly show that it is in Japan's national interest to be surrounded by prosperous and peaceful countries rather than by poor and unstable ones.[10]

10. This section is based on Kwan (1997).

The Extent of the Problem

The term *the hollowing out of industry,* as used in Japan, usually refers to rising unemployment and the weakening technology base resulting from the globalization of corporate activities. The rising scale of production activity by Japanese companies overseas is usually cited as an indicator of the seriousness of the hollowing-out problem. Overseas production of Japanese manufacturers amounted to ¥54.9 trillion in fiscal year 1999, with Asia accounting for ¥16.5 trillion.[11] The overseas production ratio of Japan's manufacturing sector (overseas production divided by domestic production) rose to a historically high level of 14.1 percent in fiscal year 1999, which was about half the corresponding level for the United States and Germany.

At the same time, deindustrialization is also often interpreted as a symptom of hollowing out in Japan. Manufacturing's share of GDP in Japan declined from a peak of 37.5 percent in 1970 to 22.6 percent in 1998. There have been two episodes of sharp decline in this ratio, one following the first oil crisis in 1973 and another accompanying the collapse of the bubble economy in the early 1990s. A similar long-term declining trend in the importance of the manufacturing sector has been observed in other major industrial countries. For example, the manufacturing sector's share of GDP in the United States is now down to 18 percent. The latest figure for Japan corresponds to the level in the United States in the early 1980s. Rather than lamenting the relative shrinking of the manufacturing sector as a symptom of hollowing out, Japan should worry that it has lagged behind other industrial countries in the transition to a service-based economy. The opportunity cost of Japan's maintaining an excessively large manufacturing sector may be high, given the rapid pace of progress in other advanced countries toward a society based on information technology.

Although the concern over Japan's hollowing out problem has not been backed by evidence (at least not at the macroeconomic level), it has persisted for several reasons. First, the benefits from the globalization of business activities are diffused (among many consumers, for example), while the costs (such as unemployment) are highly concentrated in specific industries and localities. Second, given Japan's success in transforming itself in the last postwar period from a developing country into an economic power

11. MITI, *Survey of Overseas Business Activity,* June 2000.

based on the expansion of manufactured exports, most Japanese fail to recognize the positive aspects of deindustrialization and confuse it with economic decline. Third, with the economic recession lingering, it is convenient to blame foreign countries for rising unemployment and falling investment at home.

Industrial Upgrading without Hollowing Out

Japan's economic growth has stagnated since the early 1990s, but this should be attributed largely to domestic rather than international factors (see chapter 5). Japanese companies usually move overseas to take advantage of higher rates of return abroad than at home, reflecting the differential in the (marginal) productivity of capital. If foreign direct investment is induced by an increase in foreign productivity, both Japan and the recipient countries benefit because they have a larger pie to share. On the other hand, if it is the result of a decline in Japanese productivity, foreign direct investment would be accompanied by a decline in Japanese national income. The real causes of hollowing out should therefore be found in various domestic distortions hindering productivity growth, including regulations that raise the cost of production and those that prevent the relocation of resources from declining industries to emerging ones.[12]

To achieve a more sophisticated industrial structure while avoiding hollowing out, Japan needs to facilitate the relocation of its industries that have lost their competitive edge to developing countries rather than use high tariff barriers to protect them. Such a process of positive structural adjustment should contribute not only to the economic growth of less developed countries but also to Japan's own industrial upgrading. It goes without saying that the only way to avoid the hollowing out of industry is to cultivate growth in new fields. From the long-term viewpoint, transferring declining industries overseas will release resources for the advancement of domestic industry, and the relocation of resources into high-technology and high value-added fields will increase the overall efficiency of domestic production. Japan should take the following recommendations into consideration in order to maximize the benefit from the globalization of business activities.

First, Japan needs to look beyond the manufacturing sector for new fields of growth to replace those industries that are being relocated overseas. The potential of the service sector, especially its capacity to create employment

---

12. In addition, foreign distortions likely to contribute to hollowing out include excessive exchange rate volatility and industrial policies that combine protection against imports with preferential treatments for foreign investors.

opportunities, should not be neglected. As the experience of the United States vividly illustrates, deindustrialization and the transition to a service-oriented economy accompany economic advancement and should be distinguished from the hollowing out of industry. Japan's efforts should not be confined to the conventional manufacturing industry but should take advantage of innovations in information technology and the growing importance of software and networking in economic activities. Productivity in Japan's service industry is still low in comparison with other industrialized countries, and there is much scope for improvement as deregulation proceeds. Regulations that obstruct new entry and competition should be relaxed in order to establish an environment conducive to the entry of new industries. Measures must be taken also to ensure that labor and other factors of production are able to move smoothly into new industries without being tied to the declining ones.

Second, because a nation's economic power depends more on its gross national product (GNP) than its gross domestic product (GDP), the stagnation of domestic production in a creditor nation such as Japan does not necessarily mean a decline in its standard of living. As the proportion of overseas production increases, Japanese companies should evaluate profitability on a consolidated basis that includes overseas operations, rather than only in terms of operations at home. Japan is almost certain to experience a lowering of its savings rate and growth potential as the aging of its population progresses, leading to a deficit in Japan's trade balance. Keeping the current account balance in the black would have to rely on the returns (interest income, dividends, and profits) generated by overseas assets built up thus far.

Finally, when formulating its foreign economic policy, Japan should abandon the mercantilist view that production and exports are good while consumption is bad. Direct investment overseas and the deregulation of imports will benefit both Japanese companies and consumers. Japan's terms of trade will improve as the costs of production and imports are reduced. The linkage between headquarters and overseas subsidiaries should be strengthened. Forward linkages include research and development and the export of components to support overseas production. Backward linkages include the sale of products from overseas branches and the reverse import of components produced overseas. In an optimal division of labor across national borders it is necessary to ensure that the profits acquired overseas are able to flow smoothly back into domestic research and development. This may require implementing such measures as tax incentives. Inward direct investment should also be promoted to help establish new fields. Foreign companies investing in Japan do not simply provide technology and management resources, they can also be expected to promote competition.

If the Asian countries succeed in maintaining their high pace of economic development, Japan's exports to the region will continue to increase, which will not only support the growth of Japan's economy from the demand side but also contribute to political stability in Asia, enhancing Japan's national security. The ultimate goals of the flying geese pattern of economic development are the convergence of all nations in the region to the standards of living enjoyed by industrialized countries and the development of a horizontal division of labor among Asian nations. The per capita GNP of the NIEs has already reached the level of member countries of the Organization for Economic Cooperation and Development (OECD), and the era of Japan as the only industrialized country in Asia has ended. However, a lower relative position for Japan's economy does not necessarily mean an absolute decline in its economic power. Trade and direct investment are by no means zero-sum games, and it is possible for all the economies in the region to benefit by enlarging the size of the pie.[13] The pursuit of a "prosper thy neighbor" policy has become all the more important now that the Asian economies need to further cooperation to overcome the crisis.[14]

13. MacDougall (1958).
14. See Mahathir (1997) for the phrase "prosper thy neighbor."

4

Asia in Search of a New Exchange Rate Regime

In the summer of 1997, amid intense currency attacks by speculators, many developing Asian countries were forced to abandon their traditional dollar peg system and allow their exchange rates to float. After a period of sharp depreciation accompanied by high volatility, in the autumn of 1998 exchange rates in these countries bottomed out against the U.S. dollar, thanks to the yen's rebound and a return of confidence in the economic prospects of these countries. However (with the notable exception of the Malaysian ringgit), these currencies have not restored their stability against the U.S. dollar seen before the crisis (figure 4-1). With the dust now settling, it is the right time to explore what should be done about the exchange rate system, in order to restore stable economic growth.

The latest currency crisis in Asia has raised a number of important questions relating to exchange rate management: Why has the dollar peg system, which seemed to have served Asian countries so well in the past, become so vulnerable? Is the delinking of Asian currencies from the U.S. dollar just an emergency measure, which should be reversed once the crisis is over? Finally, if the dollar peg system should be abandoned sooner rather than later, what are the alternatives? This chapter seeks to answer these questions by applying the tools of economic analysis to the current circumstances of Asian countries.

Figure 4-1. *Exchange Rates of Asian Currencies against the U.S. Dollar, 1995–2000*

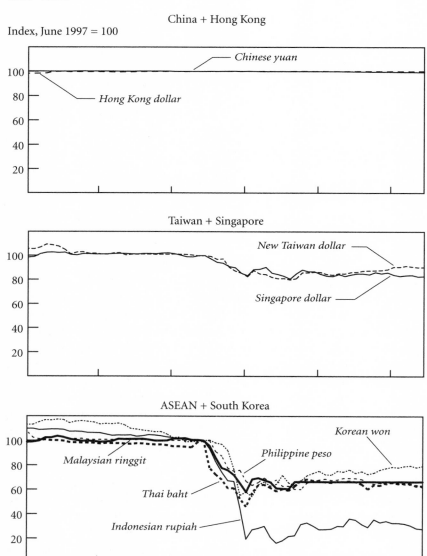

Source: Compiled by Nomura Research Institute based on Bloomberg data.

The Vulnerability of the Dollar Peg System

The latest crisis in Asia reveals some weaknesses intrinsic to the traditional dollar peg system, adopted widely by Asian countries. First, fluctuations of the yen against the U.S. dollar have led to sharp swings in export performance as well as in net capital inflow. Second, given the weakening synchronization between Asian and U.S. growth rates, leaving interest rates to be determined in the United States (as required to maintain fixed exchange rates against the dollar) has led to macroeconomic instability. Finally, countries committing to fix their exchange rates against the dollar are vulnerable to speculation. These weaknesses, which are to one extent or another common to all fixed exchange rate regimes, have been aggravated by the sharp rise in the scale of capital flows. In addition, the dollar peg system has been further strained by the growing interdependence among Asian countries (including Japan) at the expense of dependence on the United States as well as by a sharp deterioration of the U.S. balance of payments position.

Yen-Dollar Rate Fluctuations and Macroeconomic Instability

Led by the yen-dollar rate, exchange rates among the major currencies have become highly volatile since the collapse of the Bretton Woods system in the early 1970s. This has happened against a background of the sharply deteriorating U.S. balance of payments position in general and its growing imbalance with Japan in particular.

With the yen fluctuating widely against the dollar, the traditional policy of pegging their exchange rates to the dollar has led to macroeconomic instability in Asia's developing countries (see chapter 3 for details). Since the Plaza Accord in 1985, there has been a clear tendency for economic growth in Asia to accelerate when the yen appreciates and to decelerate when the yen depreciates. The downturn in Asian economic growth in 1996–97 can largely be explained by the sharp depreciation of the yen against the dollar. The weakening yen also led to a marked deterioration in Asia's export performance and current account balances, paving the way for the currency crisis.

As discussed in more detail in chapter 3, a depreciation of the yen against the dollar (and thus against the Asian currencies under the dollar peg system) affects the Asian economies mainly through the following five channels. First, a weaker yen makes Japanese exports less expensive relative to those of the Asian countries and Asian products become less competitive against Japanese products in international markets as a result. Second, with the cost of production in Japan falling relative to that of the Asian countries, the incentive for Japanese companies to relocate production to Asia is reduced, leading to a decline in the inflow of foreign direct investment from Japan. Third, the capital adequacy ratios of Japanese banks decline as the yen depreciates so that they may need to reduce their overseas lending to meet the BIS standard 8 percent minimum capital adequacy requirement. Fourth, a weaker yen reduces import prices in the Asian countries, as they are heavily dependent on Japan as a source of capital and intermediate goods. Fifth, a depreciation of the yen reduces the Asian countries' burden of repaying debts denominated in yen terms.

While the effects of the first three factors on Asian economic growth are negative, they are partly offset (and in some cases, more than offset) by the positive effects of the last two factors. The net result, which may differ from one country to another, depends on the relative magnitude of these five forces. A weaker yen is more likely to dampen economic growth in higher income countries with trade structures competitive with Japan's (South Korea, for example) than in lower income countries with trade structures that complement Japan's (Indonesia, for example). While a weaker yen has both negative and positive effects on Asia, there is strong empirical evidence that its impact is negative on economic growth in the Asian NIEs, ASEAN, and China, as a group.

Asymmetric Shocks and Loss of Monetary Autonomy

As with all fixed exchange rate systems (the extreme case being a monetary union with a single currency), pegging to the dollar under free capital mobility implies the abandonment of an independent monetary policy. Since the host country has to match domestic interest rates to the U.S. level to maintain the parity rate, it has little room to use monetary policy to restore stability when the economy is subjected to shocks. For countries whose business cycles synchronize with the ups and downs of the U.S. economy, the costs of giving up an independent monetary policy are relatively small, as they are likely to pursue a policy stance similar to that of the United States most of the time anyway. For Asian countries facing shocks that affect the two sides of the Pacific asymmetrically, however, leaving domestic interest rates to be determined in the United States may actually be destabilizing.

The synchronization between Asian and U.S. economic growth has weakened markedly since the Plaza Accord in 1985 (figure 4-2). The correlation coefficient between Asian and U.S. growth rates fell from 0.731 for the period 1971–84 to –0.193 for the period 1985–98 (table 4-1). The corresponding figure for 1985–96 was 0.175, indicating that desynchronization

Figure 4-2. *U.S. and Asian Economic Growth, 1971–99*[a]

Percent

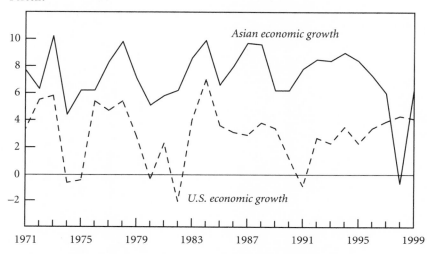

Source: Compiled by Nomura Research Institute based on official statistics of countries concerned.

a. Asia = NIEs + ASEAN + China. U.S. average economic growth is 3.0; Asia's is 7.2.

began even before the crisis.[1] This reflects both rising intraregional trade at the expense of exports to the United States and the growing importance of shocks that affect the two sides of the Pacific asymmetrically (such as fluctuations in the yen-dollar rate).

The experience of Hong Kong illustrates how pegging to the dollar can be destabilizing rather than stabilizing in this new environment (see box 8-1 for details). Thanks to the close ties through trade and investment with China developed since the 1980s, Hong Kong's growth rate now synchronizes more strongly with China than with the United States. Hong Kong thus no longer meets the conditions for forming an optimum currency area with the United States, as external shocks (the latest crisis in Asia being a typical example) do not usually affect the two economies symmetrically. The correlation coefficient between the growth rates of Hong Kong and the United

1. Of the ten major Asian countries (including Japan), all but China and the Philippines have witnessed sharp declines in the correlation between their growth rates and that of the United States. China has become more closely integrated into the global economy, thanks to the open-door policy that started in the late 1970s, while the Philippines has restored stable growth in the post-Marcos period.

Table 4-1. *Economic Growth Rates, Ten Asian Countries,*
Correlated with U.S. Economic Growth, 1971–98

Country	1971–84	1985–96	1985–98
China	0.139	0.262	0.161
Korea	0.584	−0.087	−0.298
Taiwan	0.857	0.090	−0.013
Hong Kong	0.705	0.097	−0.102
Singapore	0.461	−0.074	−0.156
Indonesia	0.436	−0.282	−0.321
Malaysia	0.537	−0.281	−0.343
Philippines	−0.189	0.243	0.204
Thailand	0.545	−0.068	−0.334
Asia	0.731	0.175	−0.193
Japan	0.616	0.066	−0.163

Source: Compiled by Nomura Research Institute based on official statistics of countries concerned.

States dropped from 0.705 in 1971–84 to 0.097 in 1985–96, and further to −0.102 when the latter period is extended to include the two crisis years. During the latest downturn prompted by the Asian crisis, the need to follow interest rates in the U.S. has deprived the government of the option of stimulating the economy through pursuing an expansionary monetary policy, resulting in a deep recession.

Destabilizing Capital Flows and Speculative Attacks

The increasing mobility of capital has accompanied advances in communications and information technology, and the deregulation of financial markets worldwide has increased the vulnerability of fixed exchange rate systems to speculative attacks. Hedge funds now have the leverage to finance very large positions in the foreign exchange market, making it more difficult for central banks to defend fixed exchange rates, as the recent experience of the Asian countries vividly illustrates.

The rising volume of international capital flows is reflected in the rapid expansion of the global foreign exchange market. The BIS estimates the daily global turnover of (traditional) foreign exchange activity at $1,490 billion in April 1998, sharply higher than the $590 billion in April 1989 when it first conducted the same survey.[2] This figure largely reflects international

2. BIS (1999).

flows of capital and dwarfs the volume of global merchandise trade, which averages about $15 billion a day (based on global export volume, which totaled $4,458 billion in 1998, according to the IMF).

Furthermore, massive inflows of capital tend to be followed by sharp reversals, and the scale of such shifts seems to have increased. Thailand, for example, experienced a net capital inflow (as approximated by the current account deficit) of 8.1 percent of GDP in 1996, before the crisis, and a net outflow equivalent to 12.3 percent of GDP in 1998, during the crisis (a net swing of more than 20 percentage points of GDP). At the same time, South Korea's net capital flow turned from a positive 4.4 percent of GDP to negative 12.5 percent (a swing of 16.9 percentage points). The magnitude of these reversals far exceeds the corresponding figures for Mexico (a swing of 10 percentage points) and Chile (a swing of 9 percentage points) between 1981 and 1983.

For countries under pegged exchange rate regimes, reversals in capital flows usually take the form of speculative attacks in the foreign exchange market when the pegged rate is judged to be out of line with economic fundamentals. The reluctance of monetary authorities to alter parity promptly in the face of misalignment tends to offer speculators a one-way bet and to increase their expected return. At the same time, countries with pegged exchange rates are also susceptible to the contagion effect of speculation in neighboring countries. This is especially true if they have close economic ties with their neighbor through trade and investment.

Defending a pegged exchange rate system can be costly in terms of the need to hold a large amount of precautionary reserves of foreign exchange and to maintain high interest rates when under speculative attack. In traditional country risk analysis, three-months' import coverage is considered a comfortable level for foreign exchange reserves in the absence of capital mobility. Amid the intense speculation of 1997, however, foreign exchange reserves well above this benchmark were not sufficient for the hard-hit Asian countries to avoid having to allow their exchange rates to float. With immense reserves—amounting to over $140 billion—and tight capital controls, China succeeded in stabilizing its exchange rate against the dollar, but the opportunity cost of maintaining this level of reserves is great. China pays much higher interest rates on its overseas borrowings than it receives on the foreign exchange reserves it maintains.

At the same time, the hikes in short-term interest rates needed to defend the parity rate raise the cost of funding and reduce loan demand, with adverse effects on profitability in the banking sector. In the absence of a well-developed bond market, corporate finance is heavily dependent on short-term bank loans, and higher lending rates bring about rising bad debts, increasing the probability of a banking crisis.

Furthermore, an unsuccessful attempt to defend a peg may be accompanied by adverse consequences. Market participants usually interpret a sharp devaluation as an indicator of failed macroeconomic management, which prompts further capital outflows. By raising the debt burden of banks and companies with foreign-currency borrowings, the devaluation may lead to serious credit crunch problems and falling domestic investment.[3]

The dollar peg system, coupled with capital account liberalization, has also been blamed for the excessive accumulation of dollar-denominated debt in the Asian countries. The long-standing stability of the Asian currencies against the U.S. dollar before the crisis had prompted both foreign investors and domestic borrowers to underestimate the foreign exchange rate risk associated with borrowing in dollars without hedging, leading to investment in excess of the optimal level and to inefficiency. Borrowers may also have difficulty repaying that debt if local currencies are forced to devalue sharply under speculative pressure, as happened during the Asian crisis.[4]

Dedollarization versus Redollarization

The weaknesses of the dollar peg system come from diverse sources, and the remedies span the gamut from moving to more flexible systems (dedollar-

---

3. Paul Krugman summarizes this argument elegantly in a simple Mundell-Fleming model that links investment not only to the interest rate but also to the real exchange rate and allows for the possibility of multiple equilibria. See "Analytical Afterthoughts on the Asian Crisis" (web.mit.edu/krugman/www/MINICRIS.htm [1999]).

4. Although both lenders and borrowers might have underestimated the foreign exchange risk because of the "exchange rate illusion," the notion that under the dollar peg system Asian governments aggravated the moral hazard problem by implicitly guaranteeing future exchange rates is misleading. Except for Hong Kong, all other major Asian countries claimed to have some kind of managed floating system and did not make any guarantee that exchange rates would not be changed. If market participants were 100 percent sure that local currencies were as safe as the U.S. dollar, local interest rates should come close to U.S. rates, but in reality the former were much higher than the latter. Conceptually, this interest rate spread can be broken down into an expected rate of depreciation, a currency risk premium, and a country risk premium. Before the Asian crisis, the country risk premium of most Asian countries should be very low, as suggested by their very favorable terms for borrowing in foreign currencies. Expectation of currency depreciation had also for a long time been negligible for most Asian countries (except for Indonesia, which was under a crawling peg system). The large spread between interest rates in Asia's developing countries and the United States therefore indicated the presence of a significant currency risk premium implicit in the loan contracts denominated in local currencies.

ization) to strengthening the dollar peg (redollarization). If the widely fluc-tuating yen-dollar rate is the root of the problem, Asian countries should peg to a basket of currencies in which the yen carries a substantial weight. If loss of monetary independence and excess borrowing are the major sources of instability, allowing the exchange rate to float is recommended.[5] If unwar-ranted speculation is blamed, the dollar peg system should be strengthened rather than abandoned for a more flexible regime.

Pegging to a Basket of Currencies

Given the very large impact on economic growth from fluctuations in the yen-dollar rate, stability of the yen-dollar rate is crucial for stability in the regional economy.[6] Unfortunately, the yen-dollar rate is beyond the control of Asia's developing countries and even of the major industrial powers, including Japan and the United States. A second-best solution for them to achieve the same goal is to stabilize their exchange rates not only against the dollar but also against the yen. As long as the yen-dollar rate fluctuates, however, it is impossible for an Asian currency to maintain stability against both the dollar and the yen at the same time. One way to compromise is to peg to a basket of currencies in which the yen carries a substantial weight.

The higher the weight assigned to the yen in the currency basket, the stronger the synchronization between the host country's currency and the yen. By allowing their currencies to follow the yen up (down) when the yen strengthens (weakens) against the dollar, pegging to a currency basket should help stabilize exports. By extension, the ups and downs in their busi-ness cycles would be moderated in magnitude, and the strong correlation between Asian economic growth and the yen-dollar rate would become a phenomenon of the past.

5. Besides exchange rate policy, a country may regain monetary independence as well as insulate itself from currency attacks by imposing capital controls, as discussed below.

6. Given that fluctuations in the yen-dollar rate are destabilizing the Asian economies, it is desirable to stabilize the yen-dollar rate itself. McKinnon and Ohno (1997) propose that the U.S. and Japan jointly announce a target zone of plus or minus 5 percent for the yen-dollar rate based on purchasing power parity. Concerted intervention should be pursued to keep exchange rates within the permissible band, which should narrow over time after confidence in the accord is established. Coordination of macroeconomic policy would be needed to ensure that stabilizing the yen-dollar rate is consistent with other domestic policy objectives. Specifically, monetary policy in the two countries should be assigned to anchor the level of tradable goods in the long run. There have also been many proposals to stabilize exchange rates among major currencies (the dollar, the yen, and the euro) based on target zones; these include Williamson (1985); Bergsten and Henning (1996); McKinnon (1988); and Bergsten, Davanne, and Jacquet (1999).

The optimal weight assigned to the yen in this currency basket should differ from one country to another, depending largely on how much the host country competes with Japan. Since higher income countries are more likely to have more competitive relations with Japan than lower income countries, South Korea should peg closer to the yen than Thailand, which in turn should assign a higher weight to the yen in its reference basket than Indonesia, for example (see chapter 7). By assigning such an optimal weight to the yen, an Asian country can minimize the ups and downs in its business cycle resulting from fluctuations in the yen-dollar rate.

Until its transition to the current managed floating system on July 2, 1997, the Thai baht was pegged to a basket of currencies with a dominant weight for the dollar. The weight of the yen was estimated at about 10 percent. Accordingly, the baht edged down by only about 4 percent against the dollar in the two years leading up to the July 1997 devaluation, during which the yen depreciated by over 30 percent against the dollar (figure 4-3). This, however, was not enough to prevent export growth from decelerating sharply in 1996. Judging by the above criterion, the weight assigned to the yen in Thailand's reference currency basket before the change to managed floating in mid-1997 was too low (and the weight assigned to the U.S. dollar was too high). Should the yen have carried a higher weight in that basket, the baht would have depreciated more sharply against the dollar as the yen depreciated after mid-1995. This in turn should have moderated the appreciation of the baht in real effective terms and helped sustain Thai export growth. In that case, the abrupt devaluation of the baht might have been avoided.

While a system of pegging to a basket of currencies with an appropriately chosen weight for the yen should contribute to macroeconomic stability in Asia, it shares with other fixed exchange rate systems shortcomings such as lack of monetary autonomy and vulnerability to speculative attacks. Compared with a system of pegging to a single currency, a basket peg system is harder to administer and the commitment to the peg is interpreted as weaker. At the microeconomic level, the cost of transactions is likely to be higher because all bilateral rates fluctuate.

Floating Exchange Rates

There is a growing recognition that more flexible exchange rates are preferable to pegged exchange rates in terms of enhancing the host country's scope to pursue an independent monetary policy and reducing its vulnerability to currency crises.

Figure 4-3. *Exchange Rates of the Baht, 1995–98*

Index, 1995:2 = 100

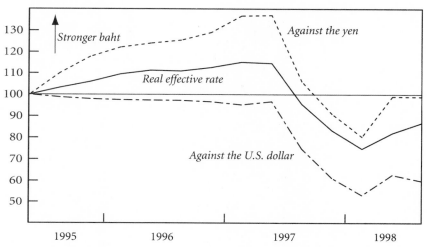

Source: Compiled by Nomura Research Institute based on official statistics and J. P. Morgan, *Trade Weighted Currency Index.*

The textbook version of the Mundell-Fleming model provides a theoretical basis for the argument that a country under a floating exchange rate system enjoys more autonomy in setting monetary policy. Although, under the assumption of perfect capital mobility, domestic interest rates are linked to the overseas level, the monetary authorities maintain control over the money supply, and monetary policy works mainly through its impact on the exchange rate. In the portfolio approach that allows for imperfect substitution between assets denominated in domestic and foreign currencies, changes in the exchange rate risk premium, which allow local interest rates to deviate from the overseas level, provide a further channel through which monetary policy works under a floating exchange rate. In the simple monetary model that assumes purchasing power parity and a stable money demand function, a floating rate regime allows the host country to choose its own level of inflation, which may differ from its trading partners.

The daily movement in the exchange rate in a floating rate regime also keeps reminding borrowers of the currency risk involved in incurring liabilities denominated in foreign currencies. By allowing its exchange rate to float, a country can thus discourage the accumulation of foreign-currency debt, making it less prone to crisis.[7] A given decline in the exchange rate is expected to have a less adverse impact on the real economy under a floating regime than under a pegged regime, as the private sector is likely to have hedged a larger portion of its foreign currency debt. A floating exchange rate regime is also less vulnerable to currency crises because it allows the exchange rate to absorb market pressure and because it presents less chance of a one-way bet for speculators.

Floating exchange rates have their own demerits, however. Exchange rate movements tend to be driven by herd behavior rather than by rational expectations, and the post–Bretton Woods period has witnessed high volatility and misalignment (chronic deviation from equilibrium rates) among major currencies that have been allowed to float. For example, the gyration in the yen-dollar rate from 80 yen to a dollar in the spring of 1995 down to 147 to a dollar in the autumn of 1998 is difficult to rationalize in terms of major changes in economic fundamentals (even ex post). Volatility of exchange rates increases the risk of cross-border transactions, with negative effects on international trade and investment. Exchange rate misalignment may aggravate business cycles at the macroeconomic level and lead to a misallocation of social resources (particularly between the tradable and nontradable sectors) at the microeconomic level.

Volatile exchange rates are particularly harmful to small and open developing countries with thin and underdeveloped financial and foreign exchange markets. Compared with the industrial countries, their exchange rates would be more volatile, and the availability of financial instruments for hedging against exchange risk would be limited. Specifically, the inability to borrow abroad in local currencies has made most developing countries vulnerable to exchange rate fluctuations.[8] Since countries whose external liabilities are necessarily denominated in foreign currencies have no way to reduce currency risk exposure at the aggregate level, most domestic borrowers would have to face currency mismatch in their balance sheets. Governments are thus unwilling to allow their currencies to float, fearing

7. If excess borrowing is the problem, however, it would better be coped with by introducing direct measures rather than by increasing exchange volatility. The latter is usually accompanied by higher domestic interest rates that reflect a higher currency risk premium, with an adverse effect on investment.

8. Eichengreen and Hausmann (1999). The inability of developing countries to borrow abroad in local currencies, together with their inability to borrow long term (even domestically), has come to be known as "original sin." The claim that currency mismatch and maturity mismatch are the major sources of financial fragility for developing countries has come to be known as the original sin hypothesis.

that a sharp depreciation may lead to bankruptcies and stagflation instead of export-led growth.[9]

While a floating exchange rate regime acts to cushion the economy from the impact of real shocks, it may actually aggravate the destabilizing effect of monetary shocks on domestic output. For example, portfolio shifts by investors (a type of monetary shock) under a floating rate system may lead not only to more volatile exchange rates but also to wider fluctuations in output than under a fixed exchange rate system. Even for shocks arising from changes in overseas interest rates, a floating exchange rate system does a better job than a fixed exchange rate system as a built-in stabilizer for domestic output only under restricted conditions. In reality, every economy faces monetary, real, and overseas interest rate shocks to one extent or another. The exchange rate regime that promises the highest degree of built-in stability is likely to be neither a purely fixed nor a purely floating regime but some managed floating regime that mixes the two.[10]

Strengthening the Dollar Peg

In contrast to basket peg and free-floating regimes, which represent steps toward dedollarization, measures to strengthen the dollar peg system (redollarization) have been proposed to avoid currency attacks in Asia's developing countries.

DOLLARIZATION. In its purest form, dollarization amounts to replacing the national currency with the U.S. dollar or simply forming a (virtual) monetary union with the United States. By eliminating the national currency, there is no longer a need to defend it (by raising interest rates or by intervention in the foreign exchange market), and domestic interest rates should therefore follow closely rates in the United States. This benefit comes at the cost of forgoing once and for all the options of changing the exchange rate or pursuing an independent monetary policy.

At the same time, dollarization also implies a loss of seigniorage for the host country, as the monetary authority needs to draw down foreign exchange reserves or borrow dollars in international markets in order to redeem the local currency in circulation. The central bank also loses its function as the lender of last resort, because it can no longer provide liquidity (by printing money) to the banking system in case of a crisis.

---

9. Calvo and Reinhart (2000) provide empirical evidence showing that the fear of floating is pervasive, even among some of the developed countries. Many countries that are classified as having a free or a managed float mostly resemble noncredible pegs.

10. See Argy (1990); Genberg (1990).

CURRENCY BOARDS. Short of eliminating the local currency, some countries have sought to enhance credibility by adopting currency boards. This involves rigidly linking the value of domestic money to that of a foreign currency (the dollar in the case of Hong Kong) and tying the domestic monetary base firmly to the level of foreign exchange reserves through legislation.[11] Unlike complete dollarization, currency boards allow the retention of seigniorage and the option of devaluation in case of emergency.

The latter may, however, turn out to be a disadvantage in some circumstances. Since countries with currency boards have not eliminated all possibility of devaluation, they are not fully immune to speculative attacks. The automatic adjustment mechanism under a currency board hinges crucially on interest arbitrage. Under normal conditions, a deterioration in the balance of payments position that puts downward pressure on the exchange rate, for example, would shrink the money supply and put upward pressure on domestic interest rates. This in turn would attract capital inflow to support the exchange rate and keep interest rates from rising.

Should confidence in the authorities' ability (and determination) to defend the official parity fade as a result of some external shocks, however, containing capital outflow would require maintaining domestic interest rates at an extremely high level, with adverse effects on economic growth and the soundness of the financial system. Furthermore, only the monetary base is supposed to be backed up by foreign exchange reserves under a currency board system, but the credit created by the banking sector is many times this amount. Hence the authorities may run out of reserves amid intense speculation and may thus have no choice but to abandon the official parity, if not the currency board system itself. Hong Kong's experience suggests that a currency board system is too rigid to allow pursuing an independent monetary policy but not rigid enough to convince speculators that the risk of devaluation is zero.

COMMITMENT TO RESTORE TRADITIONAL PARITIES. Ronald McKinnon praises the informal dollar peg system adopted by Asia's developing countries before the crisis as a form of common monetary standard that successfully insulated them from beggar-thy-neighbor devaluations and anchored their domestic prices during rapid economic growth in the 1980s

11. For a discussion of the pros and cons of currency boards, see Williamson (1995); Baliño and Enoch (1997). Ghosh, Gulde, and Wolf (1998) argue in favor of currency boards, based on the empirical evidence that countries with currency boards have lower inflation rates and higher economic growth rates on average than countries under pegged exchange rates without them.

through 1996.[12] Although he is uncomfortable with the gyration in the yen-dollar rate, he hopes that it can be stabilized through policy coordination between Japan and the United States.

McKinnon proposes a gradual restoration of the traditional exchange rate parities because he sees no fundamental flaws with Asia's dollar peg system and views the crisis as more the result of self-fulfilling speculation. Making a firm commitment to exchange rate stability would minimize a country's need to increase interest rates in the short run when the local currency is under attack, mitigate the contagion from "accidental" competitive devaluations in the medium term, and keep the domestic price level stable in the long term. The major problem with this proposal is obviously how to make such a commitment credible when there is a total loss of confidence.

Polar Regimes versus Intermediate Regimes

The selection of a country's exchange rate regime is not a dichotomous choice between fixed and floating exchange rates but involves a spectrum of options between these two polar regimes. They include (in order of descending commitment to maintain fixed rates) monetary union, currency board, adjustable peg, crawling peg, basket peg, target zone or band, managed floating, and free floating.[13]

The first two regimes belong to the fixed pole. In a monetary union, participating members share a common currency as well as a common central bank. This includes the special case of the adoption of a foreign currency as legal tender, such as official dollarization. A currency board rigidly links the value of domestic money to that of a foreign currency and ties the domestic monetary base firmly to the level of foreign exchange reserves.

The next four regimes are intermediate. The adjustable peg fixes the exchange rate but without any open-ended commitment to resist devaluation or revaluation in the presence of large balance of payments deficits or surpluses. The crawling peg includes a preannounced policy of adjusting the exchange rate bit by bit over time. The basket peg fixes not to a single currency but to a weighted average of other currencies. And with a target zone, or band, regime, there is a margin of fluctuation around a central rate.

The last two regimes belong to the flexible pole. A managed floating regime allows the exchange rate to fluctuate subject to intervention but without an explicit exchange rate target. In a free-floating regime no official

12. McKinnon (1999).
13. Categories based on Eichengreen (1994); Frankel (1999).

intervention is undertaken in the foreign exchange market, and economic policies, especially monetary policies, are pursued with benign indifference to the exchange rate.

With some pegged exchange rate systems becoming more vulnerable to speculative attacks in this age of global financial integration, the debate over the choice of exchange rate regime has shifted from fixed versus floating regimes to polar versus intermediate regimes. Although it has become fashionable to eliminate intermediate regimes with exchange rate targets as viable options in favor of either free-floating or firm-fixing regimes, neither of these polar regimes seems to suit Asia's developing countries at this stage. A more appropriate strategy is to strengthen the institutional framework to reduce the vulnerability of the intermediate regimes to speculative attacks. To this end, the option of capital controls should not be ruled out.

Polar Regimes

Based on the history of the European Monetary System, and more recently the crisis in Asia, Barry Eichengreen concludes that it has become infinitely difficult for the authorities to support a shaky currency peg.[14] This is because the volume of liquid international capital has far outstripped the reserves of even the most well-endowed central bank.[15] At the same time, progress in democratization has aggravated this problem by reducing the credibility of the government's commitment to maintain exchange rate stability over and above the pursuit of other goals. Capital mobility and democratization thus undermine the viability of contingent rules designed to hit explicit exchange rate targets such as pegged-but-adjustable rates and narrow target zones, forcing policymakers to choose between joining a monetary union and allowing exchange rates to float.

Although monetary union and free-floating regimes occupy the two ends of a spectrum of major exchange rate regimes, ranging from the strongest fixed-rate commitment to the most flexible, some free market economists believe that they share the common ground of being the "market solutions" to the currency conundrum. A floating exchange rate regime is supposed to be free from official intervention, while under an immutably fixed exchange rate regime the government puts exchange rate policy on autopilot. In contrast, with intermediate arrangements the government uses its discretion to manage the exchange rate.

---

14. Eichengreen (1994, 1999).

15. The view that fixed but adjustable exchange rates have become more difficult to maintain is supported by Obstfeld and Rogoff (1995), among others.

Eichengreen is careful to define a floating regime broadly to include managed floating, which is subject to intervention, although he insists that the authorities should avoid reference to an explicit exchange rate target. Recognizing the need to have a nominal anchor, he suggests that monetary policy should target inflation instead of the exchange rate. However, allowing the government the discretion to intervene would contradict the basic philosophy of letting the market rather than bureaucrats or politicians decide the exchange rate and would thereby disqualify it as a market solution. It is also unclear why targeting inflation is superior to targeting the exchange rate in terms of credibility and macroeconomic stability.

When applying his "going to extremes" principle to Asia, Eichengreen favors a floating regime over a monetary union regime. He doubts the possibility of Asia's developing countries forming a monetary union with the United States, Europe, or Japan, because their trade and financial flows are diversified and the political will to promote monetary integration is lacking. Even Eichengreen, however, recommends floating only with reservation, cautioning that "one must hope that the countries of the region succeed in putting in place the institutional and political prerequisites necessary to effectively manage their managed float."[16] Such prerequisites would be demanding; they include establishing credibility in monetary policy without using the exchange rate as a nominal anchor; developing liquid and efficient forward and futures currency markets so that corporations can hedge their foreign exchange positions at low costs; and preventing bureaucrats and politicians from abusing their power to influence the exchange rate to favor privileged sectors.

Intermediate Regimes

If the institutional and political prerequisites for adopting a floating exchange rate regime are lacking and costly to realize, it may be worthwhile for Asia's developing countries to reconsider the alternative of trying to achieve the prerequisites of the intermediate regimes instead. Indeed, the argument in favor of polar regimes over intermediate regimes has been based on the firm belief that intermediate regimes are not viable rather than that the polar regimes are more desirable.[17] A preferred approach is to

16. Eichengreen (1999, pp. 34–35).

17. As Frankel (1999, p. 5) puts it, "The rejection of the middle ground is then explained simply as a rejection of where most countries have been, with no reasonable expectation that the sanctuaries of monetary union or free-floating will, in fact, be any better. Therefore, a blanket recommendation to avoid the middle regimes in favor of firm-fixing or free-floating would not be appropriate."

improve the intermediate regimes with explicit exchange rate targets so as to make them less vulnerable to currency speculation.

In an attempt to combine the merits of both the fixed and floating rate regimes while minimizing their shortcomings, John Williamson proposes a crawling band, wherein a central bank undertakes a public obligation to maintain the exchange rate within a wide, publicly announced band around a parity that is periodically adjusted in relatively small steps to keep the band in line with economic fundamentals.[18] A band performs the function of guiding the market to where the equilibrium rate lies. By stabilizing expectations, it reduces the risks of volatility and misalignment that characterize floating rates.[19] While the exchange rate is free to fluctuate within the band, the central bank is obliged to intervene at the edge of the band to prevent the rate from going outside.

Consistency between the band and economic fundamentals is expected to provide the first defense against speculation. The key components of a crawling band system are the parity rate, the rate at which it crawls, and the width of the band.[20] The central parity should be managed so as to track the underlying fundamental equilibrium exchange rate (FEER). The parity rate should be defined in terms of a basket of currencies instead of a single currency, and it should be adjusted not just to offset inflation but also to reflect permanent changes in fundamentals. Since the FEER can be estimated only with imprecision, the band should be wide enough (say plus or minus 10 percent) to ensure that the "true" FEER falls within the band. By increasing the probability that the exchange rate will return to the central rate, it would also increase the risk that speculators face. At the same time, a wide band allows the authorities more room to pursue an independent monetary policy.

A number of suggestions have recently been made to improve the crawling band system in response to the criticism that it is just as vulnerable to speculation as an adjustable peg system. Williamson proposes a monitoring band that does not involve an obligation to defend the edges of the band, in the hopes that the modified system would still play a positive role in focusing market expectations on the long-term equilibrium rate.[21] Others insist that even when the exchange rate is well within the band, monetary policy

18. Williamson (1996).
19. As pointed out by Williamson (1998), the fact that a movement of the spot rate within a band is accompanied by a smaller movement in the forward rate while there is no such tendency with a floating rate is conclusive proof that a crawling band is stabilizing expectations.
20. This band-basket-crawl approach has been supported by Dornbusch and Park (1999).
21. Williamson (1998).

should be assigned to stabilize the exchange rate to enhance credibility and that the IMF should be involved in determining and supporting the band.[22] A World Bank study adds that, consistent with the insulating properties of the floating and the fixed exchange rate regimes, the band (an indicator of the degree of exchange rate flexibility) should be wide for an economy facing real shocks and narrow for an economy facing nominal shocks.[23] Within the band, nominal shocks should be coped with by intervention, while real shocks call for exchange rate adjustment.

Kenichi Ohno also favors targeting some real effective exchange rate but suggests that this is consistent with a variety of exchange rate regimes.[24] He finds no fundamental flaws with the "precrisis soft dollar zone" and detects no serious overvaluation in the developing countries in Asia during the precrisis period measured in terms of real effective exchange rates. He finds that most of these currencies were allowed to deviate from the strict dollar peg in the medium to long term in order to offset inflation gaps and movements of major currencies. His proposal for postcrisis exchange rate management involves targeting the real effective exchange rate (constructed to measure the average competitiveness of the export sector) more explicitly in normal time, to be supplemented by rules for additional adjustment and crisis management. Small adjustments in the nominal exchange rate should be made frequently against movements of other currencies as well as for inflation differentials. This can be achieved under managed floating with closer monitoring of the real effective exchange rate (REER), dollar peg with proper rate adjustment, dollar peg with inflation slide, nominal multiple currency basket with additional adjustments, and real multiple currency basket. In addition, to cope with real shocks that change the equilibrium REER and with currency attacks, monetary authorities should reserve flexibility to adjust the exchange rate by discretion (when the terms of trade deteriorate sharply, for example) and to introduce emergency measures (such as capital controls) in case of crises.

Capital Controls

Exchange rate policy does not work in isolation and should be considered in conjunction with other macroeconomic policies. Although economic theory suggests that it is difficult if not impossible for a country to achieve

---

22. Bergsten, Davanne, and Jacquet (1999).
23. World Bank (1997).
24. Ohno (1999).

Box 4-1. *The Impossible Trinity*

There is growing recognition that no country can achieve a fixed exchange rate, free capital mobility, and an independent monetary policy (the impossible trinity) simultaneously. A country maintaining a fixed exchange rate needs either to impose capital controls or to allow interest rates to follow those in the anchor currency country. If capital mobility is perfect, a fixed exchange rate and an independent monetary policy are not consistent with one another. And if the priority is to maintain an independent monetary policy, either some form of capital controls has to be put in place or the exchange rate has to be allowed to float.

Regime	Fixed exchange rate	Free capital mobility	Independent monetary policy	Examples
Monetary union	Yes	Yes	No	Hong Kong
Capital controls	Yes	No	Yes	China, Malaysia
Free floating	No	Yes	Yes	Japan

Each Asian country therefore faces three typical options. One option is to give up the freedom to pursue an independent monetary policy, the extreme case being to abandon the national currency and join a monetary union. Hong Kong's dollar peg system comes close to this. Another option is to give up free capital mobility by imposing

simultaneously fixed exchange rates, free capital mobility, and an independent monetary policy—known as the impossible trinity (box 4-1)—a country under a fixed exchange rate system can restore monetary autonomy by imposing capital controls. China's relative success in weathering the recent crisis in Asia suggests that the option of imposing capital controls should not be completely ruled out.

Capital inflow has played a major role in Asia's economic development, but with imperfect financial markets, perfect capital mobility may lead to market failures. Some form of government intervention should provide a capital controls, as in the case of China and, since September 1998, Malaysia. A third option is to give up fixed exchange rates and allow the exchange rate to float, as in the case of Japan. Unable to maintain stable exchange rates amid highly volatile capital flows, most Asian countries have been forced to allow their currencies to float.

Different policy recommendations presented to the Asian countries during the crisis correspond broadly to these three options. The IMF prescription calls for raising interest rates (abandoning monetary autonomy) to stabilize the exchange rate while maintaining the free flow of capital. Jeffrey Sachs is willing to allow the exchange rate to fall in exchange for the room to reduce interest rates. Finally, Paul Krugman favors the introduction of capital controls (abandoning capital mobility) as "extreme situations demand extreme measures."

In reality, there exist a lot more options than these three polar regimes, since the extent of exchange rate fixity, capital mobility, and freedom to pursue an independent monetary policy each ranges over a spectrum from nil to perfect. For example, a country can enhance (although not fully restore) its freedom to pursue an independent monetary policy by introducing partial capital control or by allowing its exchange range to float within a certain band. The choice of an optimal exchange rate regime, broadly defined to include choosing the degree of capital control, involves compromising the impossible trinity.

Source: Jeffrey Sachs, "The Wrong Medicine for Asia," *New York Times*, November 3, 1997; Paul Krugman, "Saving Asia: It's Time to Get Radical," *Fortune*, September 7, 1998.

second-best solution.[25] The literature on the sequencing of economic reform, which has identified the prerequisites for a successful opening up of the capital account, provides the strongest theoretical base for a developing country to impose capital controls.[26] A general consensus has

25. For a discussion of the pros and cons of capital controls, see Barry Eichengreen, "Capital Controls: Capital Idea or Capital Folly?" (elsa.berkeley.edu/users/ eichengr/capcontrols.pdf [1998]).
26. McKinnon (1991).

emerged that capital account liberalization should be preceded by the establishment of nontraditional export industries and fiscal discipline as well as by the liberalization of trade and the financial system. In particular, the latest crisis in Asia has confirmed that a developing country should not liberalize capital account transactions at a too early stage, when banks' risk appraisal is inadequate and monetary control is difficult. These conditions are more likely to be met by the more advanced countries than by the less developed ones. Premature opening up would not only lead to a misallocation of social resources but also invite speculation. The recent experience of the ASEAN countries shows that this cost can be very high. In contrast, China is fortunate that it has maintained tight controls on capital flows, which insulate it from speculative attacks and enhance the flexibility to stimulate domestic demand by pursuing expansionary fiscal and monetary policies.

Growing concern about the adverse effect of volatile short-term capital flows has given rise to proposals that they should be regulated and not left totally to the free market. For example, James Tobin challenges the claims that liberalization and globalization of financial markets are the path to prosperity and progress and reiterates his proposal to impose a tax (the so-called Tobin tax) on currency transactions.[27]

Capital controls should also be considered as emergency measures to prevent systemic risks when speculation threatens the soundness of the financial system and deprives the government of tools of macroeconomic management. Indeed, in an attempt to stabilize the exchange rate and to reclaim autonomy over its monetary and fiscal policies, Malaysia imposed drastic capital controls in September 1998.[28] In retrospect, these goals have been broadly achieved, and Malaysia has also been successful in using the breathing space to restructure its financial and corporate sectors.

27. James Tobin, "Why We Need Sand in the Market's Gears," *Washington Post,* December 21, 1997.

28. The key measures included pegging the ringgit to the U.S. dollar, imposing a twelve-month holding period on repatriations of proceeds from sales of securities, limiting capital outflow by residents, banning the trading of Malaysian shares on Singapore's over-the-counter market, and strictly limiting the use of the ringgit in international transactions.

5

*Revitalizing the
Japanese Economy*

The 1990s will be remembered as Japan's lost decade, with economic growth lagging far behind not only the high level it achieved in the past but also that of other major industrial countries. Several factors contributed to the stagnation of the Japanese economy during this period. Falling asset prices had an immense negative impact on domestic spending; macroeconomic policies failed to restore production to its potential level. The traditional "Japanese model," which worked so well when Japan was catching up with the West, became impotent once that phase was over. It is also widely recognized that structural reform is essential for Japan to cope with a new environment characterized by globalization, an aging population, and the transition to a postindustrial society.

In an attempt to revitalize the Japanese economy, in late 1996 the Hashimoto administration initiated a comprehensive reform program covering six major areas. Led by the financial Big Bang, major efforts were made to enhance competition through deregulation. Japanese companies responded by changing business practices, with more emphasis on the market mechanism as the guiding principle. Mergers and acquisitions (M&As) across corporate groups and national borders, for example, have become a common tool of restructuring. As the new millennium unfolds, there are early signs that the worst may be over for the Japanese economy, with structural reform finally bearing fruit.

The Aftermath of the Bubble Economy

The bursting of the asset price bubble was by far the most important event determining the course of the Japanese economy in the 1990s. At its trough in October 1998, the benchmark Nikkei average index was down to one-third of its peak level, recorded in late 1989 (figure 5-1). Prices of land for commercial use and residential use dropped 70 percent and 45 percent, respectively, since 1991. The government tried to boost the economy with several rounds of fiscal stimulus packages, and the Bank of Japan allowed interest rates to fall to a historic low level. The overall impact on economic growth, however, has been disappointing, with GDP expanding only 1 percent a year between 1992 and 1999 (figure 5-2).

The Disappointing Macroeconomic Performance

Ten years after the asset price bubble burst, the Japanese economy was still struggling with its aftermath. During the boom years of the late 1980s, banks and other financial institutions provided vast amounts of credit collateralized against land and stocks, whose values surged to levels totally out of line with economic fundamentals. The day of reckoning began in 1990, when stock prices plummeted, soon followed by real estate prices. Most financial institutions were left holding very large volumes of nonperforming loans, forcing them to take a much more cautious stance in extending new loans. Households and companies also suffered immense capital losses, prompting them to cut spending in an attempt to repair their balance sheets.

The Japanese economy experienced two recessions during the 1990s, interrupted by two years of relatively strong growth in fiscal year 1995 and fiscal year 1996.[1] The second recession was deeper than the first, with the banking sector driven to the brink of a major crisis. The first recession started in 1992 and lasted for three years, with the economic growth rate averaging a disappointing 0.5 percent between fiscal year 1992 and fiscal year 1994. When the economy began to show clear signs of slowing down in 1992, both the private sector and the government perceived the downturn primarily as part of a normal business cycle and expected it to be short-lived. Falling asset prices notwithstanding, capital gains (particularly on assets acquired before the bubble period) and retained earnings accumulated during boom years

---

1. The Japanese fiscal year runs from April 1 to March 31 of the following year.

Figure 5-1. *Nikkei Average, 1985–2000*

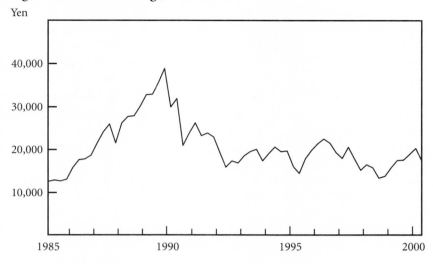

Yen

Source: Tokyo Stock Exchange.

Figure 5-2. *Japan's GDP Growth, 1985–2000*

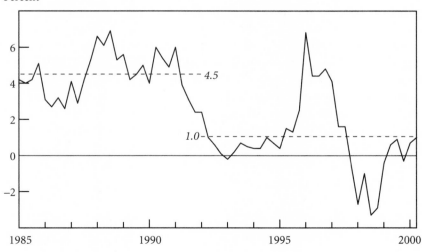

Percent

Source: EPA, *National Income Statistics.*

were still large enough at this stage for Japanese companies to take a wait-and-see stance instead of implementing drastic restructuring. Japanese banks also wrongly believed that their deteriorating bad debt problem would be easily solved as the economy recovered and asset prices picked up again. The authorities were slow in responding to the looming banking crisis partly because they failed to grasp the full extent of the problem due to inadequate disclosure by financial institutions. With hindsight the macroeconomic economic policy implemented during this period, which seemed aggressive at that time, was too little and too late.

The economy picked up in 1995 thanks to the temporary impact of two fiscal stimulation packages implemented in that year and the reconstruction demand following the Kobe earthquake in January of that year. GDP grew 3.0 percent in fiscal year 1995 and 4.4 percent in fiscal year 1996, while stock prices rose more than 50 percent between July 1995 and June 1996. However, the bad debt problem of nonbank financial institutions started to surface, with a number of small financial institutions going bankrupt.[2]

Economic performance deteriorated again in fiscal year 1997, shortly after the government shifted to a fiscal consolidation policy by raising taxes and reducing public expenditures. When Ryutaro Hashimoto took office in January 1996, he put top priority on reducing the fast-growing budget deficit. Misjudging that the economy was on its way to a robust recovery, the consumption tax rate was raised from 3 percent to 5 percent as scheduled, while the temporary tax cut amounting to ¥2 trillion implemented since fiscal year 1995 was terminated in fiscal year 1997. The Fiscal Structural Reform Act was passed in November 1997. It stipulated that the government deficit be reduced to below 3 percent of GDP by fiscal year 2003, when new issues of deficit-financing government bonds should also be terminated. These fiscal-tightening measures had adverse effects on consumption, dragging Japan's economic growth rate down to –0.4 percent in fiscal year 1997 and –1.9 percent in fiscal year 1998, its worst performance in the postwar era.

2. In 1996, public funds amounting to ¥685 billion (about $6 billion) were used to rescue troubled housing loan companies (*jusen*), which are nonbanks that do not take deposits directly from the public. It was widely believed that the government aimed to bail out the politically influential agricultural deposit-taking institutions, which had lent substantial sums to these companies. This distrust of the government's intention made subsequent use of public funds to bail out financial institutions very difficult even when the soundness of the whole financial system was at risk.

The downturn that started in 1997 was aggravated by the financial malaise at home and the currency crisis in neighboring Asian countries. Two major financial institutions, Yamaichi Securities and Hokkaido Takushoku Bank, failed in the autumn of 1997. Concerns that more Japanese bank failures might follow drove the so-called Japan premium—the interest rate premium banks paid when borrowing in dollars in international interbank markets—up to as much as one percent in late 1997. At the same time, attempts by banks to restructure their balance sheets in anticipation of the Prompt Corrective Action Plan coming into effect the following April aggravated the credit crunch problem.[3] Meanwhile, in Asia the currency crisis that started in Thailand in July 1997 quickly infected the whole region; Japan was not spared.

As the crisis deepened, the government was forced to reverse its tight fiscal policy. On April 24, 1998, it announced a stimulating package (Comprehensive Economic Measures) totaling ¥16 trillion.[4] The return to an expansionary fiscal policy stance accelerated after July 1998, when Keizo Obuchi took office as prime minister. Another fiscal package (the Emergency Economic Package) totaling ¥17 trillion was announced in November; in December the Fiscal Structural Reform Act was suspended to accommodate this major shift in fiscal policy. The expansionary initial budget for fiscal year 1999, which contained permanent tax reductions (national and local) for individuals and corporations exceeding ¥6 trillion and generous tax incentives for home purchases, was followed in November 1999 by yet another fiscal package (Policy Measures for Economic Rebirth) totaling ¥17 trillion.

The Obuchi administration also lost no time in restoring confidence in the soundness of the financial system. Major laws were enacted in October 1998 to allow the government to put failing banks under public control temporarily and to use public funds to recapitalize banks considered viable.

---

3. The Prompt Corrective Action Plan is an administrative means by which the supervisory authority, using capital-adequacy ratios as an objective indicator, issues necessary correction orders to banks in a timely and proper manner. Prompt corrective action is classified into three levels: making and implementing a plan to improve management (for institutions with a capital adequacy ratio of 4–8 percent if they have international operations and 2–4 percent if otherwise); implementing specific measures, including raising new capital and downsizing business operations (for institutions with a capital adequacy ratio of 0–4 percent if they have international operations and 0–2 percent if otherwise); and suspension of business (for institutions with a capital adequacy ratio of less than 0 percent).

4. ¥1 trillion is approximately $10 billion dollars. Japan's GDP currently stands at about ¥500 trillion.

A total of ¥60 trillion, equivalent to 12 percent of Japan's GDP, was earmarked for these schemes. Of this amount ¥17 trillion was for guaranteeing bank deposits. With the backing of these funds, all the deposits and debentures of Japanese financial institutions would be fully guaranteed until March 2001 (later extended to March 2002).[5] Another ¥18 trillion was set aside for the reorganization of failed financial institutions. The remaining ¥25 trillion was to be used for the recapitalization of viable financial institutions. The troubled Long-Term Credit Bank and Nippon Credit Bank were soon nationalized under the new framework. In addition, fifteen banks received capital injections from the government amounting to ¥7.5 trillion in March 1999, allowing them to write off bad debts at a faster pace. This financial stabilizing program has succeeded in restoring public confidence in the soundness of the financial system, as reflected in the subsequent elimination of the Japan premium as well as the recovery in the stock prices of Japanese banks.

At the same time, measures were taken to cope with the credit crunch problem plaguing small- and medium-sized companies. In addition to providing them with ample funds through government financial institutions and credit guarantees, a special credit program was set up in October 1998; total guarantee authorization amounted to ¥20 trillion and was subsequently expanded to ¥30 trillion. These measures have helped alleviate the credit crunch problem and have reduced the rate of bankruptcy of small- and medium-sized companies.

Monetary Policy

Since the bursting of the asset price bubble in the early 1990s, monetary policy has been relaxed in steps to stimulate the economy. The official discount rate has been reduced eleven times since July 1991, from its peak level of 6 percent to 0.25 percent since March 2001, while the uncollateralized overnight call rate has been kept at virtually 0 percent since February 1999 (except for a short period between August 2000 and March 2001).

While monetary relaxation has been accompanied by a sharp increase in the monetary base, it has failed to boost the broad money supply, let alone aggregate demand (figure 5-3). Two major schools of thought explain why monetary policy failed to stimulate the economy: the "liquidity trap school" led by Massachusetts Institute of Technology economist Paul Krugman, and the "credit crunch school" led by Nomura economist Richard Koo. While a

---

5. Beginning in April 2002, the amount guaranteed will be limited to ¥10 million for each person.

Figure 5-3. *Japan's Monetary Base, Money Supply, and Nominal GDP, 1980–99*

Percent

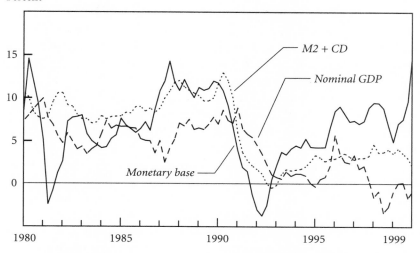

Source: Bank of Japan, *Financial and Economic Statistics Monthly;* EPA, *National Income Statistics.*

heated debate is going on between these camps, the two approaches are better interpreted as complementing, rather than competing with, one another.

The first school focuses on the interest rate channel of transmission and argues that the Japanese economy has fallen into a liquidity trap, "that awkward condition in which monetary policy loses its grip because the nominal interest rate is essentially zero, in which the quantity of money becomes irrelevant because money and bonds are essentially perfect substitutes."[6] Given the immense excess capacity in traditional industries and the slow emergence of new industries, a sharp reduction of real interest rates, probably to a negative level, would be needed to restore full employment.[7] Since

6. Krugman (1998, p. 137).

7. While Krugman attributes Japan's liquidity trap to such domestic factors as the lack of technology innovation and aging population, McKinnon and Ohno (1997) suggest that it has been externally imposed and trace its root to the "ever-higher-yen syndrome." The yen has been following an upward trend against the U.S. dollar at an average annual rate of about 4 percent, reflecting efforts by the United States to pressure Japan to allow the yen to appreciate, in an unsuccessful attempt to reduce the bilateral trade imbalance. Interest rate arbitrage based on this expectation has forced Japanese interest rates about 4 percent below U.S. rates. This was not a problem when nominal interest rates in the United States were high, due to

there is little room for nominal interest rates to fall further, Krugman advo-cates the central bank adopting a policy of managed inflation: announcing a target rate of inflation over the long term and committing to do whatever is necessary to achieve that rate. The aim is to raise inflation expectations (for example, up to 4 percent) so that, given nominal interest rates, real interest rates would decline to stimulate investment. In addition, further monetary loosening is expected to be accompanied by a sharp depreciation of the yen, with positive effects on net exports.

While Krugman's proposal has gained wide attention, if not support, from economists in both Japan and the United States, it has been rejected by the Bank of Japan on the ground that it is difficult not only to set a specific target (in terms of which price index to target and at what level) but also to achieve it.[8] With interest rates already down to a historic low level, there is little room left for further monetary loosening to raise inflation expecta-tions.[9] The Bank of Japan also worries that inflation may get out of control once it gains momentum. In that case, using monetary policy to target a higher rate of inflation may result in higher nominal interest rates and a weaker yen. Rising nominal interest rates would offset the expected reduc-tion in real interest rates resulting from higher inflation (expectations). Trying to export its way out of the recession by allowing the yen to fall is also likely to put downward pressure on the crisis-hit Asian countries and delay their export-led recovery, while at the same time heightening trade friction with the United States. By reducing the capital adequacy ratio of Japanese banks that have large exposure in dollar-denominated lending, this strategy

---

high U.S. inflation. However, in the mid-1990s when U.S. interest rates came down, Japanese interest rates were driven down to zero. McKinnon and Ohno propose a solution to Japan's liquidity trap problem consisting of two complementary policies: a commercial agreement limiting bilateral sanctions in trade disputes and ending (future) pressure from the United States to push the yen up; and a monetary accord to stabilize the yen-dollar rate over the long term. Should these bilateral commitments become credible, interest rates in Japan would rise to the levels in the United States.

8. Okina (1999). Deregulation and the ongoing information technology revolution have led to price declines through improvement in productivity and development of new products. It is difficult to distinguish these effects from deflation using traditional price indexes, which may even fail to capture fully the impact of this "new price revolution."

9. Some economists argue that there is still room for long-term interest rates to fall from the current level of over 1 percent, if the central bank buys long-term government bonds either through open-market operations or by underwriting them directly in the primary mar-ket. The Bank of Japan, however, warns that this would actually raise long-term interest rates, as investors ask for a risk premium to compensate for the resulting deterioration in the cred-itworthiness of the Japanese government.

also runs the risk of worsening the credit crunch problem facing Japanese companies (see chapter 3).

In contrast, the credit crunch school emphasizes the breakdown of the lending channel, as undercapitalized banks are unable to provide firms with adequate credit.[10] A deterioration in the quality of banks' balance sheets with the burst of the asset price bubble reduced their ability to lend. In particular, the need to meet the BIS capital adequacy ratio may act as a binding constraint on lending. Small- and medium-sized companies are particularly hurt, as they have no access to alternative sources of financing, such as issuing bonds in capital markets. The credit crunch problem cannot be solved by the central bank increasing the supply of base money, as this would result only in an accumulation of excess reserves by banks. Rather, the capital base of banks needs to be revamped by injecting public funds.

On the demand side for funds, the transmission of monetary policy through the lending channel has also been hampered by the weakening propensity and ability of companies to borrow as their net worth declines in value. Most Japanese companies have been forced to pursue a backward-looking strategy of reducing borrowings in an attempt to restructure their balance sheets. Even those with a forward-looking strategy may not be able to offer land or securities as collateral when borrowing to invest in new projects. This should be distinguished from the credit crunch problem, which reflects the supply-side problem of unwillingness or inability of banks to lend. Indeed, the injection of public funds in March 1999 has not been followed by a recovery in lending, suggesting that the current stagnation in lending can better be explained by a lack of demand for funds rather than a lack of supply.[11] This conclusion is consistent with the liquidity trap hypothesis if the "balance sheet scare syndrome," which causes stagnation in bank lending, also explains the weakness in private investment despite very low interest rates.

10. Koo (1999). The lending channel idea is based on the view that banks play a special role in the financial system because they are well suited to deal with certain types of borrowers, especially small firms in which the problems of asymmetric information (and thus adverse selection and moral hazard) are especially pronounced. An increase in money supply, by increasing bank lending, leads to an increase in output. Bernanke and Blinder (1988) show how the lending channel can be integrated into the conventional Keynesian model by abandoning the assumption of perfect substitution between bonds and bank loans.

11. In addition to capital injection, the subsequent appreciation of the yen and increase in stock prices also imply an improvement in the BIS ratios of banks and thus in their ability and willingness to lend. Indeed, the *Short-Term Economic Survey of Enterprises in Japan* (*Tankan*), published by the Bank of Japan, confirms that the lending attitude of financial institutions as seen by borrowers has turned more accommodative since early 1999.

Fiscal Policy

According to standard macroeconomic models, when the economy is under a liquidity trap, fiscal policy is supposed to be most effective in stimulating demand, because, even if the government spends more by borrowing, it will put little upward pressure on interest rates. Thus both the crowding-out effect on private investment and the negative impact on net exports as the yen rate appreciates on the back of higher interest rates (the Mundell-Fleming effect) should be minimal. The burden of repaying public debt issued now to finance the fiscal deficit should have a relatively light repayment burden due to the historic low level of interest rates. This situation represents a golden opportunity for the government to improve the country's meager infrastructure.

This optimistic scenario, however, has been betrayed by Japan's recent experience. The Japanese government has implemented a wide range of economic stimulus measures of more than ¥100 trillion since 1992, but these so far have failed to stimulate the economy. The disappointing performance of fiscal policy can be explained largely by the decline in the multiplier reflecting the following factors. First, the corporate sector's marginal propensity to invest has declined following the bursting of the asset price bubble because of excess capacity and the debt overhang problem facing Japanese companies. This is particularly true for construction companies, which are by far the largest beneficiary of fiscal stimulation. Second, the marginal propensity of the household sector to consume has also fallen (and the marginal propensity to save has increased) because of rising concern about unemployment as well as expectations of tax increases in the future to compensate for the widening fiscal deficit now (the Ricardian equivalence hypothesis). Third, the marginal propensity to import has increased in recent years because of stronger competition with developing countries in Asia. Since savings and imports by the corporate and household sectors represent leakages in the multiplier process, these changes mean that income increases have a smaller second-round effect on aggregate demand than they previously had.

Some economists argue that fiscal stimulus in the 1990s was insufficient, rather than ineffective, in restoring self-sustaining economic growth. Adam Posen, for example, dismisses the claim that the attempts at fiscal stimulus failed.[12] Rather, he argues that a serious fiscal stimulus was attempted on

12. Posen (1998).

Figure 5-4. *General Government Financial Balances,*
Japan and the United States, 1990–2000[a]

Percent of GDP

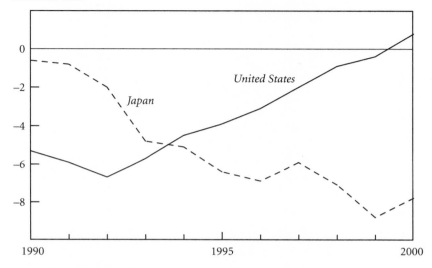

Source: *OECD Economic Outlook* 68, December 2000.
a. General government financial balances exclude social security.

only one occasion, September 1995, and that this was followed by strong growth in the next year. By contrast, misguided contractionary fiscal policies, notably the consumption tax increase in April 1997, slowed the economy. Based on this diagnosis of the prolonged recession, Posen prescribes a sizable fiscal stimulus, with income tax cuts as a major component, to bring about economic recovery.

Judging from the sharp deterioration in the government's fiscal deficit, however, it is fair to say that fiscal policy on the whole has been expansionary since 1992. According to the OECD, Japan's general government financial balance as a percentage of GDP worsened from –0.6 percent in 1990 to –8.8 percent in 1999 (figure 5-4).[13] This share was by far the highest among OECD countries and significantly higher than the peak share of –6.7 percent reached in the United States in 1992. The implementation of aggressive economic stimulus packages, coupled with the sharp decline in tax revenues

13. *OECD Economic Outlook* 68, December 2000.

Figure 5-5. *General Government Gross Financial Liabilities,*
Japan and the United States, 1990–2000

Percent of GDP

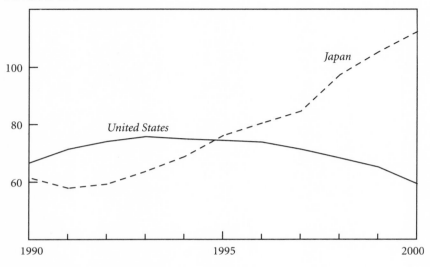

Source: *OECD Economic Outlook* 68, December 2000.

resulting from the economic slowdown, has contributed to the widening of the deficit.

The need to finance a chronic fiscal deficit has resulted in a sharp increase in public borrowing. The gross financial liabilities of Japan's public sector surged from 57.9 percent as a percentage of GDP in 1991 to 112.3 percent in 2000, the highest among all OECD countries (figure 5.5). Nominal interest rates (ten-year government bond yield) averaged 3.1 percent between 1992 and 2000, well above the 0.9 percent growth rate of nominal GDP during the same period. At these rates the debt-to-GDP ratio will continue to increase even if new borrowing is limited to financing interest payments. In addition to a recovery of the Japanese economy, drastic cuts in public spending and/or increases in taxes will be needed to redress Japan's fiscal position.

Structural Reform

As efforts to restore economic growth through fiscal and monetary expansion have failed repeatedly, the need to pursue structural reform has become more apparent. The growing concern about a hollowing out of industry (discussed in chapter 3) has added a sense of urgency. Furthermore, the prospect of a shrinking work force means that Japan will have to focus even more sharply on higher productivity through supply-side structural reform to sustain economic growth over the long term.

What Went Wrong?

Japan's economic growth rate has declined in steps since the early 1970s, from 10.4 percent in the 1960s, to 5.2 percent in the 1970s, 3.8 percent in the 1980s, and 1.7 in the 1990s. Since investment (as measured by gross capital formation) as a percentage of GDP was about the same (at about 30 percent) in both the 1980s and the 1990s, the decline in the growth rate in recent years can be attributed to a decline in investment efficiency, as reflected in a sharp increase in the incremental capital-output ratio (ICOR).[14] Indeed, the ICOR is now substantially higher, and thus efficiency of investment much lower, in Japan than in the United States (figure 5-6). Above all, the potential economic growth rate slowed as a natural result of Japan closing its technology gap with the industrial powers. The rate was further dragged down when both the government and the corporate sector failed to adapt the institutions that had contributed to the economy's past success to the new environment.

In retrospect, the postwar Japanese model played an important role in supporting Japanese industry during its catch-up phase, when technology was readily available from abroad, corporate goals were clear, and investment risk was small. A spirit of national consensus promoted close cooperation between business and government, helping to concentrate resources in promising areas that needed substantial initial investment. A high savings rate reduced the cost of capital and promoted investment, in an era when capital controls prevented domestic interest rates from converging to the overseas levels, while the emergence of new industries ensured that the marginal efficiency of investment stayed high. A cross-shareholding system centered on main banks allowed the pursuance of long-term corporate goals (including a lifetime employment system and market share maximization) instead of short-term profits. Combined with a dedication to the production of high-quality products, Japanese manufacturers quickly established themselves as a major force in international markets.

14. The ICOR is calculated by dividing gross capital formation as a percentage of GDP by the GDP growth rate. The higher its value the less efficient is investment in raising output.

Figure 5-6. *Incremental Capital-Output Ratio, Japan and the United States, 1974–99*[a]

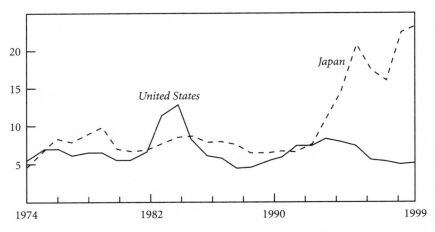

Source: Compiled by Nomura Research Institute based on IMF, *International Financial Statistics*.
a. Based on five-year moving averages of gross capital formation as a percentage of GDP and GDP growth.

Now that the catch-up process is over and Japan needs to develop its own economic frontiers, a new system that promotes competition and risk taking has become all the more important. Furthermore, Japan is facing three new challenges. First, its working population is expected to shrink as a result of an aging society and a declining birthrate. Second, the trend toward globalization implies keener international competition not only in the manufacturing sector but also in the service sector (finance, distribution, telecommunications, and so on). Third, rapid developments in information technologies call for more flexible and innovative business practices. Many of the structures and institutions that proved so valuable in helping to develop Japan's industrial power in the past are thus no longer sufficient to meet the needs of a more mature, service-oriented economy.

What Should Be Done?

To revitalize the Japanese economy in this new environment, several structural problems need be redressed.

INDUSTRIAL POLICY AND GOVERNMENT REGULATIONS. The overall thrust of Japan's industrial policy has switched from market-conforming "accelerationism" to market-defying "preservatism."[15] The purpose is to preserve existing industries to protect sunk costs, to prevent unemployment, and to maintain wage equality. The recession cartels formed under the initiative of the Ministry of International Trade and Industry (MITI) to protect declining industries have reinforced inefficiency. In the name of egalitarianism, members of a recession cartel are obliged to cut production in proportion to their share of the market or their share of capacity. To help out the weakest, the bigger or stronger firms are sometimes pressured to take an extra-large cut. Under Japan's "convoy" system, the whole convoy can move no faster than the slowest ship.

At the same time, excessive government regulations and a high corporate tax rate have sustained domestic prices at an artificially high level. The gap with overseas prices is particularly marked for public utilities charges and transportation and distribution costs. Protection of the agricultural sector has also led to higher food prices and land prices. Since services and land are important inputs for the manufacturing sector, their high prices adversely affect the competitiveness of Japanese products in international markets, forcing companies to relocate production offshore. Furthermore, constrained by the notorious Large-Scale Retail Store Law, the Japanese retail sector has traditionally been composed of small stores and complex distribution networks. The resulting inefficiency and high markups have made consumer product prices much higher in Japan than overseas.

BANKING AND FINANCE. Until recently, the convoy system also applied to the financial sector, whereby the government ensured that no financial institutions (banks in particular) would go bankrupt. In case a bank became insolvent, the Ministry of Finance would arrange for it to merge with another bank to protect the interests of depositors and borrowers. This safety net created moral hazard problems, prompting banks to take excessive risks (as in the late 1980s), sowing the seeds of the bad debt problem that emerged with the bursting of the asset price bubble in the 1990s.

Japan needs to establish a financial system capable of allocating funds based on the market mechanism instead of direction by the government. The traditional financial system was established to assist the formation of a mass production society, soaking up funds from the public at large to lend them to standardized mass production industries. The uniform interest rates and government protection adopted for this system meant that major corporations could rely on low-cost borrowing from commercial banks.

15. Katz (1998).

This system, however, encouraged inefficient uses of capital, rewarding marginally profitable firms by penalizing more efficient competitors. It also limited the access of Japanese consumers to a full range of competitive financial products. In addition, under the traditional system venture businesses have difficulty borrowing from banks because they do not have land to offer as collateral. To develop new industries, Japan should take steps to facilitate venture businesses to raise funds through capital markets, including listing on stock markets, to ensure that savings are channeled to industries that may involve high risks.

At the same time, there is an urgent need to reform the postal savings system, which is the largest deposit-taking institution in the world. This state-run system enjoys a competitive advantage over private banks because it does not have to pay corporate taxes or deposit insurance premiums and is not subject to reserve requirements. Postal savings are used to finance policy loans (channeled automatically through the Ministry of Finance and then through government-related financial institutions) based more on political than economic considerations. Some of these borrowers are public corporations that are running very large deficits, raising doubt about their ability to repay without additional financial support from the government.

PUBLIC FINANCE. The immense amount of public expenditures, including those incurred in the name of pump-priming fiscal expansion, may not have been efficiently used. At 6.0 percent of GDP in fiscal year 1998, public fixed capital formation was significantly higher than in other industrial countries (it was 1.9 percent for the United States, for example). The lack of transparency in awarding contracts has provided fertile soil for corruption and collusion among construction companies to raise prices. Public works have also been used to create jobs and transfer income (to the construction sector and to the countryside) rather than as investments to yield a return. Making matters worse, under a very rigid budget system, public expenditures continue to be channeled into declining sectors while such new areas as information infrastructure receive insufficient public funds. This backward-looking public spending strategy has led to a misallocation of social resources and retarded economic growth.

CORPORATE GOVERNANCE. The Japanese corporate system, characterized by long-term relations, has led to inefficiency, as companies come to be plagued by excess capacity, overemployment, and debt overhang. The lifetime employment system and corporate groupings (*keiretsu*) centered on main banks played important roles in the development of Japan's manufacturing industry, which requires on-the-job training, technology transfer to subcontractors, and a stable supply of low-cost funds. However, flexibility in combining various factors of production is more important in new areas such as information and finance. To facilitate industrial restructuring, the government should eliminate obstacles to mergers and acquisitions, the mobility of labor, and the development of venture capital.

In recent years, the supervisory function of the main banks has greatly weakened. There is an urgent need to rebuild corporate governance based on market principles. As part of that process, it is necessary to form a mobile market of senior executives to replace the present practice of promoting managers from within the corporate hierarchy. In addition, managers ought to be monitored using objective market indicators, and one way to achieve that is to link their compensation to company share prices by granting them stock options.

Recent Attempts at Reform

Although the structural problems facing the Japanese economy are well known, attempts at reform have always met with resistance from vested interests. In a sharp break from its traditional gradual and piecemeal approach, in December 1996 the Japanese government under Prime Minister Ryutaro Hashimoto adopted a comprehensive reform program that covers six key areas: economic structure, finance and banking, public finance, health and welfare, public administration, and education. The aim of this reform program is to revitalize the economy and to create a free and fair socioeconomic system that is fully open to the international community and is based on the rules of accountability and market principles. This is to be achieved by eliminating or relaxing regulations and transferring the responsibilities of the government to the private sector. The regulatory role of the government will be shifted from ex ante approval to ex post monitoring of compliance with general rules in this process.

Among the six key areas, reform of economic structure, which aims at shifting resources to growth areas that will underpin domestic employment over the long term, will have the largest direct impact on productivity growth. The government aims to facilitate corporate restructuring by reducing restrictions that hinder mergers and acquisitions, cross-border investments, alliances, and financial transactions both within and across national borders. Specifically, ongoing reform and deregulation initiatives include the following measures.

—Changes in corporate taxation. The government implemented a permanent tax cut in fiscal year 1999, reducing the corporate tax rate from

46 percent to 40 percent, making it competitive with tax rates in the United States and Germany.

—Promotion of new industries. The government is supporting the creation of new industries and business start-ups by private entrepreneurs. To this end, it is implementing deregulation, technological development, and human resource development to create a business environment conducive to the growth of fifteen industries selected for their high growth potential in the next generation.[16]

—Changes in antimonopoly regulations. Japan's antimonopoly law has been revised to facilitate mergers and acquisitions. The ban on pure holding companies (companies with more than half of their assets being shares of other companies) was lifted (effective from December 1997 for nonfinancial firms and March 1998 for financial firms). In addition, where once all mergers and acquisitions were required to be reported to the Fair Trade Commission, now only those transactions above a certain amount need to be registered.

—Changes in commercial law. Corporate acquisitions by stock transfer rather than cash purchases have been approved. Regulations concerning the legal structure of Japanese companies, including rules governing corporate spin-offs and divestitures, are now being reviewed and altered.

—Changes in corporate pension systems. A new pension contribution system modeled after the 401(k) plan in the United States is to be introduced in 2001. The scheme allows employees to contribute a portion of their compensation, before income taxes, to a company-sponsored retirement plan. Under the new scheme, employees decide how the contributions are to be invested, and continuity is guaranteed when they change jobs.

—Changes in accounting regulations. To improve transparency and disclosure, beginning in fiscal year 2000, Japanese companies are required to report market-value–based consolidated financial statements that cover subsidiaries. Under the new rules, the Japanese accounting system has become consistent with international standards.

Early Signs of Change

Thanks to the ongoing efforts toward reform, the Japanese economy has shown positive signs of change. Japanese corporations are responding to

---

16. The fifteen targeted fields are medical care and welfare; lifestyle and culture; information and telecommunications; new manufacturing technology; distribution and logistics; environment; business supporting services; oceanic and maritime industries; biotechnology;

keener competition resulting from globalization and deregulation, and consumers have benefited from this process in terms of lower prices and better services.

Progress in Corporate Restructuring

Japanese corporations are undergoing a restructuring process that involves not only downsizing but also drastically changing their traditional business practices. Greater emphasis is given to profitability than to market share. Labor mobility is increasing, and merit is gradually replacing seniority as the basis of remuneration. The main bank and *keiretsu* systems are also losing their influence, and mergers and acquisitions among companies belonging to different corporate groups have become a common means of restructuring.

First, Japanese companies are paying more attention to the rate of return on their investment, with return on equity and return on assets followed closely by both managers and investors. During the bubble period, fueled by very low-cost capital, Japanese corporations actively increased their asset portfolios with little regard to profitability. The subsequent recession, rising debt and bankruptcies, and inefficient use of management resources further reduced corporate profits and prompted a change in corporate strategy. A survey by the Economic Planning Agency confirms that an increasing share of Japanese corporations is focusing on the rate of return rather than the absolute levels of sales and profits (figure 5-7). The same survey shows that many corporate managers see both the cross-shareholding system and the main bank system weakening. From now on, their investment decisions will be closely monitored by shareholders and creditors, who are demanding a rate of return commensurate with the risk to their investment. At the same time, more corporate managers have been granted stock options in recent years, so that they now have a stronger incentive to maximize profit.

Second, the lifetime employment system is giving way to a more flexible one. During the recent recession many companies restructured through layoffs, early retirement, and limiting hiring. As a result, the unemployment rate has reached a historic high level; the government responded by launching diverse initiatives to create employment. The former government employment policy was designed to maintain workers at their present jobs, but the emphasis has shifted to promoting the transfer of human resources to new growth areas. Higher labor mobility in turn has made it difficult for

---

urban environment; aviation and space; new energies and energy conservation; human resource development; economic globalization; and housing and construction.

Figure 5-7. *Focus of Japanese Corporate Strategy, 1998*

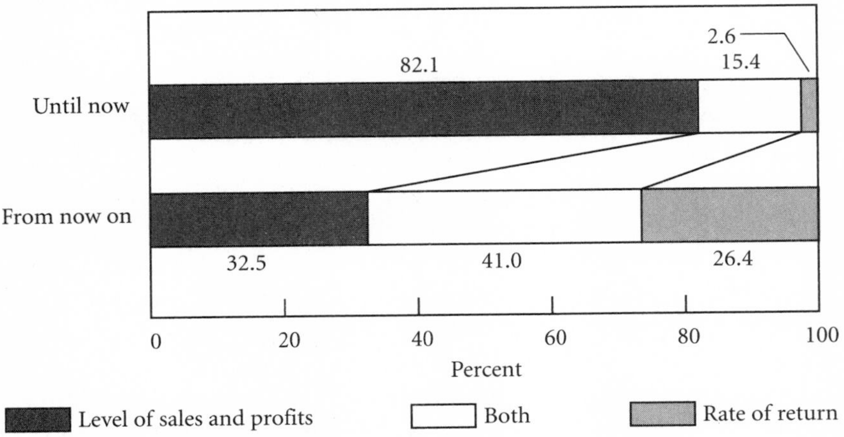

Source: EPA, *1998 Survey of Corporate Behaviors,* April, 1999.

Japanese companies to sustain a remuneration system based on seniority, prompting them to shift to a new system based more on merit. This is particularly true for financial institutions, which are losing some of their brightest professionals to foreign competitors that are expanding their operations in Tokyo.

Third, mergers and acquisitions have become widely used in corporate reorganization and restructuring to achieve economies of scale and economies of scope. M&A activity is increasing not only in the service sector, which is responding to deregulation, but also in the manufacturing sector, which is facing keen competition in the global market. The increase in M&As has been led by the banking sector. Following the merger between Mitsubishi Bank and Tokyo Bank in 1996, Dai-ichi Kangyo Bank, Fuji Bank, and Industrial Bank of Japan joined hands to form the Mizuho Financial Group in the autumn of 2000. Subsequently, alliances were formed between Sanwa Bank, Tokai Bank, and Toyo Trust Bank, and between Sumitomo Bank and Sakura Bank in the spring of 2001. At the same time, Bank of Tokyo-Mitsubishi was joined by Mitsubishi Trust Bank and Nippon Trust Bank. As a result, Japan's largest banks will effectively be consolidated into four major groups.

In many cases, recent M&As in the financial sector have involved foreign partners eager to cash in on the Big Bang. When Yamaichi Securities was liquidated in 1998, Merrill Lynch took over its branch network. GE Capital acquired Toho Life Insurance Company and then Japan Lease Corporation, Japan's fifth-largest consumer finance company. In 1998 Traveler's Group invested in Nikko Securities, one of the Big Three in Japan's securities industry, by purchasing 25 percent of its stock. More recently, Ripplewood, a U.S.-led investment group that includes General Electric and the Mellon Bank as major partners, acquired the temporarily nationalized Long-Term Credit Bank from the government.[17]

Japan is also part of the global wave of M&As in the automobile industry. Renault of France invested $5.3 billion in Nissan in 1998, giving it a 36.8 percent ownership share of Japan's second-largest automaker. This was followed by General Motors's investment in Fuji Heavy Industry in 1999 and DaimlerChrysler's acquisition of a 33.4 percent stake in Mitsubishi in 2000. As a result, seven of Japan's eleven major automakers have come under the control of foreign companies. Of the remaining four, Toyota now has majority holding of Daihatsu and Hino, and only Honda has decided to go it alone.[18]

The rise in cross-border M&A activity is reflected in a sharp increase in foreign direct investment into Japan. According to the Ministry of Finance, inward foreign direct investment doubled in fiscal year 1999, reaching $21.5 billion. The current pace of investment in Japan by foreign companies is more than five times as high as that five years ago.

Consumers Benefiting from Deregulation

Meanwhile, Japan's deregulation program is moving steadily ahead in accordance with the original schedule. In addition to the changes in the financial sector noted earlier, the positive effects of deregulation have been most apparent in the retail and telecommunications sectors.

---

17. Nippon Credit Bank, another major bank temporarily nationalized, was sold to an investment group led by Masayoshi Son, who is the chairman of Softbank and by far Japan's most successful venture capitalist.

18. Other examples of recent M&As in the manufacturing sector include the merging of Nippon Oil and Mitsubishi Oil in April 1999; and Japan Tobacco acquiring Asahi Chemical's food business in January 1999 and Asahi Beer's pharmaceutical subsidiary in November 1998. In addition, General Electric, Hitachi, and Toshiba agreed in April 1999 to create an international atomic fuel company, and Toshiba and Mitsubishi Electric established an industrial motor company in October 1999. Nippon Paper and Daishowa, the nation's second- and fourth-largest paper firms, also merged under a holding company in the spring of 2001. In the telecommunications sector, DDI, KDD, and IDO merged on October 1, 2000, to challenge NTT, Japan's largest telecom group. Meanwhile, NKK and Kawasaki, Japan's second- and third-largest steelmakers, have agreed to integrate their operations in October 2002.

Following two major amendments implemented in 1992 and 1994, the Large-Scale Retail Store Law was finally abolished in June 2000. As a result of the sharp reduction in entry barriers, the number of large-scale retail stores increased by 41.1 percent between 1991 and 1997, compared with only 16.7 percent in the previous six years, despite a sharp slowdown in economic growth. Keener competition is raising the efficiency of the retail sector, presenting Japanese consumers with lower prices and a greater array of choices than before. The Large-Scale Retail Store Law has been replaced by the Large-Scale Retail Store Location Law, which stipulates that regulation of large stores will no longer be based on supply and demand considerations but on the degree to which a large store opening or expansion affects the local environment.

In the telecommunications sector, deregulation allows businesses and consumers to access a far wider range of services at reduced prices. For example, long-distance telephone rates have fallen by more than 75 percent since 1985. Cellular telephone subscriptions also increased rapidly, from 2.13 million in 1993 to 62.2 million in October 2000, since reform efforts allowed the introduction of a new sales system in 1994.[19] The expanding scope and size of the market not only lowered telecommunication costs drastically but also provided opportunities to a number of foreign firms such as Nokia and Motorola to enter the Japanese market. Investors also recognize the emerging opportunities, as reflected in the highly successful public offering of NTT Mobile Communications Network (DoCoMo) in October 1998.

The Unfinished Agenda

Although there are early signs of change, Japan's transition to a market economy is far from complete, and many barriers hindering reform remain to be overcome.[20]

THE TRADE-OFF BETWEEN SHORT-TERM AND LONG-TERM GROWTH. Reform in some areas has been delayed because of the need to maintain employment and financial stability. In addition to roads being built to nowhere, using taxpayers' money, there are more implicit forms of serious resource misallocation. Subsidizing money-losing banks and companies has

---

19. Before that, users could only subscribe on a rental basis and were required to pay a lump-sum deposit. Subsequent innovations that allow direct access to the Internet have also boosted subscriptions.

20. For a critical view of Japan's reform process, see Lincoln (1998).

the adverse effect of locking resources in stagnant sectors instead of shifting them to more dynamic ones. Guaranteeing bank loans to small- and medium-sized companies and bailing out troubled financial institutions, in particular, have led to immense moral hazard problems.

Moreover, the current level of fiscal deficit is certainly too high to be sustainable. The frozen Fiscal Structural Reform Act should be revived once private demand is back in the driver's seat. It is necessary not only to increase tax revenues and reduce expenditures but also to improve the fiscal structure itself. This requires redefining the division of labor between the public and the private sectors as well as between the national and local governments based on cost-benefit calculations.

RESISTANCE FROM VESTED INTEREST GROUPS. Resistance from vested interest groups has remained a major barrier to reform. Administrative reform, for example, has so far achieved no more than a nominal reshuffling of the ministries. In addition to allowing the private sector and local governments to play a more important role in providing public services, a lot more needs to be done in improving administrative transparency, accountability, and adaptability. Japan suffers from a deeply conservative policy process, which slows decisionmaking, discourages open debate, encourages clientelism, and allows special interests to block needed changes.[21] New incentives, participants, and controls in the regulatory processes are needed to reorient old relationships with producer groups, to break up information monopolies in the bureaucracy, and to narrow administrative discretion to regulate in the name of the public interest.

The failure to privatize the postal savings system provides a typical example of where vested interests continue to obstruct the reform process. As proposed in the interim report of the Administrative Reform Council, an ad hoc panel headed by Ryutaro Hashimoto when he was prime minister, there is a broad consensus that the postal savings system should be privatized to improve the allocation of financial resources. With strong opposition from the Post and Communications Ministry, however, the plan has not been realized.

THE EGALITARIAN WAY OF THINKING. The egalitarian way of thinking remains deep rooted in the current debate on economic reform, even though the importance of competition has been greatly emphasized. For example, many people are concerned that competition may increase income inequality, with adverse effects on social stability. Since probably nowhere in

21. OECD, *Regulatory Reform in Japan, 1999.*

the world is the income distribution as equitable as it is in Japan, however, the efficiency gain that competition creates is likely to be much greater than any harm it causes by increasing income inequality. Japan needs a change of mind-set: a shift from pursuing equality of outcome to equality of opportunity, so as to provide more rainbows to chase for those who wish to put their talents to work.

Two

Forming a
Yen Bloc
in Asia

6

A Japanese Perspective

M y study of the possibility of forming a yen bloc from a Japanese perspective focuses on the implications for Japan itself of forming a monetary union with Asia.[1] If the benefits exceed the costs, then Japan would be likely to pursue it as a policy objective and try to remove barriers hindering its realization. With Asia now replacing the United States as Japan's largest trading partner, stabilizing the yen's effective exchange rate through the formation of a yen bloc should help insulate the Japanese economy from the adverse effects of fluctuations in the yen-dollar rate. In addition, increasing the use of the yen as an international currency should make it easier for Japanese companies and banks to manage their foreign exchange risk in international transactions and facilitate the development of Tokyo as an international financial center. Growing recognition of these benefits has prompted the Japanese government to adopt ambitious measures to reform and liberalize its financial system.

The Internationalization of the Yen

The Japanese government's stance on the internationalization of the yen has shifted from reluctance to approval. At the same time, more emphasis is

---

1. This chapter draws heavily from the official report of the Council on Foreign Exchange and Other Transactions on the internationalization of the yen. See MOF (1999).

placed on promoting the use of the yen in Asia. However, incommensurate with Japan's status as an economic power and the world's largest creditor country, the use of the yen as an international currency lags far behind the dollar and the deutsche mark.

From Reluctance to Approval

Throughout the 1970s and 1980s, Japan's official stance on the use of the yen as an international currency can at best be described as neutral if not passive. While accepting the international use of its domestic currency as a "natural development," the authorities were concerned that the massive inflow and outflow of funds would destabilize the yen in foreign exchange markets as well as undermine the effectiveness of monetary policies by weakening their control over the domestic money supply. It was only under U.S. pressure in the 1980s that concrete steps were taken to promote the international use of the yen. However, major changes in the economic environment toward the end of the 1990s prompted the government to pursue the internationalization of the yen as a policy priority based on its own cost-benefit considerations.

Interest in the international role of the yen was first sparked in the discussion seeking a new international monetary system in the wake of the collapse of the Bretton Woods system in the early 1970s. Cross-border capital account transactions, including those involving the use of the yen, were liberalized to a large extent in December 1980, when the Foreign Exchange and Foreign Trade Control Law was substantially revised for the first time in thirty years. Subsequently, the U.S. trade deficit surged on the back of a strong dollar under President Ronald Reagan's policy mix of tight monetary policy and loose fiscal policy in the first half of the 1980s. It was against this background that the U.S. government put pressure on Japan through the Yen-Dollar Committee to promote the use of the yen as an international currency, hoping that the resulting increase in the demand for the yen would keep it from falling further against the dollar. An agreement was reached in May 1984 between the two governments concerning the liberalization of Japan's financial and capital markets, the internationalization of the yen, and the lowering of the barriers to access for foreign financial institutions participating in Japan's financial and capital markets.

As a follow-up to the Yen-Dollar Agreement, in March 1985 the Council on Foreign Exchange and Other Transactions proposed the following specific measures for promoting the internationalization of the yen: financial liberalization (particularly the continued liberalization of interest rates and the further development and expansion of open short-term money markets); liberalization of Euro-yen transactions as the first step toward improving the convenience of the yen for nonresidents; and establishment of a Tokyo offshore market to facilitate Euro-yen transactions in Tokyo.[2] Subsequently, these measures were implemented as scheduled but with only limited success in achieving their goal.

It was not until the implementation of Japan's financial Big Bang, the onset of the Asian currency crisis, and the introduction of the euro as the common currency in Europe in the late 1990s that policymakers became really serious about the idea of promoting the yen as an international currency. The publication of the official report of the Council on Foreign Exchange and Other Transactions in April 1999 symbolizes a major shift in Japan's official stance on the issue from a passive one to an active one.[3] This report emphasizes the benefits of a more important role for the yen as an international currency not only for Asian countries and the stability of the global monetary system but also for Japan itself.

From a Functional Approach to a Regional Approach

Studies on the internationalization of the yen used to be formulated in terms of "Japan versus the rest of the world" and offered no regional dimension, but this has changed in recent years against a background of deepening interdependence between Japan and Asia through trade and investment. The functional approach that focuses on the yen as an international currency used in denominating trade and capital transactions and as a reserve asset for foreign central banks is giving way to a regional approach that emphasizes the increasing role of the yen in Asia.

The first signs of change appeared in 1994, when both the MITI and the MOF published reports on the internationalization of the yen, with focus on its role in Asia.[4] The package of economic and currency measures announced by the EPA in April 1995 to cope with the yen's sharp appreciation also contained a section on the internationalization of the yen.[5] Besides articulating the traditional view that efforts by companies to denominate their transactions in yen should be welcomed because invoicing in yen terms helps companies avoid exchange rate risk, the package also suggested that from the standpoint of promoting the use of the yen as an international currency and

2. Euro-yen transactions refer to borrowing and lending in yen terms in offshore markets (notably London). The term *Euro* here should not be confused with the euro, Europe's newly introduced common currency.

3. MOF (1999).

4. MITI (1994); MOF (1994).

5. EPA (1995).

stabilizing foreign exchange markets, Japan should work to establish close cooperative relations with the monetary authorities of other Asian countries.

The shift to a regional approach has become even more apparent since the onset of the Asian crisis. The 1999 report of the Council on Foreign Exchange and Other Transactions makes it clear that the internationalization of the yen in Asia should be pursued as a policy objective in itself as well as a step toward a more important global role for the yen. Recognizing the vulnerability of the traditional dollar peg system as revealed by the Asian currency crisis, the report suggests that wider use of the yen in Asia may contribute to the stable economic development of the region, which in turn is a vital concern for Japan. It also advocated that "in promoting the internationalization of the yen, it is most realistic to begin with efforts aimed at boosting the use of the yen in Asia, which shares very strong economic ties with Japan. The active use of the yen in the process of Asia's recovery from the currency crises and its return to its stable growth path would provide a potent impetus to enhancing the international position of the yen."[6]

Limited Use of the Yen as an International Currency

During the second half of the 1980s, confidence in the yen and its international use were boosted by progress toward financial liberalization and a booming economy in Japan. However, with the collapse of the bubble economy in the 1990s and the low economic growth in Japan that accompanied it, the international role of the yen has stagnated or receded in trade, capital account transactions, and foreign exchange reserves of overseas central banks. At present, the yen lags far behind the dollar and the deutsche mark (to be replaced by the euro) in its role as an international currency. Japan today accounts for about 15 percent of world GDP and ranks as the world's largest net creditor country, but Japan's economic power so far has not been reflected in a more important role of the yen as an international currency.

The ratio of yen-invoiced exports from Japan has remained essentially unchanged: between 35 percent and 40 percent for more than ten years (figure 6-1). More than 80 percent of Japanese exports to the United States are invoiced in dollars (table 6-1). By comparison, the majority of Japanese exports to Europe is invoiced in yen (about 35 percent) or various European currencies (more than 50 percent), while the share of the dollar is low at 13 percent. Approximately half of Japanese exports to Asian countries (excluding China) are invoiced in yen, with the remaining half invoiced in dollars.

6. MOF (1999, p. 11).

Figure 6-1. *Yen-Invoiced Transactions, Japan's Trade, 1986–98*

Percent

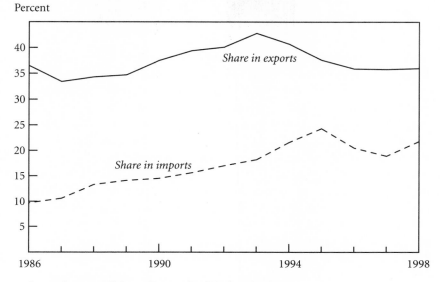

Source: Japanese Ministry of International Trade and Industry.

The share of Japanese imports invoiced in yen is only slightly more than 20 percent, although it has been gradually rising as a result of increases in imports from overseas subsidiaries by Japanese companies. The bulk of Japan's imports from the United States is invoiced in dollars (more than 80 percent). On the other hand, the yen is widely used in

Table 6-1. *Japan's Trade, Invoicing Currencies by Region, March 1998*

Percent share

Region	Exports			Imports		
	Yen	*U.S. dollar*	*Others*	*Yen*	*U.S. dollar*	*Others*
United States	15.7	84.1	0.1	16.9	83.0	0.1
European Union	34.9	13.2	51.9	44.3	14.3	41.4
Asia[a]	48.4	48.7	2.9	26.7	71.6	1.7
World	36.0	51.2	12.9	21.8	71.5	6.7

Source: Japanese Ministry of International Trade and Industry.
a. Asia excludes China.

imports from Europe and accounts for 44 percent of this trade, with various European currencies accounting for nearly the same ratio. Dollar-invoiced goods make up a very high ratio of Japan's imports from Asia (more than 70 percent).

Japan's pattern of trade invoicing is consistent with the observations that trade of homogeneous primary commodities and raw materials such as crude oil has been traditionally conducted in dollars, while trade in differentiated manufactured goods tends to be carried out in the currency of the exporting country. The fact that the share of manufactured products in Japan's total imports is low compared to other major industrial countries partly explains why the share of yen-invoiced imports is low. On the other hand, the ratio of yen invoicing is higher for Japanese exports than Japanese imports because they are largely composed of differentiated manufactured goods. In particular, Japanese products that are highly competitive in international markets tend to be invoiced in yen, as in the case of machinery in general and cars in particular.

In addition to Japan's unique trade structure among the industrial countries, three factors contribute to the low ratio of yen invoicing in Japan's external trade. First, Japanese companies prefer to use the dollar in intrafirm cross-border transactions so as to shift foreign exchange risk from overseas subsidiaries to headquarters. Second, Japanese exporters use a pricing-to-market policy in an attempt to maintain market shares.[7] Third, many Asian countries that peg their currencies loosely against the dollar favor invoicing in dollars in their trade with Japan.

Yen-denominated bonds accounted for only 9.8 percent of international bonds outstanding in March 2000, down from 15.8 percent at the end of 1994.[8] Until recently, growth of the international yen bond market has been hindered by restrictions on cross-border capital transactions, limited means for holding and managing yen assets by nonresidents, and the withholding tax on interest income and securities transaction tax.[9]

The yen's share of outstanding foreign currency denominated cross-border liabilities of all BIS reporting banks stood at 6.7 percent at the end of 1999, far behind the dollar (43.4 percent) and euro area currencies (24.4 per-

---

7. Fukuda and Ji (1994). With their emphasis shifting from market share to profitability, however, from now on Japanese companies may prefer invoicing in yen instead of pricing to the market.

8. BIS (2000, table 13B).

9. These barriers have been substantially reduced since the introduction of the revised Foreign Exchange and Foreign Trade Control Law in April 1998 and the fiscal year 1999 revisions to the taxation system.

cent).[10] The share of yen-denominated loans of Japanese banks' overseas lending is a bit higher at about 20 percent, a level that remained essentially unchanged throughout the 1990s.[11] Demand for yen-denominated loans is low, reflecting the slow growth in yen-invoiced current account transactions. At the same time, thanks to the development of swap markets for yen-dollar transactions, there seems to be no specific disadvantage in conducting business in dollars.

The use of the yen as a reserve currency has been even more disappointing. The yen's share of global reserves dropped steadily to 5.1 percent in 1999, down from 8.5 percent in 1991.[12] The high volatility of the yen against major currencies has reduced the incentives for foreign central banks to maintain a higher percentage of these foreign reserves in yen.[13] At the same time, shallow money markets, distorted by a complex system of withholding tax, have made it difficult for foreign central banks to park liquid working balances in yen-denominated short-term instruments.[14]

The Benefits to Japan

The MOF sees two principal benefits to Japan from increasing the use of the yen as an international currency: Japanese companies and other economic agents will find it easier to manage their foreign exchange risk in international transactions, and the development of Tokyo as an international financial center will be facilitated.[15] The same benefits would no doubt flow from the establishment of a yen bloc, which would be a major step in this direction. In addition, with Asia now replacing the United States as Japan's largest trading partner, stabilizing the yen's effective exchange rate through the formation of a yen bloc should help insulate the Japanese economy from the adverse effects of fluctuations in the yen-dollar rate.

Macroeconomic Stability

The yen has been more volatile than either the U.S. dollar or the deutsche mark in effective terms, as no countries today are attempting to stabilize

---

10. BIS (2000, table 5A).

11. MOF (1999, p. 23).

12. IMF, *Annual Report 2000.*

13. Generally low interest rates in Japan have also been cited as a factor restraining the use of the yen as a reserve currency. However, this disadvantage should have been largely (if not more than) offset by the high rate of expected appreciation of the yen against the dollar.

14. Garber (1996).

15. MOF (1984).

Figure 6-2. *The Effective Exchange Rates of the Yen, the Deutsche Mark, and the U.S. Dollar, 1974–99*

1974 = 100

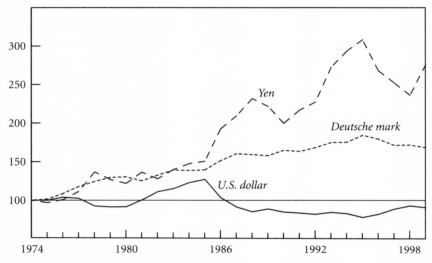

Source: Compiled by Nomura Research Institute based on IMF, *International Financial Statistics.*

their currencies against the yen (figure 6-2). A yen bloc would give the yen a certain built-in stability against other Asian currencies, since countries participating in it would seek to maintain stable exchange rates against the yen. As a group, the countries of Asia are now Japan's single largest export market and source of imports. If the yen were to remain stable against other Asian currencies, then its effective exchange rate against the currencies of major trading partners would fluctuate less. In fact, a yen bloc in Asia would eliminate exposure to fluctuations in the yen-dollar rate for nearly 40 percent of Japan's exports and imports.[16]

16. Instead of forming a yen bloc, a more orthodox approach to stabilizing Japan's effective exchange rate would be to stabilize the yen against major currencies through the coordination of monetary policy among the major industrial countries. Given the Asian countries' current foreign exchange policy of a loose peg to the dollar, this would also help to achieve the stability of the yen against Asian currencies indirectly. However, the experience since the Plaza Accord in 1985 shows just how difficult it is to maintain stable exchange rates among the major currencies. Therefore, at least as a second-best solution, the option of forming a yen bloc in Asia should not be ruled out.

By stabilizing the yen's effective exchange rate, a yen bloc would contribute to macroeconomic stability in Japan. Germany has set an example for Japan to follow. Through monetary integration with its European neighbors and the establishment of a de facto deutsche mark bloc, Germany has been able to minimize the adverse domestic economic impact of changes in the deutsche mark's exchange rate against the U.S. dollar. Japan's trade and investment ties with other Asian countries have been growing rapidly in recent years, and if Japan could form a similar yen bloc with these countries, its economy would no doubt become less vulnerable to fluctuations in the yen-dollar rate.

Most Asian countries loosely peg their currencies to the U.S. dollar, so that their currencies fall against the yen whenever the yen rises against the dollar. As a result, an appreciation of the yen boosts the competitiveness of Asian products at Japan's expense. It also creates deflationary pressures in Japan (leading to lower production and prices) but pushes up demand in Asia (leading to higher production and prices). If Asian countries joined the yen bloc and began to peg their currencies to the yen, however, the relative prices between products made in these countries and those made in Japan would become less volatile, and changes in the yen-dollar rate would have less impact on Japan's domestic economy.

With the formation of a yen bloc, a rise in the yen's value against the dollar would mean that the currencies of participating countries would also rise against the dollar at the same time and by the same degree. As the yen appreciates, Japan's competitiveness would still decline against countries outside the yen bloc (such as the United States) but would remain stable against countries inside (such as South Korea). In neither Japan nor in other Asian countries or third countries (such as the United States), then, would the stronger yen cause demand to shift from Japanese products toward products made in other Asian countries. The deflationary impact of yen appreciation on Japan would therefore be smaller if other Asian countries were part of a yen bloc. If the yen were to fall against the dollar, so too would other Asian currencies in the yen bloc. Japanese industries would as a result become more competitive only against industries in countries outside the yen bloc, and the resulting stimulus to the Japanese economy from growing net exports would be diminished. In this way, a yen bloc serves as a built-in stabilizer that reduces the impact of fluctuations in the yen-dollar rate on output and prices in Japan.

A yen bloc can be said to already exist but with only one member—Japan itself. Different regions within this bloc share a common currency and the flows of labor, capital, and goods are not exposed to exchange rate risk. If this yen bloc were to expand in size through the additional participation of other Asian countries, it would strengthen Japan's economic ties with these nations while contributing to a more stable domestic economy in Japan.

For instance, the exchange rate between the Tokyo yen and the Osaka yen is always one to one. Trade and investment between the two cities are therefore neither subject to exchange rate risk nor directly affected by fluctuations in the yen-dollar rate. Exporters in the two cities do not have to worry about losing export markets to each other as a result of exchange rate fluctuations. Should Korea join this yen bloc, the economic relations between Korea and Japan would become similar to those between Osaka and Tokyo. An appreciation of the yen against the dollar, for example, would not lead to a substitution of Korean products for Japanese products either in the two countries or in third-country markets (such as the United States).

The impact of the formation of a yen bloc on Japan's macroeconomic performance can be analyzed in terms of the supply and demand framework (figure 6-3). As the yen rises, the demand curve will naturally shift to the left along the plane of prices (in yen terms) and output, reducing both output and domestic prices. In the presence of a yen bloc, however, the shift is smaller in size: output and domestic prices would fall less. The larger the market size of the countries participating in the yen bloc and the stronger their competitive relationships with Japan, the smaller the shift in the demand curve that results from a change in the yen-dollar rate and the greater the yen bloc's stabilizing effect on Japan's economy.

In this way, the formation of a yen bloc (or an increase in the use of the yen as an international currency in general) will enable the Japanese economy to cope more effectively with fluctuations in the yen-dollar rate. In the short term, however, it could have just the opposite effect because overseas demand for yen (as a reserve asset, for example) could rise, pushing up the yen rate. Even so, over the long term the supply of yen assets may also increase as more yen-denominated financial instruments are issued by foreign companies and governments. The total impact on the yen rate can therefore be either positive or negative, depending on the new balance between demand and supply.

Microeconomic Considerations

The formation of a yen bloc would help Japan reduce the volatility of exchange rate movements (the irregular short-term ups and downs) while ameliorating the misalignments of exchange rates from equilibrium levels (the longer term deviations). Exchange rate volatility increases the risk of

Figure 6-3. *The Effect of a Yen Bloc on Japan*[a]

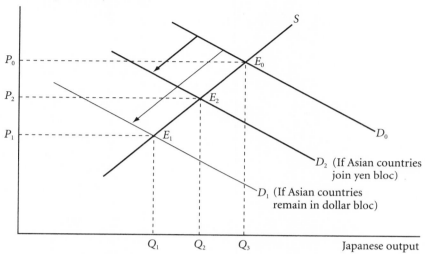

Domestic prices (in yen terms)

P_0

P_2

P_1

S

E_0

E_2

E_1

D_0

D_2 (If Asian countries join yen bloc)

D_1 (If Asian countries remain in dollar bloc)

Q_1 Q_2 Q_3 Japanese output

Source: Nomura Research Institute.
a. The case of a stronger yen.

cross-border transactions and impedes international trade and capital flows. Currency misalignments, by distorting the relationship between domestic and international prices, cause the relocation of labor, capital, and other economic resources, which can result in temporarily higher unemployment and less efficient utilization of capital invested in plant and equipment. Even if the currency misalignment disappears, once resources are misallocated it takes time for the economy to return to an optimal allocation of resources because of fixed costs and other factors. For instance, if an overvalued yen causes companies to shift certain production operations offshore, it is unlikely that this production will move back to Japan after the yen weakens to a more appropriate level.

Japanese companies try to deal with the adverse impact of exchange rate movements by using currency futures as a hedge, by writing yen-denominated export and import contracts, and by procuring their financing in yen and keeping their financial investments in yen. They also try to establish complete production and marketing capabilities in each of the major markets in which a different currency is used. Forming a yen bloc with other Asian countries would mean that more of Japan's trade would be denominated in yen and would help reduce the costs accompanying such actions to hedge against exchange rate fluctuations. Some observers argue that denominating more trade in yen would hurt Japan's trading partners. This argument, however, does not apply to members of a yen bloc, as they peg their currencies to the yen so that invoicing in yen actually helps reduce their foreign exchange risk.

Japan's expanding role as a net creditor nation also makes wider use of the yen, and thus the formation of a yen bloc, desirable, as it would help Japan stabilize the value of its overseas assets. Japanese investors have suffered huge capital losses as a consequence of the yen's appreciation since the Plaza Accord. Based on the latest level of net foreign assets of $819 billion (end of 1999), every 1 percent appreciation of the yen against the dollar implies a reduction in their total value in yen terms by $8.19 billion. The formation of a yen bloc should help Japan hedge against such foreign exchange risk, as most of its capital transactions with Asian countries would become denominated in yen.

The prospect of an aging population suggests that it may be difficult for Japan to sustain its high savings rate, and the day may soon come when it needs to borrow from abroad to finance a current account deficit. Already, the Japanese government is issuing a very large amount of bonds to finance its immense fiscal deficit. The costs of borrowing (in terms of interest rates) would become lower if the yen were in high demand as an international currency, the savings being the seigniorage that would accrue to Japan.[17] As in the case of overseas assets, Japan can also minimize exchange risk by borrowing in yen.

The flow of capital and goods should accelerate among countries participating in the yen bloc because of the diminished foreign exchange risk. This would bring Japanese financial institutions new business opportunities in financing yen-denominated trade transactions, in developing their brokerage business in Asian securities, in underwriting yen bonds issued by companies in other Asian countries, and in listing Japanese companies on Asian stock exchanges. Japanese banks and other financial institutions have a natural advantage in dealing with products denominated in yen over their foreign competitors because of familiarity with domestic macroeconomic policies and the legal and regulatory environment. They also have better

17. As the key-currency country, the United States has long been able to finance its current account deficit and overseas investment by borrowing at low costs from overseas (Japan in particular). This situation has continued despite the sharp deterioration of its net external position. In contrast, Japanese banks, ironically, have to pay a "Japan premium" when borrowing in dollar terms, although Japan is by far the largest creditor country in the world.

knowledge of the functioning of local financial markets, long-standing relationships with a large yen-based client base, and easy assess to the domestic payment and settlement systems.

Promoting the use of the yen as an international currency should also reduce the vulnerability of Japan's banking sector to fluctuations in the yen-dollar rate. With the bulk of their overseas lending denominated in the dollar, a weaker yen, for example, would force Japanese banks to reduce lending in order to meet the BIS minimum capital adequacy ratio (capital divided by risk assets) of 8 percent (see chapter 3). This constraint on Japanese bank lending can be avoided if overseas lending is mostly denominated in yen. Indeed, U.S. banks can afford to pay much less attention to exchange rate movements because most of their major balance sheet items are denominated in dollars, so that there is no mismatch in terms of currency denomination between the numerator and the denominator of the BIS ratio.

Promoting the Yen as an International Currency

When promoting the yen as an international currency, Japan should begin by concentrating its efforts in Asia, with which it shares very strong economic ties. More stable exchange rates between the yen and Asian currencies, together with progress in Japan's financial reform and liberalization, are the preconditions for wider use of the yen in the region.

Financial Reform and Liberalization

The formation of a yen bloc implies that the macroeconomic performance of the Asian countries would depend very much on that of Japan. Ten years after the bursting of the asset price bubble, Japan is still suffering from its aftermath. It goes without saying that if the yen is to play the role of Asia's key currency Japan needs first to put its own house in order. The success of current efforts in financial reform and liberalization under the Big Bang would be essential to enhance the attractiveness of the yen as an international currency (box 6-1). Conversely, actively promoting wider international use of the yen in Asia and elsewhere should enhance the quality and sophistication of the Tokyo market.

As the forerunner of the Big Bang, the Foreign Exchange and Foreign Trade Control Law was drastically revised in April 1998 to foster an environment that facilitates free cross-border transactions. It involves expanding the choice of financial instruments for investment and borrowing for both residents and nonresidents by liberalizing cross-border securities

Box 6-1. *Japan's Financial Big Bang*

The financial Big Bang aims to transform Tokyo into an international financial center on par with New York and London by the year 2001. The three underlying principles are free (toward a free market in which the market mechanism prevails), fair (toward a transparent and reliable market), and global (toward an international market ahead of its time). The Big Bang covers all major areas of the financial sector, including banking, securities, and insurance. It drastically reduces restrictions on products, services, and organizational structures and tries to improve fair trading rules for customer protection and to provide the framework for dealing with failures. While the measures to stabilize the financial system implemented since October 1998 aim at remedying problems inherited from the past, the Big Bang represents a forward-looking strategy preparing for the future.

The financial Big Bang was initiated in November 1996 and formulated into a formal agenda in June 1997. As the first step, the Foreign Exchange Law was revised in April 1998 to completely liberalize cross-border transactions. In December 1998 the Financial System Reform Law, a package of revisions of laws including the Banking Law, the Securities and Exchange Law, and the Insurance Business Law, came into effect. Almost all measures were implemented as planned, bringing drastic changes to the financial sector.

Efforts were made to provide attractive services by enhancing competition. Major measures include promoting entry of banks, securities companies, and insurance companies into each other's business, switching from the licensing system to a registration system for securities companies, liberalizing cross-border capital transactions and foreign exchange business, and liberalizing brokerage commissions

transactions and foreign deposits. Permission and prior notification requirements were abolished for external settlements and capital transactions. In addition, the "foreign exchange bank system" was abolished and restrictions on foreign exchange business were lifted to allow free entry (even by nonfinancial institutions). The resulting competition should lead to lower costs and better services in foreign exchange transactions.

The following aspects of the latest revision of the Foreign Exchange and Foreign Trade Control Law are particularly relevant for enhancing the use of and insurance premium rates. Many new securities companies including foreign ones have been established since switching to a registration system. (Thirty-two companies were newly registered during the thirteen months beginning with December 1998.) Furthermore, the liberalization of brokerage commissions has led to expansion of securities trading through the Internet (online trading). Financial institutions have also taken advantage of deregulation to increase the range of financial instruments and services available to investors, including financial derivatives and new investment trusts and over-the-counter sales of investment trusts by banks and other financial institutions.

New markets and channels for raising funds were created by abolishing the requirement to trade equities only through stock exchanges and by introducing electronic trading systems. In November 1999 the Tokyo stock exchange opened a new market for promising start-ups: "MOTHERS" (market of high-growth and emerging stocks). This was followed in May 2000 by the establishment of NASDAQ-Japan at the Osaka Stock Exchange.

Finally, a framework for prudential surveillance was established by improving the disclosure system, setting up fair trading rules (such as stricter insider trading control), and protecting customers when financial institutions fail. Since the accounting period ending March 1999, financial institutions have been required by law to disclose information on their nonperforming assets on a consolidated basis, according to standards equivalent to the ones set by the U.S. Securities and Exchange Commission.

Source: Japan's Ministry of Finance, "Japanese Big Bang" (www. mof.go.jp/english/big-bang/ebb37.htm [2000]).

the yen as an international currency. First, residents can now hold yen-denominated bank accounts overseas, making the yen a more convenient currency to use as a means of payment. Second, on the fund-raising side, residents are now free to issue yen-denominated bonds (Euro-yen bonds) overseas while nonresidents are free to issue yen-denominated bonds (samurai bonds) in the Tokyo market. Finally, regarding the use of funds, nonresidents can now invest in Japanese certificates of deposit and commercial paper without restrictions.

In December 1998 the Japanese government announced additional measures to facilitate the internationalization of the yen. They include the issuing of financing bills through competitive price auctions instead of underwriting by the Bank of Japan, exempting withholding tax on original issue discounts for treasury bills and financing bills, and exempting nonresidents and foreign corporations from tax on the interest from government bonds.

In the April 1999 report of the Council on Foreign Exchange and Other Transactions further measures were recommended to enhance the attractiveness of yen-denominated financial instruments. First, to promote nonresident participation in Japan's repo market, the transaction scheme should be promptly adjusted to promote transactions based on repurchase agreements adopted in the United States and Europe instead of collateralized lending and borrowing. Second, to fill in a major gap in the yield curve, five-year interest-bearing government bonds should be introduced to serve as a medium-term benchmark issue. Third, further diversification of available products in government bond markets should be pursued to match the various needs of investors. Introduction of the Separate Trading of Registered Interest and Principal of Securities program, which has already been introduced in government bond markets in the United States and Europe, should be considered. Fourth, the settlement system should be upgraded from the current Bank of Japan financial network system to a real-time gross settlement system. Fifth, it is necessary to expand yen-denominated facilities offered by the Bank of Japan to foreign central banks, to expand international commodity trading in Japan, to review Japanese accounting rules and standards, and to improve bankruptcy laws. These proposals are now being implemented step by step.

There has also been an ongoing debate over whether redenomination should be undertaken to promote the internationalization of the yen. Redenomination involves replacing the current "old yen" with "new yen" at a rate of 100 to 1, so that a new ¥100 note has the same value as an old ¥10,000 note.[18] As a result, exchange rate calculation will become simpler as one new yen would be worth approximately one dollar or one euro. This change should also give Japan a chance to proclaim to the world its intention to promote the yen as an international currency. On the negative side, however, the costs involved in printing the new notes, as well as in changing

18. The current ¥10,000 note carries the portrait of Yukichi Fukuzawa (1834–1901), a sage who popularized Western ideas in Japan during the Meiji era. Although Fukuzawa played a key role in the modernization of Japan, he may not be the right person to symbolize a yen bloc because he is famous for recommending that Japan should give up its Asian identity and become a member of the West.

the software and hardware of millions of automatic teller machines, computers, and cashier and vending machines to accommodate them, will be immense.[19]

At a more fundamental level, restoring the stability of the financial system that has been suffering the aftermath of the bursting of the asset price bubble is essential for the success of both the Big Bang and the internationalization of the yen. Fortunately, much progress has been made since the government committed ¥60 trillion for this purpose in October 1998, as we saw in chapter 5.

Issues Specific to Asia

A major factor restraining the use of the yen in Asia is the high volatility between the yen and Asian currencies. Japan can help reduce this volatility both by stabilizing the yen-dollar rate in coordination with the United States and by encouraging other Asian countries to peg closer to the yen.[20]

Increasing the trade between Japan and its neighbors should enhance the use of the yen in the region. While Japan's dependence on the Asian market has increased in recent years, the Asian countries' dependence on the Japanese market has actually declined due to the sharp slowdown in economic growth. Japan should therefore seek to revitalize its economy and to open its market further to imports.[21]

However, it is incorrect to attribute Japan's chronic trade surplus with its Asian neighbors per se as a major barrier to the formation of a yen bloc, as the capital account provides an alternative channel through which international liquidity can be easily raised. This is in sharp contrast to the situation under the Bretton Woods system, when international capital flows

---

19. These costs could be partly offset by the additional demand created by re-denomination. Although such demand is likely to be concentrated in specific industries, such as paper and pulp and office machinery, some economists argue that redenomination should create enough demand to bring the Japanese economy out of its prolonged recession.

20. The former is less favorable to wider use of the yen as an international currency than the latter. By minimizing the volatility of the yen-dollar rate, it may actually reduce the incentive for the Asian countries to diversify from the dollar to the yen in an optimal portfolio that seeks to balance between risk and return.

21. While Japan has expressed clearly its intention to promote the internationalization of the yen in Asia, there remain doubts over its ability to do so. Edward Lincoln of the Brookings Institution questions Japan's ability to play a leader's role in the region, based on his pessimistic view of the country's long-term economic outlook. This reservation is echoed by his colleague Barry Bosworth, who wonders why Asian countries should tie their fortune to a sinking ship, the "Nippon Maru." Meanwhile, Takatoshi Ito, deputy vice minister of the MOF, regrets that Japan did not promote the use of the yen as an international currency in the 1980s, when Japanese financial institutions were playing a leading role in international financial markets.

were tightly controlled so that, as the key-currency country, the United States could provide international liquidity only by importing more than it exports.[22] Improvement in Tokyo's financial markets should therefore provide opportunities for Asian countries to increase the weight of the yen on both sides of their balance sheets. Indeed, being the largest investor in Asia, Japan now runs an immense capital account deficit with Asia. Japanese banks, for example, account for 30 percent of bank lending to the region from OECD countries. Japan is also the most important source of official development assistance for Asia. In addition to the regular aid program, Japan has played a key role in granting financial support to the troubled countries in Asia to help them recover from the recent crisis. It has so far committed approximately $80 billion, including $30 billion under the new Miyazawa initiative announced in October 1998.[23]

So far, the idea of a yen bloc in Asia has been widely dismissed as premature, if not irrelevant, for political reasons. Most Asian countries, remembering their harsh experiences under Japanese occupation during World War II, are reluctant to give Japan a more prominent role in the region. The Japanese government, for its part, also seems unwilling to assume a higher profile in Asia or in the world at large. However, the recent monetary integration between Germany and France and the formation of a de facto deutsche mark bloc in large parts of eastern Europe, much of which suffered

22. During the 1960s, the need to supply international liquidity by running a large trade deficit led to a rapid deterioration in the U.S. net foreign position, which in turn reduced the credibility of the dollar as the key currency. This dilemma (known as the Triffin dilemma, named after Robert Triffin of Yale University) was one of the major factors leading to the demise of the Bretton Woods system.

23. Between July 1997 and November 1998 Japan committed emergency assistance for Asia totaling $44 billion, including bilateral cooperation (in the context of the IMF-led assistance package): $4 billion for Thailand, $5 billion for Indonesia, and $10 billion for South Korea. Also included in the $44 billion figure were funds for the facilitation of trade financing and assistance for private investment, for the socially vulnerable, for economic structural reforms, and for human resources development. In October 1998 Japan announced a "new initiative to overcome the Asian currency crisis," more commonly known as the New Miyazawa Initiative, with financial commitments totaling $30 billion. Of this, $15 billion was to be made available for the medium- to long-term financial needs for economic recovery in Asian countries; another $15 billion was to be set aside for these countries' possible short-term capital needs while implementing economic reform. Japan has also proposed an "Asian currency crisis support facility" totaling about $3 billion. This facility provides guarantees for private bank loans, bond insurance, and interest subsidies. Finally, at the December 1998 ASEAN + 3 (China, Japan, South Korea) Informal Summit Meeting, Japan committed to establishing a Special Yen Loan Facility totaling ¥600 billion (about $5 billion) over three years to promote economic recovery, employment creation, and structural reforms in Asian countries. Concessional terms include a low interest rate of 1 percent, with repayment in forty years. Information from Japan's Ministry of Foreign Affairs.

at Germany's hands in both world wars, suggest that such political barriers are surmountable. By enhancing economic interdependence, monetary integration is expected to play a positive role in preventing member countries from fighting one another again in the future.

Indeed, the political cost of a yen bloc in Asia seems to be falling, while the potential economic benefit is rising. The idea of a yen bloc will mature when the economic benefit surpasses the political cost. Malaysia's proposal to form an East Asian Economic Caucus, with Japan playing a leading role and the United States being excluded, suggests that this time may not be far away. The recent improvement in Japan-Korea relations is also encouraging. By burying past animosity between the two countries, President Kim Dae Jung's visit to Japan in October 1998 paved the way for a Korea-Japan partnership in the twenty-first century. As a major step in this direction, the possibility for the two countries to form a free trade area is now under serious discussion.

7

An Asian
Perspective

A yen bloc would not be formed to suit only Japan's own interest. To deepen understanding of the issue, we need to add the perspective of the Asian countries, which would be potential members of the bloc.[1] Pegging exchange rates closer to the Japanese yen should contribute to macroeconomic stability in Asia's developing countries (see chapter 4). This is particularly true for the Asian NIEs, which compete with Japan in international markets. By reducing the foreign exchange risk associated with yen-based transactions, such a major shift in Asia's exchange rate policy should promote wider use of the yen as a regional currency and capital inflow from Japan into the Asian countries, paving the way for the formation of a yen bloc.

In Search of Stability against the Yen

The latest crisis in Asia vividly illustrates that the traditional exchange rate policy of pegging to the U.S. dollar is no longer compatible with macroeconomic stability in the Asian countries (see chapter 3). To insulate themselves from the adverse effect on macroeconomic stability of a widely fluctuating yen-dollar rate, these countries should peg their currencies closer to

1. The chapter is based on Kwan (1992, 1994).

the Japanese yen by targeting a basket of currencies in which the yen carries a substantial weight.

Asia as a de Facto Dollar Bloc

Consistent with global trends, since the breakdown of the Bretton Woods system in the early 1970s the exchange rate regimes of most of the Asian countries have gradually shifted from pegging to a single currency (predominantly the dollar) to more flexible arrangements. To one extent or another, however, these countries continue to emphasize stability against the U.S. dollar in managing their foreign exchange rates. This can be confirmed by noting that the Asian currencies have been less volatile against the U.S. dollar than against other major currencies.[2]

The volatility of currency A (the yen, for example) against currency B (the dollar, for example) can be measured by the standard deviation of the month-to-month percentage change in the bilateral rate between A and B. The volatility among the Asian currencies, the dollar, the yen, and the deutsche mark is calculated for the period January 1991 to December 1994 (tables 7-1 and 7-2). The lower the volatility in the bilateral rate between two currencies, the more synchronized are their exchange rates (against third currencies).

The volatility of the Asian currencies has been much lower against the dollar than against the yen, which in turn has been marginally lower than against the deutsche mark. The volatility of the Chinese yuan against the dollar has been about the same as against the yen. This largely reflects the sharp devaluation of the yuan in January 1994, when China's dual exchange rates were unified. Excluding this outlier from the calculation, the volatility of the yuan has been much lower against the dollar than against the yen, as in the case of other Asian currencies. The volatility among the Asian currencies is low, but the volatility of these currencies against the dollar is even lower. It is therefore fair to say that the Asian countries belong to a de facto dollar bloc.

In contrast, despite a series of currency crises since 1992, the volatility among currencies of the western European countries has been much lower than their volatility against the dollar and the yen. These European currencies have been most stable against the deutsche mark, which has played the role of the anchor currency in the region. Among countries that adopted the euro as their common currency in 1999, exchange rate volatility has virtually disappeared.

2. Kwan (1998b).

Table 7-1. Volatility Matrix, Nine Asian Currencies, 1991–94[a]

Currency	Korea	Taiwan	Hong Kong	Singapore	Indonesia	Malaysia	Philippines	Thailand	China
Korean won	...	0.010	0.005	0.010	0.005	0.014	0.015	0.006	0.059
New Taiwan dollar	0.010	...	0.008	0.010	0.009	0.015	0.017	0.008	0.061
Hong Kong dollar	0.005	0.008	...	0.010	0.002	0.013	0.015	0.004	0.059
Singapore dollar	0.010	0.010	0.010	...	0.009	0.013	0.018	0.006	0.058
Indonesian rupiah	0.005	0.009	0.002	0.009	...	0.013	0.015	0.004	0.059
Malaysian ringgit	0.014	0.015	0.013	0.013	0.013	...	0.019	0.012	0.051
Philippine peso	0.015	0.017	0.015	0.018	0.015	0.019	...	0.016	0.060
Thai baht	0.006	0.008	0.004	0.006	0.004	0.012	0.016	...	0.059
Chinese yuan	0.059	0.061	0.059	0.058	0.059	0.051	0.060	0.059	...
(except January 1994)	0.007	0.010	0.007	0.010	0.006	0.010	0.015	0.007	...
Japanese yen	0.022	0.022	0.022	0.018	0.021	0.023	0.029	0.018	0.059
U.S. dollar	0.004	0.008	0.001	0.009	0.002	0.013	0.015	0.004	0.059
Deutsche mark	0.029	0.027	0.029	0.022	0.028	0.028	0.031	0.026	0.062

Source: Kwan (1998b).

a. Standard deviation of month-to-month rate of change for the period January 1991 to December 1994.

Table 7-2. *Volatility Matrix, Fifteen European Currencies, 1991–94*[a]

Currency	United Kingdom	France	Italy	Belgium	Nether-lands	Denmark	Ireland	Spain	Portugal	Greece	Austria	Sweden	Finland	Norway	Switzer-land
Pound sterling	...	0.020	0.018	0.020	0.020	0.021	0.021	0.018	0.022	0.018	0.021	0.027	0.022	0.019	0.021
French franc	0.020	...	0.020	0.005	0.006	0.006	0.018	0.015	0.014	0.007	0.006	0.021	0.026	0.007	0.011
Italian lira	0.018	0.020	...	0.020	0.020	0.021	0.027	0.020	0.022	0.017	0.021	0.021	0.022	0.017	0.022
Belgian franc	0.020	0.005	0.020	...	0.007	0.006	0.018	0.014	0.014	0.008	0.008	0.022	0.026	0.009	0.012
Dutch guilder	0.020	0.006	0.020	0.007	...	0.009	0.018	0.015	0.015	0.007	0.002	0.023	0.027	0.008	0.010
Danish krone	0.021	0.006	0.021	0.006	0.009	...	0.018	0.015	0.014	0.010	0.009	0.022	0.026	0.009	0.014
Irish pound	0.021	0.018	0.027	0.018	0.018	0.018	...	0.020	0.021	0.019	0.018	0.028	0.028	0.019	0.020
Spanish peseta	0.018	0.015	0.020	0.014	0.015	0.015	0.020	...	0.014	0.015	0.015	0.026	0.026	0.014	0.020
Portuguese escudo	0.022	0.014	0.022	0.014	0.015	0.014	0.021	0.014	...	0.015	0.015	0.024	0.025	0.015	0.020
Greek drachma	0.018	0.007	0.017	0.008	0.007	0.010	0.019	0.015	0.015	...	0.008	0.021	0.024	0.007	0.013
Austrian schilling	0.021	0.006	0.021	0.008	0.002	0.009	0.018	0.015	0.015	0.008	...	0.023	0.027	0.008	0.011
Swedish krona	0.027	0.021	0.021	0.022	0.023	0.022	0.028	0.026	0.024	0.021	0.023	...	0.025	0.018	0.024
Finish markka	0.022	0.026	0.022	0.026	0.027	0.026	0.028	0.026	0.025	0.024	0.027	0.025	...	0.024	0.027
Norwegian krone	0.019	0.007	0.017	0.009	0.008	0.009	0.019	0.014	0.015	0.007	0.008	0.018	0.024	...	0.013
Swiss franc	0.021	0.011	0.022	0.012	0.010	0.014	0.020	0.020	0.020	0.013	0.011	0.024	0.027	0.013	...
Japanese yen	0.033	0.027	0.032	0.028	0.026	0.028	0.034	0.033	0.029	0.026	0.027	0.033	0.035	0.028	0.028
U.S. dollar	0.032	0.028	0.033	0.029	0.029	0.029	0.033	0.033	0.031	0.027	0.029	0.034	0.035	0.028	0.032
Deutsche mark	0.020	0.006	0.021	0.008	0.001	0.009	0.018	0.015	0.015	0.007	0.001	0.023	0.027	0.008	0.011

Source: Kwan (1998b).

a. Standard deviation of month-to-month rate of change for the period January 1991 to December 1994.

Figure 7-1. *A Dollar Bloc and a Deutsche Mark Bloc, with No Yen Bloc*[a]

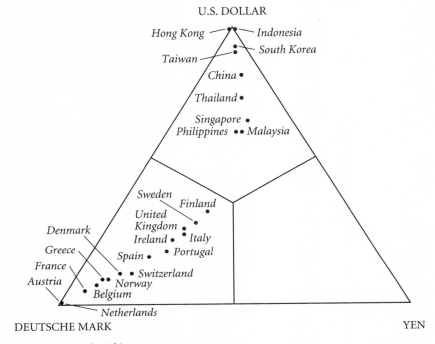

Source: Kwan (1998b).

a. For each country, distance from the corners shows the (relative) volatility of the home currency against the U.S. dollar, the deutsche mark, and the Japanese yen. Volatility is measured as the standard deviation of month-to-month rate of change for the period January 1991 to December 1994. Devaluation of the Chinese yuan in January 1994 is excluded from the calculation.

When the volatility of bilateral exchange rates is expressed as the "distance" among the currencies concerned, the relations of the Asian currencies and the European currencies with the dollar, the yen, and the deutsche mark appear as in figure 7-1. The three corners denote the dollar, the yen, and the deutsche mark. For any Asian or European currency, the distance from each corner is proportional to the currency's relative volatility against each of these three major currencies. The Asian currencies are located closer to the dollar than to the yen and farthest from the deutsche mark. The Hong Kong dollar, which is pegged to the U.S. dollar, virtually overlaps the corner denoting the U.S. dollar. In contrast to the Asian currencies, the European currencies tend to gather around the deutsche mark. This analysis confirms that while the Asian countries (excluding Japan) belong to a dollar bloc, European countries (members of the European Union in particular) belong to a deutsche mark bloc. On the other hand, any currency whose exchange rate synchronizes with the yen cannot be identified, showing that a yen bloc does not exist.[3]

Pegging to a Basket of Currencies

A country choosing to adopt a fixed exchange rate system needs to decide which currency or basket of currencies should serve as the anchor for its monetary policy. For a small economy closely linked to a single country, the obvious choice is to peg to the currency of that major trading partner. At the macroeconomic level the cost of abandoning an independent monetary policy would be small as the synchronization in the business cycles between the host country and the anchor-currency country is likely to be strong. At the microeconomic level, the benefit of exchange rate stability in terms of reductions in risk and transaction costs will also be large. An economy with a more diversified trade pattern may not meet the conditions for forming an optimum currency area with any single country. In that case, it is advisable to peg to a basket composed of the currencies of its major trading partners.

A currency basket can be considered a currency unit (or composite currency) formed by combining a number of existing currencies. There is no limit to the number of currencies composing a currency basket, although their weights together should add up to 100 percent. Typical examples of currency baskets are the special drawing right (SDR) created by the IMF and the European currency unit (ecu) created by the European Union to facilitate the transition toward a single currency. The SDR is made up of the U.S. dollar, the yen, the deutsche mark, the franc, and the pound sterling, while the European currency unit is composed of major European currencies.

A country can stabilize the value of its currency (in terms of purchasing power or export competitiveness) by pegging to a basket of currencies instead of a single currency. For a country pegging its currency to a basket of currencies comprising the yen and other currencies, the higher the weight assigned to the yen, the stronger the synchronization between the host country's currency and the yen. Suppose the yen carries a weight of 70 percent (and the dollar carries the remaining 30 percent) in Korea's reference basket. The won would then be allowed to appreciate (depreciate) by 7 percent against the dollar when the yen strengthens (weakens) 10 percent against the dollar (figure 7-2). Compared with the dollar peg system, the

---

3. Alternatively, Frankel and Wei (1994) show that the weights of the dollar in the Asian countries' reference baskets (as implied by the degree of exchange rate synchronization) are much higher than the weights of the yen.

Figure 7-2. *Movements of the Won-Dollar Rate under a Basket Peg and a Dollar Peg*[a]

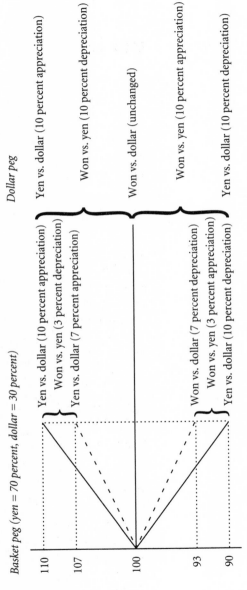

Basket peg (yen = 70 percent, dollar = 30 percent)

Dollar peg

Yen vs. dollar (10 percent appreciation)

Yen vs. dollar (10 percent appreciation)
Won vs. yen (3 percent depreciation)
Yen vs. dollar (7 percent appreciation)

Won vs. yen (10 percent depreciation)

Won vs. dollar (unchanged)

Won vs. yen (10 percent appreciation)

Won vs. dollar (7 percent depreciation)
Won vs. yen (3 percent appreciation)
Yen vs. dollar (10 percent depreciation)

Yen vs. dollar (10 percent depreciation)

110

107

100

93

90

Source: Compiled by Nomura Research Institute.

a. Based on the assumption that the yen appreciates (or depreciates) by ten percent against the dollar.

won would be more stable against the yen (plus or minus 3 percent instead of plus or minus 10 percent, given a plus or minus 10 percent fluctuation in the yen-dollar rate), although it would become more volatile against the dollar (plus or minus 7 percent instead of plus or minus 0 percent). By design, the weighted average of the won rate against the yen and the dollar would remain unchanged (− 3 percent × 70 percent + 7 percent × 30 percent = 0 in the case of a 10 percent yen appreciation, and 3 percent × 70 percent − 7 percent × 30 percent = 0 in the case of a 10 percent yen depreciation). A basket peg should therefore be understood as a fixed exchange rate system, although the value of the currency concerned fluctuates against all other currencies (both the yen and the dollar in this case). It should be noted that the currency basket discussed here is a policy rule determining exchange rates and should be distinguished from the currency composition of the foreign exchange reserves of central banks.

The effective exchange rate, which is a widely used measure of export competitiveness of nations, can be considered a basket composed of the currencies of major trading partners, with the weight of each currency proportional to the issuing country's share of the host country's total trade. Pegging to a basket of currencies carrying trade weights is therefore equivalent to pursuing an exchange rate policy that seeks to stabilize the effective exchange rate.

The Criteria for Choosing an Optimal Currency Basket

The meaning of a currency basket should be clear by now, but a question remains as to how its composition should be determined. As in the case of choosing an appropriate exchange rate regime in general, the optimal composition of the currency basket for a country hinges on the structure of its economy, the nature of the shocks facing it, and the objectives of the policy authorities.[4] Stanley Black, for example, suggests pegging the local currency to a basket based on the direction of total trade in goods and services in order to stabilize the relative price between tradable and nontradable goods.[5] Others, however, argue in favor of pegging to a basket weighted to reflect market power in export and import markets so as to stabilize the terms of trade (and thus real income).[6]

---

4. For a survey of the literature on the optimal composition of currency baskets, see Williamson (1982).

5. Black (1976).

6. Branson and Katseli-Papaefstratiou (1980).

When applied to Asia, most studies have in common the understanding that the major shock comes from fluctuations in the yen-dollar rate. Accordingly, they focus on determining the optimal weight of the yen in those baskets with the objective of stabilizing some macroeconomic variable, such as output or the balance of payments.

In a model that focuses on the dual role of Japan as a competitor in international markets and a major source of imports, I derive an optimal peg for an Asian country that seeks to stabilize output amid a widely fluctuating yen-dollar rate.[7] For an Asian country under a dollar peg system, a stronger yen boosts demand by enhancing export competitiveness against Japanese products but suppresses supply by increasing the cost of imports from Japan. The net result depends on the degree of competition (or complementarity) between Japan and the country concerned. Countries having competitive relations with Japan are more likely to benefit from a stronger yen, while those having complementary relations with Japan are more likely to be hurt. To stabilize output, the monetary authorities should allow the local currency to follow the yen up when the yen appreciates against the dollar (and to follow the yen down when the yen depreciates against the dollar). Accordingly, the optimal weight assigned to the yen in a currency basket should be high for countries competing with Japan in international markets and low for countries with trade structures complementary to that of Japan.[8] Given the clear tendency for the trade structures of Asian countries to approach that of Japan as their economies develop, it follows that the higher income countries such as the Asian NIEs should assign a greater weight to the yen than do lower income members of ASEAN (Indonesia and the Philippines, for example) and China.[9]

Agnès Bénassy-Quéré estimates the optimal weight of the yen in a basket for a country that seeks to stabilize its balance of payments (as a percentage of GDP).[10] Fluctuations in the yen-dollar rate affect the balance of payments

7. Kwan (1992, 1994). The model is elaborated further in the next section and the appendix to this chapter.

8. Ito, Ogawa, and Nagataki-Sasaki (1998) estimate the optimal weight of the yen in a currency basket for an Asian country that seeks to stabilize the trade balance amid a fluctuating yen-dollar rate, again emphasizing the dual role of Japan as a competitor in international markets and as a major source of imports. Their estimation confirms that higher income countries with competitive relations with Japan should assign higher weights to the yen.

9. This contrasts sharply with a weighting scheme based on the regional composition of trade, in which case the ASEAN countries, rather than the Asian NIEs, should peg closer to the yen.

10. Bénassy-Quéré (1996).

not just through the trade account but also through altering the burden of debt service. (While interest payment is counted as a current account item, changes in repayment of principal affect the capital account.) Under normal conditions (when the Marshall-Lerner condition is met), the trade balance improves as the yen appreciates against the local currency, with the magnitude dependent on the host country's competition-complementarity relation with Japan. However, the debt burden increases so that the capital account deteriorates, with the magnitude proportional to the size of yen-denominated debt. The total impact on the balance of payments is therefore ambiguous. Assuming that the impact on the trade account dominates so that the balance of payments improves with a stronger yen, the total improvement in the balance of payments would be smaller the larger the size of yen-denominated debt. In this case, the weight of the yen in the currency basket that seeks to stabilize the balance of payments would be inversely proportional to the size of the yen-denominated debt. Accordingly, lower income countries with large yen-denominated debt (such as China and Indonesia) should not peg their currencies too close to the yen, although at the microeconomic level raising the share of yen-denominated assets (foreign exchange reserves of central banks) would reduce the exposure to foreign exchange risk.[11]

An Optimal Peg for an Asian Country

In this section I derive an optimal peg for an Asian country that seeks to stabilize output, using a model that focuses on the relationship between exchange rate changes and output fluctuations in Asian countries. Besides the exchange rate against the dollar, the yen-dollar rate and oil prices are emphasized. Specific attention is given to Japan's dual role as the major competitor and supplier of imports for the Asian countries. The model is then tested using Korean data.[12]

11. Complementary to exchange rate policy, a country with a significant amount of yen-denominated debt can also reduce its exposure to foreign exchange risk by matching it with yen-denominated assets in its foreign exchange reserves. However, in contrast to the composition of the currency basket, where the optimal weight of the yen is inversely proportional to the size of yen-denominated debt, the weight of the yen in the optimal composition of foreign exchange reserves is proportional to the size of yen-denominated debt.

12. This section is more technical than the rest of the book and can be skipped without affecting the flow of the argument. For a mathematical formulation of the model, see the appendix to this chapter.

Exchange Rate Fluctuations and Short-Term Economic Growth

In a small open economy typical of developing Asian nations, the level of output in the short run is to a large extent determined by the terms of trade (the ratio between export prices and import prices) and the real wage rate (the ratio between the nominal wage rate and output prices, both measured in the same currency unit). For developing Asian nations, export prices correspond broadly to output prices (as a large proportion of output is exported), while import prices are a major determinant of input prices (as these countries depend heavily on imported intermediate goods). Other things being equal, an improvement in the terms of trade or a decline in real wages implies higher profits, leading to an expansion of output.

Fluctuations in the yen-dollar rate are a major determinant of the terms of trade for Asian countries. An appreciation of the yen raises Japanese export prices in dollar terms, which in turn raises import and export prices in other Asian countries. The impact on the terms of trade depends on the structure of the host country, particularly its trade relations with Japan. In the Asian NIEs, for which Japan is more a competitor than a supplier on the import side, higher Japanese export prices tend to raise their export prices more than their import prices so that their terms of trade improve. To give a specific example, a stronger yen raises the prices of Japanese cars in dollar terms, allowing Korean automakers to act as price followers to raise their own export prices by the same extent. Although Korean automakers also import parts and components from Japan, the increase in overall import prices should be limited because prices of imports from other countries are not affected directly. As a result, for Korean automakers higher import prices can be translated into even higher export prices so that profitability improves and output expands as the yen appreciates.

In contrast, an appreciation of the yen tends to depress the terms of trade of lower income members of ASEAN and China, reflecting the fact that for these countries Japan is more a supplier than a competitor. These countries cannot take advantage of a stronger yen to raise their export prices because their products do not compete directly with Japan in international markets. Yet they suffer an increase in the prices of their imports because they depend heavily on imports from Japan for capital and intermediate goods. The resulting squeeze in profits induces a fall in output.

Assuming that the nominal wage rate is rigid in the short run, an increase in export prices (output prices) resulting from the yen's appreciation also boosts output by reducing the real wage rate. This effect is expected to be larger for the Asian NIEs, whose export prices are more sensitive to changes in the yen-dollar rate, than for lower income members of ASEAN and China.

Taken together, a stronger yen tends to raise output in the Asian NIEs by improving their terms of trade and reducing their real wage rates. In contrast, it tends to reduce output in lower income members of ASEAN and China as the negative effect on output from a deterioration in the terms of trade is likely to exceed the positive effect from a decline in real wage rates.

Besides the yen-dollar rate, oil prices are a major determinant of short-term output fluctuations in the Asian countries. An increase in oil prices, which is analogous to an appreciation of OPEC currencies, boosts output in oil-exporting countries by improving their terms of trade (and depressing their real wage rates). Conversely, it depresses output in oil-importing countries by worsening their terms of trade.

The model can be tested using data from South Korea. The results support the formulation of the relationship between exchange rate and output fluctuations (table 7-3). The following points are worth noting. First, Korean output (as measured by industrial production) tends to be more sensitive to changes in the terms of trade than changes in the real wage rate, rising 1.071 percent with a 1 percent improvement in the terms of trade, versus only 0.399 percent with a 1 percent decrease in the real wage rate. Second, an appreciation of the yen against the dollar tends to raise both export prices and import prices in Korea, with the impact on the former larger than on the latter. A 1 percent appreciation of the yen raises export prices by 0.394 percent and import prices by 0.261 percent, boosting the terms of trade by 0.133 percent. This result reflects the fact that Japan is more a competitor than a supplier for South Korea. Third, reflecting the fact that South Korea is a net importer of oil, an increase in oil prices tends to raise Korean import prices more than export prices, thus worsening its terms of trade.

Exchange Rate Policy and Output Stabilization

The model just described can be used to examine the role of exchange rate policy in output stabilization and to derive the optimal currency peg for an Asian country seeking to minimize output fluctuations that result from changes in exchange rates (and oil prices).

The domestic currency's exchange rate against the dollar can be considered a policy variable at the government's disposal. Changes in the domestic currency's exchange rate against the dollar affect output through their impact on the real wage rate. Given the nominal wage rate, a devaluation of the local currency raises output prices in local currency terms and reduces

Table 7-3. *Major Determinants of Korean Output and Prices, 1980–90*[a]

Dependent variable	Time	Terms of trade	Real wage rate	Yen-dollar rate	Oil prices	Adjusted R^2	Durbin-Watson statistic
Industrial production	0.029 (52.47)	...	...	...	...	0.985	0.390
Industrial production	0.030 (20.68)	1.071 (5.25)	−0.399 (−5.10)	...	...	0.989	0.761
Industrial production	0.025 (34.48)	...	...	−0.220 (−6.28)	−0.141 (−2.81)	0.993	1.064
Export prices	0.003 (3.88)	...	...	−0.394 (−10.54)	0.322 (6.07)	0.936	0.730
Import prices	−0.002 (−2.92)	...	...	−0.261 (−6.43)	0.416 (7.16)	0.754	0.945
Terms of trade	0.005 (8.03)	...	...	−0.133 (−4.07)	−0.094 (−2.01)	0.926	1.377

Source: Kwan (1992).

a. Except for time trend, all variables are in log form so that coefficients correspond to elasticities. Shiller lags of appropriate length used in estimation and figures show cumulative effect. Since a larger number for the yen-dollar rate denotes a weaker yen, the negative coefficients show the negative impact of a weaker yen (or the positive impact of a stronger yen) on Korean output and prices. Figures for industrial production are seasonally adjusted; figures in parentheses denote *t*-values.

the real wage rate, which in turn boosts output.[13] Asian governments can therefore offset changes in output resulting from fluctuations in third currencies such as the yen-dollar rate by manipulating the exchange rates of their local currencies. This case can be illustrated by referring to a situation involving an appreciation of the yen.

In the case of the Asian NIEs, an increase in output resulting from a stronger yen can be offset by revaluing the local currency, which reduces output through raising the real wage rate. In contrast, for the lower income members of ASEAN and China, a decrease in output resulting from an appreciation of the yen can be offset by devaluing the local currency.

The direction and magnitude of the exchange rate adjustment needed to achieve output stability in the face of a changing yen-dollar rate depends on the following four parameters: the responsiveness (elasticity) of output to changes in the terms of trade (a); the responsiveness (elasticity) of output to changes in the real wage rate (b); the responsiveness (elasticity) of export prices to changes in the yen-dollar rate (α); and the responsiveness (elasticity) of import prices to changes in the yen-dollar rate (β).[14] These four parameters (a, b, α, β) summarize the economic structures of the host country relevant to the formulation of exchange policy. The value of α reflects more the degree of competition between the exports of the host country and Japan than Japan's share of the host country's exports. By contrast, the value of β comes closer to Japan's share of the host country's imports. The asymmetry here reflects the fact that international prices are more highly dependent on the exchange rates of exporting countries than those of importing countries, since countries usually have more monopoly power on the export side than on the import side in international trade.

The impact of fluctuations in oil prices on output can also be offset by manipulating the exchange of the local currency. As explained above, an increase in oil prices boosts output in oil-exporting countries and reduces output in oil-importing countries through its impact on the terms of trade. To stabilize output, an oil-importing country should devalue its currency to stimulate production as oil prices increase, while an oil-exporting country should revalue its currency to suppress production. The direction and magnitude of the exchange rate adjustment that is needed to achieve output

---

13. In contrast to changes in foreign exchange rates (such as the yen-dollar rate), changes in the domestic currencies' exchange rates through the terms of trade have a negligible effect on the Asian countries because they are too small to have price-setting power in international markets (the small-country assumption).

14. The parameter b is defined as the responsiveness (elasticity) of output to a fall in the real wage rate so that, like other parameters, it has a positive value.

stability in the face of changing oil prices will again depend on the four parameters cited above, with α and β representing, respectively, the responsiveness of export and import prices in the host country to changes in oil prices.

Choosing the Optimal Peg

Pegging to a basket of currencies provides an automatic way for Asian countries to stabilize output fluctuations resulting from changes in third-country exchange rates, such as the yen-dollar rate. The weight θ_i of currency i in the optimal basket that stabilizes output depends on the elasticity of output with respect to currency i's exchange rate (against the U.S. dollar) and the elasticity of output with respect to the exchange rate of the domestic currency (against the dollar). In what follows, currency i refers to the yen, so that θ_i denotes the weight of the yen in the optimal basket of the host country.

The elasticity of output with respect to the yen-dollar rate can be calculated as the sum of two products: the product of the elasticity of the terms of trade with respect to the yen-dollar rate ($\alpha_i - \beta_i$) and the elasticity of output with respect to the terms of trade (a); and the product of the elasticity of export prices (and thus the real wage rate) with respect to the yen-dollar rate (α_i) and the elasticity of output with respect to the real wage rate (b).

The elasticity of output with respect to the domestic exchange rate is equal to the elasticity of output with respect to the real wage rate (b).

The optimal weight of currency i (the yen in the present case) in the currency basket is given by the elasticity of output with respect to currency i's exchange rate divided by the elasticity of output with respect to the host country's exchange rate. That is,

$$\theta_i = [a\,(\alpha_i - \beta_i) + b\alpha_i]\,/\,b.$$

A country whose terms of trade benefit from an appreciation of the yen (with $\alpha_i - \beta_i > 0$) should include a substantial weight for the yen in the basket. Conversely, in a developing country that depends on Japan heavily for imports but does not compete with it directly (with $\alpha_i - \beta_i < 0$), the optimal basket may involve a very low weight for the yen.[15]

When currency i refers to oil prices, the above equation suggests that an oil-importing country should assign a negative weight to oil prices when considering pegging to a basket of currencies. In contrast, an oil-exporting

---

15. In extreme cases, the optimal weight of the yen may be negative, as a decline in output resulting from a stronger yen needs to be offset by a devaluation of the local currency.

Figure 7-3. *The Output Stabilizing Effect of Pegging the Korean Won to a Basket of Currencies*[a]

Percent change in Korean output

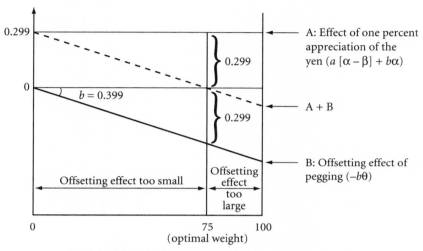

Yen's weight in basket, percent

Source: Kwan (1992).
a. Based on the assumption that the yen appreciates by one percent.

country should peg to a basket of currencies that involves a large positive weight for oil prices.

The South Korean case illustrates how pegging to a basket can help stabilize output (figure 7-3). Using the parameter estimated above, the optimal peg for the Korean won is composed as follows: 75 percent weight for the yen ($\alpha = 0.394$, $\beta = 0.261$, $a = 1.071$, $b = 0.399$), –8 percent weight for oil ($\alpha = 0.322$, $\beta = 0.416$, $a = 1.071$, $b = 0.399$), and 33 percent weight for the dollar (100 percent – 75 percent + 8 percent).

When the yen appreciates by 1 percent against the dollar, for example, South Korea's export prices and import prices rise by 0.394 percent and 0.261 percent, respectively, so that the country's terms of trade improve by 0.133 percent. At the same time, given the nominal wage rate and the won rate against the U.S. dollar, the real wage rate drops by 0.394 percent. As a result, output rises by 0.299 percent (0.133 percent × 1.071 = 0.142 percent through an improvement in the terms of trade, plus 0.394 percent × 0.399 = 0.157 percent through a decline in the real wage rate). To reduce output by the same amount requires raising the real wage rate by 0.75 percent (0.299 percent / 0.399), which can be brought about by revaluing the won against the dollar by 0.75 percent. This result could be achieved automatically by pegging the won to a basket of currencies in which the yen carries a weight of 75 percent (the optimal weight of the yen as calculated above). Likewise, when the yen depreciates against the dollar by 1 percent, the negative impact on Korean output can be offset by devaluing the won by 0.75 percent. Or again, the same result can be achieved by pegging to a basket of currencies in which the yen carries a weight of 75 percent.

When the won is pegged to this optimal basket of currencies, a 10 percent appreciation of the yen against the dollar would automatically lead to a 7.5 percent appreciation of the won against the U.S. dollar. The positive effect of this 10 percent appreciation of the yen on Korean output would then be just offset by the negative effect of the 7.5 percent appreciation of the won. Assigning any other weight to the yen would imply a counterbalancing force too small (when the weight is less than 75 percent) or too large (when the weight of the yen is over 75 percent) to offset the initial effect.

So far I have concentrated on the policy objective of stabilizing output, but in reality other macroeconomic objectives need to be taken into consideration. If the objective is to stabilize domestic prices, for example, the optimal peg would involve assigning a weight equal to α_i for currency i. For an oil importer this would magnify the decline (increase) in output as oil prices rise (decline). Since these objectives may contradict one another, the final choice involves striking an optimal trade-off between them.

The Yen as an Anchor

The use of the yen as a regional currency has been constrained by the volatility of Asian currencies against the yen. This picture will change drastically, however, if the Asian countries choose to use the yen instead of the dollar as their anchor currency.

Macroeconomic Considerations

The Asian countries have up to now focused on the bilateral rates between their local currencies and the dollar in formulating their exchange rate policies. However, as discussed above, they have experienced wide fluctuations in economic growth brought about by the wide swings in the yen-dollar rate since 1985. To adapt to the new international environment, the traditional exchange rate policy of a loose peg to the dollar may have to be amended to put more emphasis on the yen.

When the policy objective is to stabilize output, a country should peg its currency to a basket with large weights for competitors' currencies and small or even negative weights for major suppliers' currencies. When applied to the Asian countries, this principle suggests that the Asian NIEs (Korea and Taiwan in particular), which have export structures similar to that of Japan, may benefit by pegging closer to the yen. The reverse may be true for primary commodity exporters that rely heavily on Japan as a source of imports (lower income members of ASEAN and China, for example). Other things being equal, the Asian NIEs have more incentive than other Asian developing countries to peg their exchange rates to the yen or to join a yen bloc.

The argument that the Asian countries should peg their currencies to the dollar because the United States is their largest export market can be challenged on two grounds. First, the major market for a country's exports is not necessarily a competitor or an unimportant supplier of the export country, so there is no inherent reason for a trading partner's currency to be given a weight proportional to its share of the country's exports. Second, the share of Asian countries' exports to the United States has been declining rapidly since 1986. This trend is expected to continue in the future, in view of the need for the United States to reduce its trade deficit. In its place, the share of intraregional trade among Asian countries is expected to increase.

The rapid pace of industrialization in the Asian countries is likely to continue, thereby favoring a more important role for the yen in the management of their exchange rate policies. The commodity composition of exports in the Asian NIEs will become increasingly similar to that of Japan, while export composition in the ASEAN countries will approach that of the Asian NIEs. As a result, there will be an increase in the benefits in terms of output stability should Asian countries peg their currencies closer to the yen.

Indeed, some Asian currencies have shown stronger synchronization with the yen following the onset of the latest crisis. In addition to the market-imposed contagion effect, this may also reflect the closer attention that monetary authorities paid to the stability of their currencies against the yen. Based on the hypothesis that the Asian countries peg their exchange rates to specific baskets of currencies (albeit loosely), the stronger synchronization between the Asian currencies and the yen can be interpreted as the result of monetary authorities increasing the weight of the yen in those baskets. The Monetary Authority of Singapore (Singapore's central bank) estimates that the implicit weight of the yen in the currency basket increased sharply for the

Table 7-4. *Asian Currencies' Linkage with the Yen,*
July 1995 to September 1999[a]

Currency	January 2, 1995–July 1, 1997			July 2, 1997–September 30, 1999		
	Weight of yen	R^2	Durbin-Watson statistic	Weight of yen	R^2	Durbin-Watson statistic
Thai baht	0.110 (2.98)	0.016	2.495	0.375 (4.65)	0.049	1.798
Malaysian ringgit	0.097 (7.77)	0.095	2.292	0.593 (5.16)	0.079	1.964
Philippine peso	0.003 (0.19)	0.000	2.129	0.146 (3.06)	0.015	1.895
Indonesian rupiah	0.000 (0.01)	0.000	2.166	0.656 (4.40)	0.025	1.860
Korean won	0.018 (1.12)	0.002	2.201	0.019 (0.31)	0.000	1.638
Taiwan dollar	0.054 (2.71)	0.028	2.218	0.089 (5.32)	0.036	1.733
Singapore dollar	0.169 (12.00)	0.245	2.349	0.317 (8.52)	0.211	2.141

Source: MAS (2000).

a. Figures in parentheses are *t*-values adjusted for heteroskedasticity using the White procedure.

five major ASEAN countries after the onset of the Asian crisis in July 1997 (table 7-4). This major shift in exchange rate policy in the Asia countries may herald Asia's transition from a dollar bloc to a yen bloc.

Microeconomic Considerations

For Asia's developing countries, choosing a currency to use in international transactions can be considered conceptually as a two-stage process. The first stage involves choosing an exchange rate regime, thereby determining the relationship between the domestic currency and foreign currencies. This decision is usually undertaken by the government, with its policy objectives taken into consideration. The second stage involves the actual choice of which currency (or currencies) economic agents are to use in denominating trade and capital account transactions under the given exchange rate regime.[16] While the decision at the first stage usually involves macroeco-

16. This is analogous to the two-stage "world money game," with the first stage of the game being an agreement on an international monetary regime and the second stage being monetary interplays under given sets of rules. See Hamada (1985).

nomic objectives as discussed above, that at the second stage is mainly based on microeconomic considerations involving balancing between risk and return (or cost).

Foreign exchange rate risk is no doubt a major factor determining the outcome in the second stage. Should the Asian countries peg their currencies closer to the yen, the foreign exchange risk involved when using the yen in international transactions will be reduced and that associated with using the dollar will increase. The cost-benefit calculation at the microeconomic level will therefore likely shift in favor of wider use of the yen in denominating trade, capital account transactions, and foreign exchange reserves of central banks in Asia. Barry Eichengreen estimates that the dollar's share of total foreign exchange reserves tends to be 19.1 percentage points higher and the yen's share 7.5 percentage points lower in countries with exchange rates pegged to the dollar than in countries in which exchange rates are not pegged to the dollar.[17]

Some observers argue that denominating more trade in yen would hurt Japan's trading partners because they will have to assume more of the foreign exchange risk. This argument, however, would not apply to members of the yen bloc, as they would peg their currencies to the yen so that invoicing in yen actually would help reduce their foreign exchange risk. By lowering the risk associated with exchange rate fluctuations, pegging to the yen may also benefit the Asian countries by expanding their trade with, and capital inflows (foreign direct investment in particular) from, Japan. Strengthening ties with Japan has become all the more important now that the United States can no longer play the role of sole economic locomotive for the Asian countries.

Appendix

The earlier analysis can be formalized in mathematical form using the following simple macroeconomic model (figure 7-4).

(7-1) $$y = a\,(p_x - p_m) - b\,(w - e - p_x);$$

(7-2) $$p_x = -\sum_{i=1}^{n} \alpha_i\, e_i;$$

(7-3) $$p_m = -\sum_{i=1}^{n} \beta_i\, e_i;$$

17. Eichengreen (2000).

Figure 7-4. *The Impact of Exchange Rate Fluctuations on Economic Growth*[a]

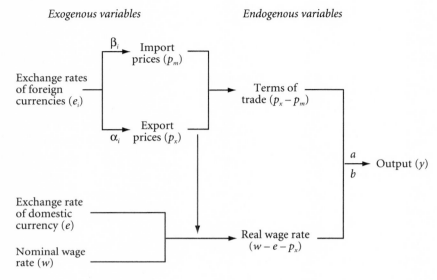

Source: Kwan (1992).

a. Variables expressed in natural log form. Exchange rates measured in terms of domestic currencies per U.S. dollar. Import and export prices measured in terms of U.S. dollar. Nominal wage rate measured in terms of domestic currency. Parameters a and b measure elasticity of output with respect to terms of trade and real wage rate, respectively, while α and β_i measure elasticity of export prices and import prices with respect to the exchange rate of foreign currency i.

with $a > 0$, $b > 0$, $\alpha_i > 0$, and $\beta_i > 0$ for all i. The exchange rate of the U.S. dollar (the numeraire, or unit of account) against itself is 0 in log form (that is, when the United States is taken as country n, $e_n = 0$). By the small-country assumption, $\Sigma\alpha_i = 1$, and $\Sigma\beta_i = 1$ (where i includes the United States). Output y can be obtained as a function of the exogenous variables by substituting (2) and (3) into (1) and rearranging. That is

$$(7\text{-}4) \qquad y = -\sum_{i=1}^{n} e_i \left[a\left(\alpha_i - \beta_i\right) + b\alpha_i \right] + be - bw.$$

Equation 7-4 furnishes the starting point of the analysis of output volatility under alternative pegging schemes—pegging to the dollar and pegging to the yen. For simplicity, changes in the nominal wage rate are neglected, and the yen and the dollar are taken as the only two foreign currencies. Equation 7-4 can be simplified to

$$(7\text{-}4a) \qquad y = -e_j\,[a\,(\alpha_j - \beta_j) + b\alpha_j] + be,$$

where e_j denotes the yen-dollar rate and α_j and β_j denote the yen-dollar rate elasticities of export prices and import prices, respectively.

First consider the case of pegging to the yen, that is $e = e_j$. Equation 7-4a can then be simplified to

$$y = -e_j[a\,(\alpha_j - \beta_j) + b\alpha_j - b].$$

The volatility of y in terms of its variance is given by

$$(7\text{-}5) \qquad \text{Var}(y) = \{- [a\,(\alpha_j - \beta_j) + b\alpha_j - b]\}^2\,\text{Var}(e_j).$$

When the domestic currency is pegged to the dollar, that is $e = 0$, equation 7-4a becomes

$$y = -e_j\,[a\,(\alpha_j - \beta_j) + b\alpha_j],$$

and

$$(7\text{-}6) \qquad \text{Var}(y) = \{- [a\,(\alpha_j - \beta_j) + b\alpha_j]\}^2\,\text{Var}(e_j).$$

For a given $\text{Var}(e_j)$, pegging to the yen would imply a smaller $\text{Var}(y)$ than pegging to the dollar when

$$|a\,(\alpha_j - \beta_j) + b\alpha_j - b| < |a\,(\alpha_j - \beta_j) + b\alpha_j|.$$

The Asian NIEs, which are competitors of Japan (with large α_j), are likely to meet this condition. On the other hand, for lower income members of ASEAN and China, which do not compete much with Japan but depend heavily on it for imports (with small α_j but large β_j), pegging to the dollar may be more commensurate with output stability.

The exchange rate of the domestic economy is a policy variable at the government's disposal to stabilize the economy. On the one hand, an appreciation of currency i against the dollar can either raise or lower output of the host country, depending on the relative values of α_i and β_i, as summarized in equation 7-4. On the other hand, an appreciation (a depreciation) of the domestic currency lowers (raises) output by raising (lowering) the real wage rate. Output fluctuations resulting from changes in foreign exchange rates can thus be offset by manipulating the exchange rate of the domestic currency. Pegging to a basket of currencies provides an automatic way in which this can be achieved.

When the host country chooses to peg its currency to a basket of currencies by assigning a fixed weight of θ_i in the basket to currency i, the exchange rate of the local currency against the dollar is given by the weighted average of the exchange rates of all other currencies against the dollar, with the weights given by θ_i. That is,

$$(7\text{-}7) \qquad\qquad e = \sum_{i=1}^{n} \theta_i e_i.$$

Substituting equation 7-7 into equation 7-4 and neglecting the nominal wage rate gives

$$(7\text{-}8) \qquad y = -\sum_{i=1}^{n} e_i \left[a\,(\alpha_i - \beta_i) + b\alpha_i \right] + b\sum_{i=1}^{n} \theta_i e_i.$$

Assuming that foreign exchange rates are not correlated with one another, minimizing the variance of y can be achieved by setting $y = 0$ in equation 7-8. This condition is met when the weight for each foreign currency θ_i is set so that

$$(7\text{-}9) \qquad\qquad \theta_i = \left[a\,(\alpha_i - \beta_i) + b\alpha_i \right] / b,$$

which gives the optimal weight for currency i. Equation 7-9 shows that the weight assigned to one currency in the optimal peg may differ from one host country to another, reflecting the difference in their economic structures (as summarized by a, b, α_i, and β_i).

8

A Regional Perspective

The theory of optimum currency areas considers which countries should come together to form a monetary union. When applied to the possibility of monetary integration in Asia centering upon Japan, it provides a regional perspective of a yen bloc.[1]

The major cost associated with monetary integration arises from the abandonment of an independent monetary policy. Countries with similar economic structures can respond to a common shock with a common monetary policy, and the costs of giving up an independent monetary policy are relatively small. At the same time, the larger the differential in inflation rates among members, the more difficult it is to maintain fixed exchange rates, and countries with similar inflation rates are therefore more likely candidates for a monetary union. Both the economic structure and the level of inflation in the Asian countries are closely related to the level of economic development. A yen bloc centering on Japan should therefore start with the participation of the Asian NIEs, to be followed by Malaysia and Thailand as they reach a higher level of economic development. Countries still at an early stage of economic development, such as China, Indonesia, and the Philippines, fail to meet the conditions for forming an optimum currency area with Japan.

1. This chapter is based on Kwan (1998b).

The Theory of Optimum Currency Areas

The traditional approach to the theory of optimum currency areas tries to single out a crucial economic characteristic that supposedly indicates where the lines between different blocs should be drawn.[2] Studies so far have focused on the costs involved in abandoning an independent monetary policy. Here, I also touch upon the benefits in terms of enhancing the usefulness of money.

The decision to participate in a monetary union can be broken down conceptually into a two-step process. The first step involves choosing between fixed and flexible exchange rates (that is, whether to join any monetary union at all); the second step consists of determining the members of the union. Accordingly, the criteria for optimum currency areas can be divided into two groups, one involving characteristics of individual countries and the other involving economic relations among the countries concerned.[3]

To Peg or Not to Peg

A monetary union is composed of countries that adopt (genuinely) fixed exchange rates among themselves, while allowing flexible rates with the rest of the world.[4] An optimum currency area refers to the combination of countries that enjoy net gains by forming a monetary union.[5]

---

2. For a survey of the literature on the theory of optimum currency areas, see De Grauwe (1992).

3. Drawing an analogy between monetary integration and marriage, the former corresponds to the factors determining whether one should marry or not, while the latter corresponds to factors determining whom one should marry.

4. As pointed out by Corden (1972), the distinction between a pseudo exchange rate union and a complete monetary union should be made when considering the costs and benefits of monetary integration. A pseudo exchange rate union is based on fixed but adjustable exchange rates among participating countries, while a complete monetary union has a single currency issued by a single central bank. Both the costs of giving up an independent monetary policy and the benefits of enhancing the usefulness of the money are much smaller for the former than for the latter. In a pseudo exchange rate union, international trade and investment are still subject to the risk of exchange rate changes, and the transaction costs of changing from one currency to another remain. For the sake of simplicity, I concentrate on the complete monetary union.

5. According to this definition, it is likely that a country belongs to several different optimum currency areas at the same time. Conceptually, given the optimality conditions, there should exist a single optimal way (number of monetary unions and their composition by country) of classifying all nations of the world into mutually exclusive optimum currency areas. Unfortunately, studies so far have failed to identify conditions for determining optimum currency areas in this strict sense. Also, for the sake of simplicity, the term *coun-*

The major benefits of monetary integration (or participation in a monetary union) are enhancement of the usefulness of money, the "import" of stable monetary policy from abroad, reduction in currency speculation, and saving on foreign reserve holdings. Among them, the enhancement of the usefulness of money seems to be the most important. Thus the elimination of exchange rate volatility within the monetary union, by reducing foreign exchange risk, should promote trade and investment as well as the optimal allocation of resources. In addition, the transaction costs accompanying the exchange of currencies would be reduced and the usefulness of money enhanced if the same currency circulates in a larger area due to economies of scale.

The major cost accompanying monetary integration is the abandonment of an independent monetary policy needed to achieve internal equilibrium (full employment and price stability) and external equilibrium (balance in the current account).[6] In a monetary union, monetary policy is unified: participating countries have to relinquish autonomy in pursuing monetary policy because it is difficult, if not impossible, to achieve a fixed exchange rate, perfect capital mobility, and an independent monetary policy at the same time.[7] As interest rates among member countries cannot deviate from one another under the pressure of arbitrage, joining a monetary union implies giving up not only the option of adjusting the exchange rate but also the pursuit of an independent monetary policy. Hong Kong's experience under the linked exchange rate system shows that the cost involved may be very high (box 8-1).

The choice between a fixed exchange rate system and a floating exchange rate system depends on a variety of factors, including economic structures, nature of shocks, and credibility versus flexibility.[8]

The major economic structures relevant to the choice between a fixed and a floating exchange regime are the need to have an independent monetary

---

tries is used here to denote the basic units forming an optimum currency area, although theoretically the boundary of an optimum currency area does not necessarily coincide with national borders.

6. Mundell (1961), who emphasizes the abandonment of an independent monetary policy as the major cost of joining a monetary union, defines an optimum currency area as the domain of a monetary union where participating countries can attain internal and external balances simultaneously.

7. For a discussion of this impossible trinity, see box 4-1.

8. These are well documented in Aghevli, Khan, and Montiel (1991); IMF (1997); Richard N. Cooper, "Exchange Rate Choices" (www.economics.harvard.edu/faculty/cooper/papers/frbb_full.pdf [1999]).

Box 8-1. *The Cost of Abandoning Monetary Autonomy:*
The Case of Hong Kong

Hong Kong decided to peg its currency to the U.S. dollar under a currency board system in October 1983, when the Hong Kong dollar fell sharply amid heightening political uncertainty over the return of Hong Kong to China. The Hong Kong dollar has never deviated significantly from its official parity against the U.S. dollar, despite numerous external shocks to the economy (such as Black Monday in October 1987, the Tiananmen incident in June 1989, the contagion effect of the Mexican crisis in early 1995, and the 1997–98 Asian crisis).

This stability of the Hong Kong dollar against the U.S. dollar, however, has been achieved at the expense of macroeconomic stability. For example, Hong Kong's inflation rate has been much higher on average, and has fluctuated more widely, than the inflation rate in Singapore, which has a more flexible exchange rate regime. Also, the downturn in economic activity during the latest crisis was much sharper for Hong Kong than for Singapore, with Hong Kong's 1998 GDP declining by 5.1 percent and Singapore's rising by 0.3 percent.

Under the dollar peg system, Hong Kong's monetary authorities lose the flexibility not only to change the exchange rate but also to adjust domestic interest rates when the economy faces shocks. In normal times when exchange rate risk is considered negligible, domestic interest rates closely follow their U.S. counterparts, as the force of arbitrage tends to eliminate spread between the two markets. When there is a downward pressure on the Hong Kong dollar, interest rates in Hong Kong tend to rise above U.S. rates, with the spread reflecting the currency risk premium. Indeed, the overnight interbank rate shot up to an annual rate of nearly 300 percent on October 23, 1997, when the Hong Kong dollar was under intense speculation. Symmetrically, domestic interest rates can fall below U.S. rates when the Hong Kong dollar is expected to be revalued, as happened in 1988 when the currencies of other NIEs were appreciating under pressure from the United States.

The latest economic crisis in Asia hurt Hong Kong more than the United States, so following the monetary policy stance adopted by the United States actually aggravated and prolonged the recession in Hong Kong. Indeed, Hong Kong fell into a liquidity trap, in which monetary policy became totally ineffective in stimulating demand because local interest rates could not fall below U.S. rates, which were far above the "natural" floor of 0 percent.

Making things worse, real interest rates in Hong Kong rose sharply during the Asian crisis on the back of a falling inflation rate. Excluding the option of a devaluation, Hong Kong was on the horns of a dilemma: on the one hand, deflation in prices and wages was needed to restore export competitiveness; on the other, this process pushed up real interest rates, restraining domestic demand. Indeed, the real interest rate in 1999, measured in terms of the difference between the best lending rate (8.5 percent) and the consumer price index (−4.2 percent) averaged 12.7 percent [8.5 percent − (−4.2 percent) = 12.7 percent]. The adverse effect of rising real interest rates on domestic demand acted largely to offset the positive effect of deflation (through stimulating exports) on economic growth. This situation contrasted sharply with the precrisis period, when negative real interest rates (reflecting high inflation) fueled the bubble economy. In this way, under Hong Kong's dollar peg system, the countercyclical movement in real interest rates (that is, the tendency for real interest rates to decline during a boom and to rise during a recession) has made the economy inherently unstable.

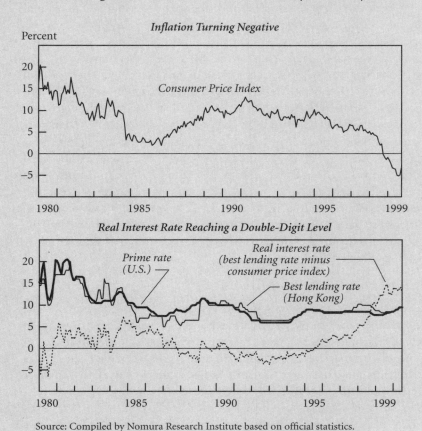

Source: Compiled by Nomura Research Institute based on official statistics.

policy, the effectiveness of monetary policy, and the volatility of exchange rates under a flexible regime and its consequences. First, if the market mechanism works smoothly, the cost of abandoning an independent monetary or exchange rate policy is low because there is little need to use these tools for the sake of stabilization. Specifically, if wages and prices are flexible, adjustment in their levels would help maintain internal and external balances. Second, in highly open economies, changes in exchange rates would sooner or later be reflected in offsetting changes in domestic price levels. Flexible exchange rates are therefore not only ineffective in achieving external balance targets but also harmful to price stability. Finally, in developing countries where capital markets are rudimentary, allowing exchange rates to fluctuate involves high volatility and a high cost of hedging through forward market transactions.

The fixed exchange rate system and the floating exchange rate system enjoy different comparative advantages as a built-in stabilizer for various shocks facing the economy. A fixed exchange rate regime, which allows anchoring to a stable price level, is desirable if monetary shocks are common. Conversely, a floating exchange rate regime, which eases adjustment costs in the presence of stickiness of wages and prices, is more desirable for an economy facing real shocks (terms of trade or productivity shocks).

A major objective in adopting a fixed exchange rate system is to enhance the credibility of economic policy, even at the cost of sacrificing flexibility. The need to maintain exchange rate parity will impose monetary and fiscal discipline on the government, and by providing a clear and transparent nominal anchor, the adoption of a fixed exchange rate may help to establish the credibility of a stabilization program. However, short of fixing the exchange rate permanently by joining a monetary union, countries adopting some form of fixed exchange rate system may end up losing flexibility without gaining credibility.

Criteria for an Optimum Currency Area

The criteria in the narrow sense for an optimum currency area involve the economic relations among potential members. They include the presence of mechanisms that reduce the need to use the exchange rate as an instrument for redressing macroeconomic imbalances; symmetry between shocks affecting member countries; similarity of policy objectives among member countries; and a high degree of intraregional economic interdependence.

The costs of joining a monetary union will be small when there exist mechanisms other than exchange rate changes to redress macroeconomic imbalances arising from asymmetric shocks. Specifically, high mobility of capital and labor as well as fiscal transfers can help finance trade imbalances among members of a monetary union automatically, and synchronization of business cycles implies that internal balance (full employment and price stability) can be achieved using a common monetary policy. Thus the higher the mobility of capital and labor and the larger the scope for fiscal transfers among member countries, the more likely that they form an optimum currency area. In reality, for a monetary union that transcends national borders, it is unlikely that mobility of labor and fiscal transfers can play a significant role in the adjustment process. Fiscal transfers among nations may infringe upon national sovereignty and may be possible only with some form of political integration. Labor mobility is limited not only by immigration laws but also by barriers resulting from differences in languages, employment practices, and social security systems, which are difficult to change in the short run.

When the shocks common to two countries are symmetrical, they can be offset with a similar stance of monetary policy, and the need to pursue (and the costs of giving up) an independent monetary policy will be small. To a large extent, whether shocks are symmetrical or not reflects whether or not the two countries share similar economic structures. For example, an increase in oil prices will have similar effects on major macroeconomic variables (such as output, inflation, and balance of trade) of oil-importing countries (such as Japan and South Korea), which can therefore respond with the same monetary policy stance. In contrast, an increase in oil prices will increase output in an oil-exporting country (such as Indonesia) while reducing output in an oil-importing country (such as Japan), making it unwise for them to adopt a common monetary policy stance.

Fixed exchange rates will be difficult to maintain if policy objectives differ widely among members of a monetary union, even if they share similar economic structures and symmetric shocks. For example, to cope with an increase in oil prices, some importing countries may prefer monetary tightening to maintain price stability while others may choose monetary relaxation to stimulate economic growth. The law of one price is likely to hold for tradable goods in a monetary union, so that prices (and thus inflation rates) tend to synchronize across member countries.[9] As a result, in the

---

9. Since the law of one price does not apply to nontradable goods (services, for example), inflation can differ from one country to another in a monetary union. Productivity growth in the tradable sector raises the price level in the nontradable sector through pushing up wages. As a result, a high-growth country (with higher productivity growth in its tradable goods sector) will tend to have a higher inflation rate than a low-growth country (with lower productivity growth in its tradable sector).

short run, when there exists a trade-off between inflation and unemployment, members of a monetary union cannot attain their own optimal combinations of these two variables at the same time (as long as they do not share exactly the same Phillips curve and social preferences). Thus it is more likely for countries to form an optimum currency area if they have similar preferences for unemployment and inflation than if they differ widely. In the long run, when the trade-off between inflation and unemployment no longer exists, the optimal inflation rate will largely reflect the preference for inflation tax (or seigniorage) as a source of public revenue. Countries at lower levels of development, given their underdeveloped taxation systems, will be more likely to depend on this inflation tax than the developed countries. If a high-inflation country tries to reduce its inflation rate in order to join a monetary union, it would have to seek alternative sources of revenue to make up for the loss of the inflation tax.

The three criteria discussed so far are concerned with the costs of abandoning an independent monetary policy; the fourth criterion is related to the benefits of fixed exchange rates. The more tightly a country is integrated with other members of the monetary union in terms of trade, labor movements, and capital flows, the higher the benefits of joining the union.

When the criteria for optimum currency areas discussed above are taken into consideration, the costs and benefits of joining a monetary union can be depicted as functions of the degree of dependence on intra-union (or intraregional) trade (figure 8-1). The costs of joining a monetary union are inversely proportional to the dependence on intra-union trade because the need to pursue, and the effectiveness of pursuing, an independent exchange rate policy would be small if the country concerned is heavily dependent on other members of the monetary union for trade. On the other hand, the benefits of joining a monetary union increase with the degree of dependence on intra-union trade, reflecting the reduction in transaction costs and exchange rate risk. The net benefits (benefits minus costs) of joining a monetary union therefore increase with the size of intra-union trade relative to GDP. A country should join when the net benefits are positive (that is, when the size of intra-union trade relative to GDP lies to the right of the intersection of the two curves).

The positions of these two curves are determined by factors other than the degree of dependence on intra-union trade, however. For example, for a country having an inflation rate or an economic structure significantly different from other members of a monetary union, the position of the curve showing the costs of joining that union will be high. As a result, the level of intra-union trade critical for joining will be higher. On the other hand, if

Figure 8-1. *Costs and Benefits of a Monetary Union*

Costs and benefits (percent of GDP)

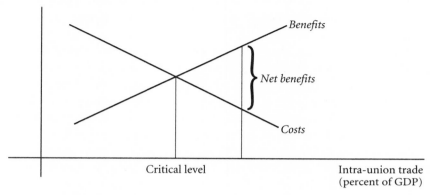

Source: Krugman (1990).

capital and labor are highly mobile among member countries, the position of the cost curve will be low and the net benefit of joining a monetary union is likely to be large even at a relatively low level of intraregional trade.

Is Asia an Optimum Currency Area?

A number of studies apply the theory of optimum currency areas to the case of Asia. However, no consensus on whether the region satisfies the criteria of an optimum currency area has been reached, as different criteria give contradicting results.

A Brief Review of the Literature

Jeffrey Frankel and Shang-Jin Wei show empirically that a yen bloc does not exist in Asia in terms of both monetary and trade ties and that the dollar still plays the dominant role in the exchange rate policy of the Asian countries.[10] Although, as in the case of the Western Hemisphere, Asia has also shown bias toward intraregional trade, this can mostly be explained by such geographic and economic factors as distance and GNP size. There is little evidence of joint policy efforts among Asian nations in forming a trading bloc.

Drawing from the European experience, Nigel Holloway identifies a common tariff wall; the free movement of goods, services, labor, and capital

10. Frankel (1991, 1993); Frankel and Wei (1994).

within a common market; and rough parity among members in their level of economic development as the major preconditions for the successful formation of a monetary union.[11] Since these preconditions are not currently met in Asia, he concludes that the formation of a yen bloc is unrealistic at this stage.

Yung Chul Park and Won-Am Park are skeptical about the formation of a yen bloc between Japan and the Asian countries for the following reasons.[12] First, Asian countries are still highly dependent on the U.S. market, while Japan lacks the capacity and willingness to absorb more imports from Asia. Second, Japan's lead in technology and high savings rate necessitate frequent devaluation of Asian currencies against the yen to prevent deterioration in their current accounts. Third, Asian countries are unwilling to cede monetary autonomy and to tolerate a worsening of the inflation-unemployment trade-off. Fourth, a monetary union centering on the yen is unlikely to narrow inflation differentials among members. Finally, Asian countries worry that the formation of a monetary union could pave the way for the formation of a political union.

While most studies following the optimum currency area approach have been descriptive, Junichi Goto and Koichi Hamada go one step further by providing a more formal statistical analysis.[13] Using principal component analysis, they find that major economic indicators such as money supply, interest rates, consumer price index (CPI), real GNP, and investment-to-GNP ratio are as highly correlated among the Asian countries as among western European countries. Again, based on principal component analysis, they find real shocks to be more symmetrical for Asia than for western Europe, while monetary shocks show about the same degree of symmetry for both regions.[14] Based on these results, they conclude that Asia satisfies the criteria of an optimum currency area. However, they have not included Japan in the study, making it difficult to draw direct implications for the possibility of forming a yen bloc.

To test the symmetry of exogenous shocks on Asian countries, the United States, and Japan, Hiroo Taguchi calculates correlation coefficients for interest rates, stock prices, and the CPI among major countries in the three

11. Holloway (1990).
12. Park and Park (1990).
13. Goto and Hamada (1994).
14. Real shocks are measured by the change in investment that cannot be explained by changes in income and interest rates, while monetary shocks are measured in terms of the change in money demand that cannot be explained by changes in income and interest rates.

regions.[15] He finds that the CPIs of Asian countries correlate more strongly with the CPI of Japan than with that of the United States. In contrast, interest rates and stock prices in Asian countries correlate more strongly with their counterparts in the United States, but the correlation coefficients with the corresponding figures for Japan increased in the latter half of the 1980s. He concludes that although the criteria for forming an optimum currency area in Asia are not fully satisfied at this stage, the possibility of monetary integration may increase as intraregional economic interdependence continues to deepen.

Tamin Bayoumi and Barry Eichengreen distinguish between demand and supply shocks statistically and estimate the respective bilateral correlation coefficients among Asian countries.[16] Supply shocks are found to be symmetrical among Japan, South Korea, and Taiwan and also among Hong Kong, Indonesia, Malaysia, and Singapore. Demand shocks are also found to be highly symmetrical for the latter group of countries. Based on the criterion of symmetry in exogenous shocks, it is likely that these two groups of countries form separate optimum currency areas.

Additional Empirical Analysis

Most empirical analyses based on the theory of optimum currency areas (including Goto and Hamada, Taguchi, and Bayoumi and Eichengreen cited above) focus on the costs of monetary integration and study the correlation of various macroeconomic variables among the Asian countries. These studies are based on historical data before monetary integration, when exchange rates are allowed to fluctuate. However, the correlation relations may change after monetary integration, when exchange rate fluctuations are eliminated. This in turn may alter the behavior of economic agents, including the government. Thus a negative correlation between a major macroeconomic variable in two countries does not necessarily mean that external shocks are asymmetrical or that the two countries fail to meet the criteria to form an optimum currency area.

This can be illustrated by noting the relations between Japan and South Korea. With South Korea belonging to the dollar bloc, fluctuations in the yen-dollar rate affect South Korea and Japan asymmetrically. An appreciation of the yen, for example, is inflationary for South Korea (raising inflation and economic growth) but deflationary for Japan (reducing inflation and economic growth). If Japan and South Korea form a monetary union,

---

15. Taguchi (1994).
16. Bayoumi and Eichengreen (1994).

however, this asymmetric shock would be eliminated, and the correlation of economic growth rates and of inflation rates between the two countries would actually increase.

Taking into consideration the fact that the correlation of macroeconomic variables among nations may change sharply with a shift in the exchange rate system, I focus instead on the correlation of economic structures and of policy objectives, which are less dependent on the exchange rate system. For the sake of comparison, data for the European countries based on the same methodology are also presented. Furthermore, to take into account the benefit of monetary integration, I also touch upon recent trends in intraregional trade and investment.

The degree of similarity in the economic structures of two countries can be quantified in terms of the correlation coefficient between vectors showing their respective share composition of trade (imports and exports) classified by product. This index takes a value between minus 1 and plus 1. The larger its value (closer to plus 1) the more similar the trade structures of the two countries and the more they compete with one another; the smaller its value (closer to minus 1) the more the trade structures diverge and the more they complement one another. The correlation coefficient so calculated can therefore be used as an indicator of the degree of competition (or complementarity) in the trade structures of two countries.

The matrix of bilateral correlation coefficients for the trade composition of Japan, the four Asian NIEs, the four major ASEAN countries, China, and the United States is calculated based on a three-category classification for exports and imports: primary commodities, machinery, other manufactures (a total of six categories). The same procedure is repeated for eleven western European countries (with Luxembourg included in Belgium). The results are shown in tables 8-1 through 8-4.

Since trade structure is closely related to the level of economic development, countries with similar per capita incomes tend to have similar trade structures as shown by the correlation matrixes. Reflecting the diversity in per capita income among Asian countries, their trade structures in general are less similar than the trade structures of western European countries. The forty-five correlation coefficients for the ten Asian countries including Japan average 0.28, much lower than the average correlation of 0.52 for the eleven western European countries (fifty-five coefficients). In particular, the average correlation between the trade structure of Germany and the other ten western European countries is 0.53, far higher than the –0.1 average correlation between Japan and the other nine Asian countries.

Table 8-1. *Trade Structures, Ten Asian Countries and the United States, 1993*
Percent

	Exports			Imports		
Country	Primary commodi- ties	Other manu- factures	Machin- ery	Primary commodi- ties	Other manu- factures	Machin- ery
Korea	7	51	43	37	29	34
Taiwan	7	53	40	24	36	40
Hong Kong	7	67	26	11	56	33
Singapore	20	25	55	20	31	49
Indonesia	47	48	5	24	34	42
Malaysia	35	24	41	15	30	54
Philippines	24	58	19	25	43	32
Thailand	28	45	28	20	36	45
China	19	65	16	16	43	42
Japan	3	29	68	52	32	17
United States	18	33	49	19	38	43

Source: Compiled by Nomura Research Institute based on World Bank, *World Development Report*, 1995.

To consider the similarity of policy objectives among nations, let us compare inflation rates. In the short run, a country's inflation rate depends on factors ranging from various shocks to economic structures and policy responses, but in the long run it largely reflects the preferences of the policy authorities. Based on average inflation rates between 1982 and 1999, Asia can be divided into a low-inflation group (Japan, Singapore, Taiwan, Malaysia, Thailand, and South Korea) and a high-inflation group (Hong Kong, China, the Philippines, and Indonesia). Countries with high per capita income tend to have lower inflation rates than those with low per capita income (figure 8-2).[17]

A cross section comparison among the Asian countries shows that there is a stable trade-off relation between inflation rates and exchange rates (figure 8-3). Countries with currencies appreciating against the dollar, such as Japan, Taiwan, and Singapore, have low inflation rates, while countries with currencies depreciating against the dollar, such as China, Indonesia, and the Philippines, have high inflation rates.

Between 1982 and 1999, the inflation rate of the Asian countries averaged 5.7 percent a year, similar to the 5.4 percent annual average for the western European countries (figures 8-4 and 8-5). The standard deviation showing

17. A negative correlation between the inflation rate and the level of economic development has also been observed in western Europe (figure 8-5).

Table 8-2. Correlation of Trade Structures, Ten Asian Countries and the United States, 1993

Country	Korea	Taiwan	Hong Kong	Singapore	Indonesia	Malaysia	Philippines	Thailand	China	Japan	United States
Korea	1.00										
Taiwan	0.89	1.00									
Hong Kong	0.57	0.82	1.00								
Singapore	0.34	0.46	0.08	1.00							
Indonesia	−0.33	−0.09	0.28	−0.53	1.00						
Malaysia	−0.17	0.11	−0.05	0.78	0.01	1.00					
Philippines	0.43	0.63	0.90	−0.29	0.59	−0.26	1.00				
Thailand	0.32	0.68	0.76	0.28	0.57	0.46	0.72	1.00			
China	0.45	0.71	0.91	−0.07	0.61	0.01	0.96	0.89	1.00		
Japan	0.63	0.35	−0.02	0.39	−0.92	−0.26	−0.27	−0.43	−0.33	1.00	
United States	0.51	0.71	0.46	0.92	−0.42	0.63	0.07	0.48	0.25	0.39	1.00

Source: Compiled by Nomura Research Institute based on World Bank, *World Development Report*, 1995.

Table 8-3. *Trade Structures, Eleven Western European Countries, 1993*
Percent

Country	Exports			Imports		
	Primary commodities	*Other manufactures*	*Machinery*	*Primary commodities*	*Other manufactures*	*Machinery*
Germany	10	42	48	24	44	33
United Kingdom	19	40	41	22	39	39
France	22	40	38	25	41	34
Italy	10	52	37	31	39	29
Netherlands	36	40	24	29	41	30
Belgium[a]	19	54	27	26	49	25
Denmark	33	40	27	24	46	29
Ireland	25	46	29	18	45	37
Greece	47	49	5	29	38	34
Spain	22	36	41	30	35	35
Portugal	17	62	21	25	37	38

Source: Compiled by Nomura Research Institute based on World Bank, *World Development Report*, 1995.
a. Belgium includes Luxembourg.

the dispersion of inflation rates among countries is also about the same for Asia and western Europe. Thus by the similarity-in-inflation-rate criterion, Asia qualifies as an optimum currency area as much as western Europe. It should be noted, however, that inflation rates among the European countries have shown signs of convergence in recent years as these countries move closer to a monetary union, with the standard deviation falling sharply in the latter half of the period under consideration. Such a trend has not been observed among inflation rates in the Asian countries.

From a microeconomic perspective, the major benefit of forming a monetary union is to reduce the costs and uncertainty involved in transactions among member countries by the elimination of foreign exchange risk. With intraregional trade and investment in Asia surging since the 1985 Plaza Accord, the potential benefit of monetary integration has increased. A look at the exports of the Asian countries (including Japan) shows that the share of intraregional trade rose from 30.9 percent in 1986 to 48.7 percent in 1996, immediately before the Asian crisis. In contrast, the share of exports to the United States fell from 34.0 percent to 22.0 percent over the same period. In the sphere of foreign direct investment, in addition to Japan, the Asian NIEs, led by overseas Chinese, have emerged as major investors in the region.

Table 8-4. *Correlation of Trade Structures, Eleven Western European Countries, 1993*

Country	Germany	United Kingdom	France	Italy	Netherlands	Belgium	Denmark	Ireland	Greece	Spain	Portugal
Germany	1.00										
United Kingdom	0.93	1.00									
France	0.95	0.95	1.00								
Italy	0.85	0.75	0.84	1.00							
Netherlands	-0.04	0.02	0.23	0.21	1.00						
Belgium[a]	0.63	0.58	0.77	0.84	0.70	1.00					
Denmark	0.33	0.37	0.57	0.38	0.90	0.80	1.00				
Ireland	0.63	0.77	0.84	0.64	0.65	0.83	0.83	1.00			
Greece	-0.44	-0.29	-0.17	-0.09	0.85	0.35	0.56	0.37	1.00		
Spain	0.96	0.91	0.86	0.78	-0.28	0.44	0.07	0.47	-0.59	1.00	
Portugal	0.48	0.58	0.64	0.78	0.56	0.83	0.55	0.80	0.48	0.39	1.00

Source: Compiled by Nomura Research Institute based on World Bank, *World Development Report*, 1995.

a. Belgium includes Luxembourg.

Figure 8-2. *Inflation and Level of Economic Development,*
Ten Asian Countries, Average for 1982–99

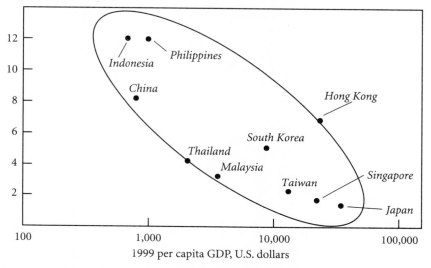

Inflation, percent per year

1999 per capita GDP, U.S. dollars

Source: Compiled by Nomura Research Institute based on official statistics.

The Key Currency for an Asian Monetary Union

The theory of optimum currency areas is useful in identifying potential members for monetary integration, but it has little to say about which currency should serve as the common currency. Should Asia (or part of it) satisfy the criteria for forming an optimum currency area, the question remains as to which currency should be assigned this role. At present, Asian currencies are loosely pegged to the dollar, and as a result, interest rates in these countries are highly responsive to U.S. monetary policy. In what follows, I examine the Japanese yen, the U.S. dollar, the Chinese yuan, and some form of composite currency similar to the European currency unit as potential candidates for a common currency for Asia.

The Possibility of Forming a Yen Bloc

I here explore the possibility of forming a monetary union in Asia centering on Japan (that is, a yen bloc), based on optimum currency area considerations. As noted, the major criteria for an optimum currency area are strong

Figure 8-3. *Correlation between Inflation and Exchange Rates, Ten Asian Countries, 1982–99*

Inflation, percent per year

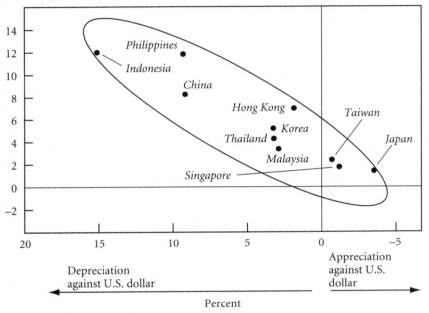

Source: Compiled by Nomura Research Institute based on official statistics.

economic linkages and similarity of economic structures and policy objectives. I examine to what extent these conditions are met between Japan and the Asian countries.

First, the repositioning of Japan toward Asia has become apparent in trade and foreign direct investment. However, the Asian countries' dependence on Japan has actually declined due to the rise of China as a major trading partner and the emergence of the Asian NIEs as major investing countries. To promote the transformation of Asia from a dollar bloc to a yen bloc, Japan needs to open its market further to absorb more Asian exports.

Second, as shown in tables 8-1 and 8-2, Japan's trade structure is similar to those of the Asian NIEs, which have reached a relatively high level of economic development, but differs significantly from those of the ASEAN countries and China. Based on the criterion of homogeneity in economic structure, it is unlikely that all Asian countries and Japan together form an optimum currency area. This contrasts sharply with the case of Europe, where the trade structure of Germany, the key-currency country, is similar

Figure 8-4. *Inflation Rates, Ten Asian Countries, 1982–99*

Percent per year

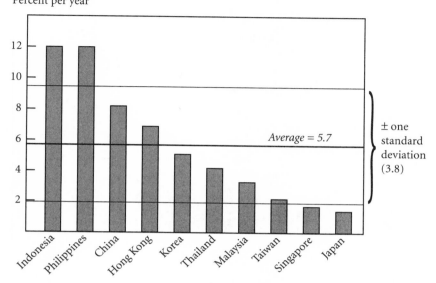

Source: Compiled by Nomura Research Institute based on IMF, *International Financial Statistics.*

to that of neighboring countries. However, given their very rapid pace of economic development, the trade structures of the Asian countries are expected to converge with Japan's in the years ahead.

Third, the inflation rate in Japan is lower than in all other Asian countries. By the criterion of similarity in inflation rate, low-inflation countries such as Singapore, Taiwan, Malaysia, Thailand, and South Korea are more appropriate candidates for forming a yen bloc. On the other hand, Indonesia, China, and the Philippines, which have high inflation rates, would find it difficult to maintain stable exchange rates against the yen.

In view of the diversity among these countries, it is unrealistic that Japan, the Asian NIEs, the ASEAN countries, and China together and at once form a monetary union. A more recommendable strategy is to follow a multitrack approach, in which countries join only when they satisfy the above conditions. To sum up, it is more likely that Japan and the Asian NIEs form an optimum currency area, with potential membership extended to include Malaysia and Thailand as they reach a higher level of economic development. Countries still at an early stage of economic development such as China, Indonesia, and the Philippines fail to meet the conditions for forming

Figure 8-5. *Inflation Rates, Twelve European Countries, 1982–99*

Percent per year

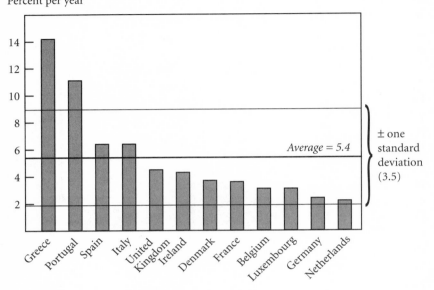

Source: Compiled by Nomura Research Institute based on IMF, *International Financial Statistics.*

an optimum currency area with Japan. Leaving their monetary policies to be determined by the Bank of Japan would be destabilizing rather than stabilizing. This confirms the conclusion reached in chapter 7, which derives an optimal peg for an Asian country that seeks to stabilize output.

Other Options for Monetary Integration

At present the Asian countries stabilize their currencies against the dollar and can be said to belong to a de facto dollar bloc. To a large extent, this reflects the fact that the Asian countries broadly satisfy the criteria for forming an optimum currency area with the United States. First, the United States has remained the single largest market for the Asian countries, although its share of Asian exports has declined. Second, the U.S. inflation rate, which averaged 3.4 percent between 1982 and 1999, is close to the median inflation rate of the Asian countries. Third, as shown in the correlation coefficients in table 8-2, with the exception of South Korea, the trade structures of Asian countries are more similar to that of the United States than to that of Japan. The preconditions for the transformation of Asia from a dollar bloc to a yen bloc therefore include a sharp increase in U.S. inflation resulting from a sharp depreciation in the dollar, in addition to deepening economic integration and a shrinking gap in the level of economic development between the Asian countries and Japan.

Meanwhile, China's rapid economic growth and expanding links with neighboring countries have given rise to speculation that it will sooner or later replace Japan as the leading economic power in Asia, and the Chinese yuan, instead of the Japanese yen, will play the role of the key currency in the region. An analysis based on optimum currency area considerations, however, suggests that such a scenario is unlikely in the foreseeable future. First, although lower income countries such as Indonesia and the Philippines share similar economic structures and inflation rates with China, their economic links with China through trade and investment are rather weak. On the other hand, Hong Kong and Taiwan, which have developed strong economic ties with China, fail to meet the criteria of similarity in economic structures and in inflation rates. Second, China's inflation rate is among the highest and most volatile in Asia. Should the Asian countries peg to the yuan, they would have to accept high and fluctuating inflation rates. Third, although China accepted the IMF Article VIII obligation to allow free convertibility of current account transactions in December 1996, it still maintains tight controls over capital flows. China's underdeveloped and strictly regulated financial system and capital markets also discourage the use of the yuan as an international currency. Indeed, China should have learned from the bitter experience of other Asian countries that it is unwise to liberalize capital account transactions prematurely. China thus lacks both the will and the ability to promote the yuan as an international currency.

Instead of forming a yen bloc, monetary integration in Asia could also be achieved by pegging exchange rates of member countries to an Asian currency unit (acu), analogous to the European currency unit (ecu).[18] The currency composition of the European currency unit is broadly in line with the relative economic power of European Union members, with the weight of the deutsche mark reaching 30.1 percent (table 8-5). Japan's share of the Asian economy reached 65.0 percent in terms of GDP and 28.4 percent in terms of trade in 1999. If the European rule applies to the Asian currency unit, the Japanese yen should have a weight of over 50 percent.

18. Williamson (1999).

Table 8-5. *Relative Economic Size of Participating Countries and Composition of the Common Currency Basket, 1999*

Units as indicated

Country	GDP or GNP		Per capita annual income (U.S. dollars)	Exports + Imports		Weight in ecu (percent)[a]
	Billions of U.S. dollars	Percent		Billions of U.S. dollars	Percent	
Germany	2,112.0	26.8	25,729	1,013.1	25.7	30.1
France	1,434.0	18.2	24,264	585.1	14.8	19.0
Italy	1,162.0	14.7	20,393	446.8	11.3	10.2
United Kingdom	1,423.0	18.1	24,022	589.1	14.9	13.0
Spain	590.7	7.5	14,986	254.4	6.5	5.3
Netherlands	394.8	5.0	25,150	393.0	10.0	9.4
Belgium (+ Luxembourg)	265.7	3.4	24,998	353.5	9.0	7.9
Denmark	173.5	2.2	32,619	91.1	2.3	2.5
Portugal	110.7	1.4	11,093	61.1	1.5	0.8
Greece	124.7	1.6	11,880	41.4	1.0	0.8
Ireland	90.7	1.2	24,219	115.2	2.9	1.1
Western Europe	7,881.8	100.0	22,348	3,943.8	100.0	100.0

Japan	4,370.4	65.0	34,518	730.1	28.4	...
NIEs	939.0	14.0	11,792	1,078.7	42.0	...
Korea	406.9	6.0	8,684	264.0	10.3	...
Taiwan	288.6	4.3	13,097	232.7	9.1	...
Hong Kong	158.6	2.4	23,171	356.5	13.9	...
Singapore	84.9	1.3	21,817	225.6	8.8	...
ASEAN	420.6	6.3	1,142	399.0	15.5	...
Indonesia	141.0	2.1	678	72.4	2.8	...
Malaysia	78.9	1.2	3,622	150.0	5.8	...
Philippines	76.5	1.1	996	67.6	2.6	...
Thailand	124.3	1.8	2,011	109.0	4.2	...
China	996.8	14.8	792	360.7	14.0	...
Asia	6,726.8	100.0	3,669	2,568.5	100.0	...

Source: Compiled by Nomura Research Institute based on IMF, *International Financial Statistics*; OECD, *Main Economic Indicators*; World Trade Organization, *International Trade Statistics*; and official statistics of individual countries.

a. The weight of each currency in the European currency unit (ecu) is determined by its physical amount in the ecu basket (composition) and current exchange rates. Figures in the table show the weights on September 21, 1989, after the latest recomposition of the basket.

As a compromise between the yen bloc scenario and a scenario involving an Asian currency unit, we can envision a three-stage process toward monetary integration in Asia. In the first stage, each Asian country pegs its currency closer to the yen by targeting a basket of currencies in which the yen carries a substantial weight, taking into consideration its trade relations with Japan. In the second stage, Asian countries, including Japan, shift to pegging to a common basket (an Asian currency unit) and allow their currencies to float jointly against the dollar and other major currencies. In the final stage, they adopt a common currency and allow monetary policy to be determined by a common central bank. The common currency adopted may not be the Japanese yen, but as long as Japan has effective control over the common monetary policy, the monetary union behaves as a de facto yen bloc.

9

A Global Perspective

S o far I have examined the yen bloc from the perspectives of Japan itself, of Asia's developing countries, and of the Asian region as a whole, but the analysis would be incomplete without a discussion of its implications for the world economy. Analogous to the relations between regionalism and globalism widely discussed in trade policy, in this concluding chapter the question posed is whether, in the quest for a more stable international monetary order, currency blocs form building blocks or stumbling blocks. Lacking the advantage of hindsight, the answer to this question can only be based on a priori (and less ambitiously, speculative) reasoning. Fortunately, the fast-growing literature on the global implications of the euro provides precious insights into the issue at hand.

Some of the problems plaguing the current international monetary system can be attributed to the United States abusing its privileges as the key-currency country under the de facto dollar standard. Two different approaches to reform have been tried to redress the asymmetric positions between the United States and the rest of the world. The first one is the pursuit of regional monetary integration, as is taking place in Europe, and the second one is the attempt to coordinate macroeconomic policy among major industrial countries mainly through G7 summits and ministerial meetings.[1]

1. The G7 countries are the United States, Japan, Germany, France, the United Kingdom, Italy, and Canada.

The two approaches may actually complement one another if the transition to a tripolar system centering on the dollar, the euro, and the yen promotes policy coordination among the three blocs.

National Currencies as International Currencies

In the absence of a world government or world central bank, some national currencies have simultaneously performed the role of international currencies.[2] While the choice of which currencies are to be legal tender for domestic transactions is a political decision made by sovereign governments, the choice of which currencies to use in international transactions is an economic decision based on the considerations of risks and returns. Darwin's law, interpreted here as "good money drives out bad money," has been the rule in determining the winners in the competition among the world's top currencies.[3]

The Functions and Features of International Currencies

Parallel to a domestic currency, an international currency performs the functions of a medium of exchange, a unit of account, and a store of value. Corresponding to each of these three functions, an international currency has both official and private uses (table 9-1).[4] As a medium of exchange it is used in settling international transactions: as a vehicle currency for private use (to settle trade and financial transactions and to intermediate exchange between third currencies) and as an intervention currency for official use. As a unit of account, an international currency is used to invoice trade and denominate international financial instruments and to express exchange rate relationships. For a country adopting a pegged exchange rate system, it is used to define the official parity rate and serves as an anchor for monetary policy. Finally, as a store of value, an international currency is used to hold

2. Cohen (1998) distinguishes between the use of a foreign currency for domestic transactions (currency substitution) and the use of a currency for international transactions (currency internationalization). The latter category can be broken down further into international use of a currency involving the issuing country and transactions involving only third countries. While the dollar carries dominant weights in all three categories, the yen's role has been limited to transactions involving Japan.

3. This is in sharp contrast to Gresham's law (bad money drives out good money), which only holds when the "goods" and "bads" exchange for the same price so that their true (market) values deviate from their prices legally defined.

4. This classification was first used by Cohen (1971) and has been followed by Kenen (1983) and Krugman (1984), among others.

Table 9-1. *The Roles of an International Currency*

Role	Private	Official
Medium of exchange	Vehicle	Intervention
Unit of account	Invoice	Peg
Store of value	Banking	Reserve

Source: Krugman (1984).

foreign assets (cash, bank deposits, bonds) by private agents and by central banks as reserves.

While conceptually these six functions are distinct, in reality they are interwoven. For example, the currency used as a unit of account in denominating trade and financial transactions usually also performs the medium of exchange function, which in turn enhances its attractiveness as a store of value. Likewise, a central bank is likely to maintain a higher portion of its reserves in the currency it uses to intervene in foreign exchange markets. Furthermore, in a country with high inflation and political instability, a foreign currency (predominantly the dollar) may circulate side by side with the local currency and serve simultaneously as a means of payment, a unit of account, and a store of value for private domestic transactions. As an example of the interaction between private and official uses, a currency that serves as an anchor currency also enhances its uses in other functions by reducing the risk and cost of doing transactions in that currency. Conversely, a country is more likely to peg to the currency that it uses widely in other international monetary functions.

Although the lack of data precludes a detailed comparison between major currencies in performing these six major functions, as a first approximation, data in table 9-2 show that the dollar has maintained its dominant role as the key currency in all categories. In particular, it leads its rivals by a substantial margin in global foreign exchange trading and cash held outside the home country.

A broad consensus has emerged as to the characteristics of good money qualifying for international currency status. These characteristics include, among others, a large share of world output and trade, historic inertia, highly developed financial markets free of controls, and confidence in the value of the currency.[5]

The currency of a country with a large share of world output, trade, and finance has a natural advantage. An economy with deep and broad markets

5. See for example Black (1990); Bergsten (1996); Mundell (1999).

Table 9-2. *The International Use of Major Currencies on the Eve of the Introduction of the Euro*

Percent

Currency	Pegging of minor currencies	Foreign exchange reserves held by central banks	Foreign exchange trading in world markets[a]	International capital markets	International trade	Cash held outside home country
U.S. dollar	39	57	87	54	48	78
Deutsche mark	6	13	30	11	16	22
Japanese yen	0	5	21	8	5	N.A.
Pound sterling	0	3	11	8	} 15	0
French franc	29	1	5	6		0
Other European Monetary System currencies	4	N.A.	} 17	N.A.		
Ecu	0	5		1	0	0
Other/unspecified	22	15	29	12	16	N.A.

Source: *Economic Report of the President, 1999*, based on data from IMF, BIS, OECD, and other sources.

a. Shares add to 2.00 because in each currency transaction two currencies are traded.

has high liquidity for its currency and can therefore exploit the economies of scale and scope inherent in money as a public good. In addition, the larger the single-currency area, the more likely a currency can act as a cushion against shocks. No wonder the key currency has always been provided by (or at least has been the legacy of) a major power.

There is a strong bias in favor of using whatever currency that has been widely in use (historic intertia). The use of a currency as international money reinforces its usefulness, as market participants (exporters, importers, lenders, borrowers, and currency traders) are more likely to use a given currency in their transactions if everyone else is doing the same. The resulting economies of scale are particularly important for an international currency to function as a medium of exchange and a unit of account.

A country whose currency is also used internationally should possess financial markets that are broad, deep, and free of controls. Such a key-currency infrastructure is usually provided by international financial centers (New York and London, for example). Broad markets with a large assortment of financial instruments traded allow portfolio diversification (in terms of maturity, for example) within the same currency. Deep financial markets enjoy high liquidity thanks to network externality, allowing participants to buy and sell at low cost. Financial markets free of controls (capital controls in particular) allow both residents and nonresidents easy access.

Confidence in the value of the currency hinges on the ability of the issuing government to maintain its domestic and international values. As in the case of a domestic currency, a high and variable inflation rate generates exchange rate depreciation and uncertainty and reduces the attractiveness of an international currency in all its major functions. The major prerequisites for maintaining the value of a currency, in turn, are an independent central bank free of political pressure, a healthy balance of payments position, and political stability.

The Future of the Dollar, the Euro, and the Yen

The above criteria have been widely applied to explain the relative status of the dollar, the euro, and the yen as international currencies. However, the differences in emphasis on the relative importance of these criteria and the outlook for the economic fundamentals underlying these criteria have led to conflicting conclusions concerning the role these three major currencies are going to play in the future.

Representing the majority view, Jeffrey Frankel is confident that the economic size and developed financial markets of the United States, together with historic inertia, will continue to support the dollar as the key currency well into the twenty-first century.[6] Among these factors, he assigns the largest weight to historic inertia, drawing the analogy between the use of the dollar as an international medium of exchange and the use of English as the medium of international communication. Although he cautions that the chronic current account deficit of the United States may make the dollar less attractive, it seems unlikely that the Federal Reserve will succumb to the temptations or pressure to inflate away the buildup of external debt needed to finance it.

Paul Krugman also emphasizes the role of inertia in sustaining the dollar's role as the key currency, but he is concerned that the circular reasoning that the use of the dollar reinforces its usefulness may work in the opposite direction and accelerate the dollar's decline.[7] Thus the fundamental advantages of the dollar may drop to some critical point, leading to an abrupt unraveling of its international role; or a temporary disruption of world financial markets may permanently impair the dollar's usefulness, as happened to the pound sterling after World War I.

Opinions have been more divided concerning the future role of the euro as an international currency.

Optimists emphasize the size factor and credibility of the newly formed European Central Bank. C. Fred Bergsten, for example, believes that a successful euro will be the first real competitor to the dollar since the dollar surpassed sterling as the world's dominant currency during the interwar period.[8] The euro ranks on par with the dollar in terms of the size of its underlying economy and global trade. In the absence of exchange controls, European capital markets, which are small and decentralized by U.S. standards, should expand strongly in the medium term. The European Central Bank is also certain to run a responsible monetary policy and achieve rapid credibility, although Europe may not carry out the structural reforms needed to restore dynamic economic growth. Robert Mundell also finds the strength of the euro as an international currency in a large and expanding transactions size and a culture of stability surrounding the European Central Bank in Frankfurt.[9] Although he is concerned that the euro is not backed by a central state and has no fallback value in case the issuing authority collapses, he is confident that such potential weaknesses are

6. Frankel (1995).
7. Krugman (1984).
8. Bergsten (1997a).
9. Mundell (1999).

unlikely to materialize because the North Atlantic Treaty Organization (NATO) should continue to sustain the stability of Europe.

In contrast, pessimists believe that problems with euroland's fragmented financial markets and inertia will prevent the euro from rivaling the dollar as an international currency.[10] Richard Cooper, for example, doubts whether the elimination of currency differences among European countries is enough to create a widely accepted store of value.[11] Specifically, he is concerned that the stability pact (which limits the extent to which European governments issue debts through budget deficits) and the preference of European governments for long-term debts over short-term debts will slow the development of highly liquid euro-denominated securities markets. Barry Eichengreen also cautions that, because of inertia, the prospective gain of the euro as a reserve currency at the expense of the dollar will be a very slow process at best. To overcome the inertia that favors the dollar, "not just healthy growth in Europe but economic mismanagement by an erratic Federal Reserve and a protectionist U.S. president would be required— something that hardly seems likely."[12]

The implications of the determinants of international currency use for the yen are mixed.[13] Major factors supporting the yen's international use include Japan's favorable inflation performance in recent years, the substantial deregulation of Japanese financial markets and capital flows, and Japan's growing share of exports of specialized manufactured goods. Furthermore, Japan's growing trade with Asian countries suggests an enlarged role for the yen as a regional currency. On the other hand, thin and tightly regulated financial markets, high dependence on markets in developed countries (which are more likely than developing countries to denominate their imports in their own currencies), and the pricing-to-market behavior of Japanese companies to maintain market shares have restricted the international use of the yen. As a result, Japan's emergence as the world's

---

10. At a more fundamental level, some pessimists rule out the possibility that the euro will pose a challenge to the dollar on the ground that euroland is likely to be plagued by new problems created by the Economic and Monetary Union. Dornbusch (1996), for example, is concerned that Europe's labor market may be too rigid to perform the task of adjusting competitiveness and relative prices, once the option of exchange rate adjustments for member countries is ruled out. Feldstein (1997) further warns that the adverse effects on macroeconomic stability would outweigh any gains from intraregional trade and capital flows and that disagreement over the stance on monetary policy may increase conflict among member countries.

11. Cooper (1999).

12. Eichengreen (1997), p. 53.

13. Tavlas and Ozeki (1992).

largest net creditor nation as well as a major international financial intermediary has not been accompanied by Japan's transformation into a world banker that enhances the liquidity of the international monetary system in terms of the yen.[14]

When the above criteria are applied to Asia, I predict that the dominance of the dollar in the region is likely to give way to a larger role for the yen.[15] The direct reason that economic agents in Asia (importers, exporters, and financial institutions) prefer the dollar to the yen is that the exchange rates of the local currencies are loosely pegged to the dollar, resulting in yen-based transactions involving a high exchange rate risk. The decision to peg loosely to the dollar in turn reflects four considerations. First, Asian exports have been highly dependent on the immense U.S. market. Second, the widespread use of the dollar as an international currency has reinforced its usefulness. Third, the existence of well-developed and open dollar-based financial markets reduces the cost of transactions. Finally, the creditworthiness of the dollar has been supported by U.S. hegemony. These advantages of the dollar versus the yen, however, have been fading at a rapid pace. The Asian countries' dependence on the U.S. market has declined sharply since the Plaza Accord of 1985, with interdependence among themselves increasing sharply. In addition, the United States has turned from a creditor country into the world's largest debtor country, and the dollar has sharply depreciated against major currencies in this process. Although New York has so far maintained its status as the world's financial center, the situation will gradually change with the continuous decline of the dollar as the key currency. Inertia dictates that the dollar will continue to play an important role even as the relative position of the United States in the global economy declines, but there is a critical point beyond which the dollar will lose this advantage, as the pound did during the interwar period.

The Limitations of the Present International Monetary Regime

Following the collapse of the Bretton Woods system, the major currencies of the world, beginning in 1973, adopted a floating exchange rate system. Notwithstanding the "dollar crisis," symbolized by President Richard Nixon's closing of the gold window in August 1971 and repeated episodes of

14. Both a financial intermediary and a world banker import short-term capital from the rest of the world and export long-term capital (both on a net basis). A world banker is a financial intermediary that engages in this international liquidity transformation in terms of its own currency.
    15. Kwan (1996).

sharp depreciation of the dollar against major currencies that followed, the dollar has maintained its role as the key currency under the new system. The general confidence in the dollar as supported by the international political leadership exercised by the United States, and the forces of inertia generated by the convenience of the dollar as an international currency, have allowed the United States to adopt an economic policy of benign neglect toward foreign exchange markets. However, the United States continues to register a massive deficit in its current account balance and has become the world's largest net debtor country in this process. The failure of the United States to provide the public good of a stable international monetary system manifests as the disappointing performance of the floating exchange rate regime.

The Asymmetric Role of the United States

The floating exchange rate regime in place since the early 1970s has largely failed to deliver the potential advantages it promised.[16] It was believed that exchange rates would tend to move in line with long-term economic fundamentals—relative prices and balances of payments, in particular. Stabilizing speculation would quickly eliminate any deviation of exchange rates from their equilibrium levels. In reality, both nominal and real exchange rates have been more volatile than under the Bretton Woods system.

In addition, countries under a floating exchange rate regime were supposed to enjoy macroeconomic independence: autonomy in pursuing monetary policy to control the level of domestic demand and insulation from overseas disturbances. However, macroeconomic interdependence among nations has been aggravated by the increasing mobility of capital. There were to be smaller trade imbalances and therefore less political pressure for protectionism, but the persistence of the large U.S. trade deficit, particularly against Japan, has intensified trade friction between the two sides of the Pacific. Finally, with exchange rates determined by market forces under a floating exchange rate regime, there was to be no need for the monetary authorities to intervene in the foreign exchange market, thus eliminating the need for reserves. However, both international reserves and interventions have continued to play important roles under the floating exchange rate system, reflecting attempts by monetary authorities to reduce exchange rate volatility and misalignments.

Some of these problems associated with the prevailing floating rate system can be attributed to the United States abusing its privileges without fulfilling its responsibilities as a key-currency country, as manifested by the

16. Frankel and Dornbusch (1988).

wide fluctuations in the dollar's exchange rate against major currencies and by the chronic current account deficit of the United States. C. Randall Henning blames the situation on U.S. international monetary policy, which alternates between neglect and activism rather than providing stability and consistency to the international monetary system.[17]

The asymmetry between the United States and other countries under this de facto dollar standard reflects two sets of factors. The mere size of the U.S. economy means that, although changes in U.S. policies have immense effect on other countries, the domestic economy is relatively insulated from repercussions through international trade and capital flows. As the key-currency country, the United States enjoys seigniorage and more autonomy in pursuing its own economic objectives. While seigniorage is derived from the fact that the United States effectively gets zero-interest loans when dollar bills are held by foreigners, more autonomy in pursuing its own economic objectives reflects several factors.[18]

First, the United States has stronger control over its money supply because it has no obligations to intervene in the foreign exchange market to stabilize exchange rates. In contrast, for other countries, high-powered money is injected or withdrawn from the market as the monetary authorities intervene in foreign exchange markets.

Second, the United States can sustain a balance of payments deficit for a long time because it can be financed "automatically" by issuing IOUs in its own currency.[19] As long as foreign entities, both private and official, are will-

---

17. Henning (1998). Specifically, Henning identifies seven episodes in which disturbances arising from the United States shocked the international monetary system in the postwar period. They are the shift of U.S. balance of payments from surplus to deficit in 1958–61; the pursuance of a benign neglect policy amid rising inflation and a deteriorating balance of payments between 1967 and 1971; the suspension of gold convertibility in 1971 and the switch to flexible rates in 1973; the locomotive conflict of 1977–78, when the United States pressed Germany and Japan to reflate; the surge in U.S. interest rates resulting from President Ronald Reagan's policy mix of loose fiscal policy and tight monetary policy; the exchange rate realignment following the Plaza Accord of 1985 and renewed pressures on Japan and Germany to reflate; and continued fiscal deficits, renewed neglect, and pressure for policy adjustment in the late 1980s and early 1990s.

18. Foreign holdings of dollars are estimated at $265 billion, 60 percent of total dollar notes outstanding (as of mid-1998). Multiplying this figure with the interest rate on Treasury bills gives an estimate for seigniorage of about $13 billion a year. See *Economic Report of the President, 1999.*

19. It does not mean that the United States can obtain imports in excess of exports free of charge. Foreigners do not usually hold their claims to the United States in interest-free dollar notes—and keep them under the pillow—but in interest-bearing instruments such as Treasury bonds. The costs of borrowing for the United States (interest rates on Treasury bonds, for example), however, would be much higher if the dollar did not play the role of the

ing to accept payments in dollars, there is no incentive for the United States to reduce domestic demand to restore the external balance. In contrast, other countries may find it difficult to finance a balance of payments deficit by private capital inflow alone and need to draw down their foreign exchange reserves or reduce imports by cutting domestic spending.

Finally, although the role of the dollar as a store of value has been eroded by the deutsche mark (now the euro) and the Japanese yen, the dollar continues to play a dominant role as a medium of exchange. Since U.S. companies and financial institutions have most of their international transactions denominated in dollars, they do not bear the risk associated with exchange rate fluctuations. In contrast, other countries, which have the bulk of their international transactions denominated in dollars, have strong incentives to maintain a stable exchange rate against the dollar so as to reduce the foreign exchange risk facing residents as well as the adverse consequences of exchange rate fluctuations on income distribution.[20]

The United States can take advantage of the asymmetry in the international monetary system by pursuing a benign neglect policy and concentrate on achieving domestic objectives without caring about its balance of payments and its exchange rate.[21] As long as the United States pursues a policy of benign neglect, the costs of adjustment would fall on the rest of the world. Portfolio shifts into and out of the United States have led to wide swings in the business cycles in the rest of the world.[22] When there is upward pressure on the dollar as a result of capital inflow into the United States, for example, the world simultaneously tightens monetary policy to stabilize exchange rates, giving rise to global deflationary pressure. The reverse is true when the dollar is under downward pressure.

Even when the balance of payments deficit and exchange rate misalignment are judged to be excessive, the United States has the leverage to force its trading partners to bear most of the burden of adjustment. To reduce its trade deficit, for example, it can pressure Europe and Japan to expand domestic demand instead of tightening its own monetary and fiscal policies, taking advantage of its strong bargaining power at both the bilateral and multilateral levels.

---

key currency. The savings in interest payments add to the seigniorage accrued to the United States as the key-currency country.

20. Exporters gain in competitiveness, while residents with dollar assets enjoy capital gain when the local currency is weak. The reverse is true for importers and for residents with dollar liabilities.

21. McKinnon (1993).

22. McKinnon (1982, 1984).

The United States is also in a position to exploit the monopoly power enjoyed by the dollar as a medium of exchange in international transactions. The persistently higher U.S. rate of inflation compared to that of its major trading partners—and the accompanying secular depreciation of the dollar against major currencies—may reflect an attempt by the United States to maximize seigniorage.

The U.S. Current Account Deficit as a Source of Instability

The U.S. current account has been in deficit since the early 1980s, reflecting a persistent excess of investment over savings. In recent years, the private sector deficit has replaced that in the public sector as the major source of external imbalance. The U.S. current account deficit reached a historic high level of $430 billion in 2000, equivalent to 4.3 percent of GDP, surpassing the previous peak of 3.4 percent recorded in 1986. By prompting sudden shifts in U.S. macroeconomic policy as well as in private capital flows, the chronic U.S. current account deficit has been a major source of the instability plaguing the international monetary system.

The U.S. balance of payments has deteriorated in terms of not only the size of its deficit but also its composition. When the current account balance is divided into investment income balance and the balance on goods and services, the former turned into a deficit in 1998 for the first time in eighty-four years. While U.S. foreign liabilities have surpassed foreign assets since 1988, the higher rate of return on the asset side helped maintain a surplus in the investment income balance for another decade. With the investment income account turning into a deficit, the United States needs to borrow from overseas to finance not only its deficit on goods and services but also its net interest payments.

In terms of the balance of payments cycle, since 1998 the United States has degenerated into a young debtor country, with deficits in its balance of goods and services, investment income, and current account (figure 9-1, table 9-3). To restore creditor country status, it needs to turn first its balance on goods and services, then its current account balance, and finally its balance on investment income into surpluses.[23]

Indeed, borrowing from abroad—accumulated over the last twenty years to finance its chronic current account deficit—has turned the United States into the world's largest net debtor country, with overseas liabilities exceeding overseas assets by an immense $1,474 billion at the end of 1999

---

23. From the current debtor stage, the United States needs to go through the mature debtor stage and the debt reducer stage to reach the young creditor stage.

(figure 9-2). The mirror image of the deterioration of the U.S. external position is the emergence of Japan as the world's largest creditor country, with net external assets amounting to $819 billion.[24] Japan has played a dominant role in financing the U.S. current account deficit by investing its excess savings in dollar assets. Indeed, Japan owned $336 billion of U.S. treasury securities at the end of 2000, accounting for about 12 percent of the amount held outside the Federal Reserve and U.S. government accounts. This was equivalent to 28 percent of the total amount held by foreigners, making Japan by far the largest foreign holder.

Never before has the world's leading creditor country had most of its overseas assets denominated in the currency of the world's largest debtor country. This unprecedented situation has become a major source of instability in the international financial system, as symbolized by the gyration in the yen-dollar rate. Since Japan has consistently been the single major source of the U.S. trade deficit, repeated attempts by the United States to reduce the bilateral trade imbalance by allowing the dollar to fall against the yen, rectified by Japan to avoid trade frictions, have added to volatility in the yen-dollar rate.[25] In addition, should Japanese investors diversify from dollar-denominated assets for fear of further capital losses, the dollar may come under further pressure to depreciate. At the same time, the need for the United States to reduce imports may put deflationary pressure on the global economy.

Indeed, there is now rising concern that the United States may have difficulty sustaining its huge current account deficit and the resulting deterioration in its net international investment position. With imports larger than exports by a substantial margin, stabilizing the trade balance would require exports growing much faster than imports. At the same time, as long as the current account is in deficit, the resulting deterioration in the net investment position implies that the burden of interest payments will continue to increase. Based on the result of simulation that takes these factors into consideration, Catherine Mann concludes that in the absence of structural changes (such as raising the household savings rate, improving education, and liberalizing global trade in services) the prevailing path of the current account deficit is not sustainable over the long term even with a sharp depreciation of the dollar.[26] This concern is shared by Ernest Preeg, who

24. In terms of the balance of payments cycle, Japan is now a young creditor country (see table 9-3), with a surplus in the balance of goods and services, investment income, and current account.

25. McKinnon and Ohno (1997).

26. Mann (1999). Earlier studies of the sustainability problem include Krugman (1985); Marris (1985).

Figure 9-1. Stages in the U.S. Balance of Payments Cycle, 1900–99

Percent of GDP

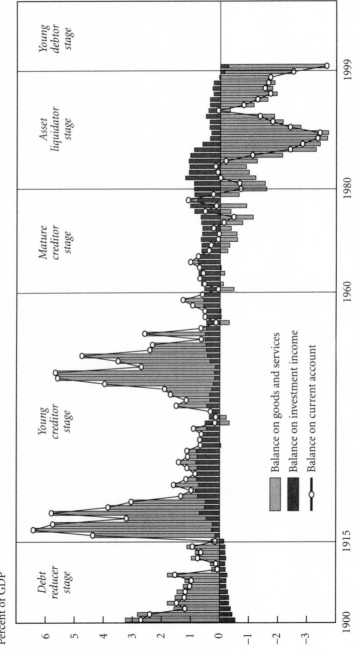

Source: Compiled by Nomura Research Institute based on U.S. Department of Commerce, *International Transactions Tables.*

Table 9-3. *The Six Stages of the Balance of Payments Cycle*[a]

Stage	Goods and services balance	Current account balance	Investment income balance
Young debtor	−	−	−
Mature debtor	+	−	−
Debt reducer	+	+	−
Young creditor	+	+	+
Mature creditor	−	+	+
Asset liquidator	−	−	+

Source: Kindleberger (1968), with adaptations.

a. By definition, balances on goods and services and investment income add up to the current account balance.

also worries that foreign governments, notably Japan and China, may use their large holdings of U.S. treasury bonds in their foreign exchange reserves as a leverage against the United States to achieve political ends.[27]

To keep the yen from rising against the dollar, the Bank of Japan has kept intervening in foreign exchange markets by buying dollars. In this process, Japan's exchange reserves have surged from about $70 billion in early 1993

Figure 9-2. *International Investment Positions, the United States and Japan, 1985–99*[a]

Billions of U.S. dollars

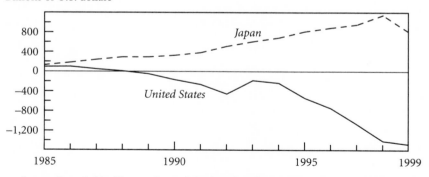

Source: Compiled by Nomura Research Institute based on Japanese Ministry of Finance and U.S. Department of Commerce statistics.

a. The direct investment position of the United States is evaluated at market value. The sharp decline in Japan's net external position in 1999 largely reflects the capital gain that accrued to foreign investors as stock prices in Tokyo rallied.

27. Preeg (2000).

to over $300 billion since early 2000. With private investors keeping an arm's length from the dollar for fear of further capital losses, the Bank of Japan is acting as the bank of last resort in supporting the "dollar standard" by absorbing excess dollars in international markets. Unfortunately, by making it possible for the United States to delay the necessary adjustment needed to redress its trade deficit, Japan's action may actually increase the risk of a hard landing of the dollar in the longer term.

Currency Blocs as Building Blocks

The theory of hegemonic stability holds that the international system is most stable when power is concentrated in one nation, the hegemon. When applied to the international monetary system, the relative stability of the gold standard in the nineteenth century and the Bretton Woods system that lasted for a quarter of a century through 1971 is attributed to the dominance of, respectively, Britain and the United States. By contrast, the instability of the interwar period is explained in terms of "the inability of the British to continue their role of underwriter to the system and the reluctance of the United States to take it on until 1936."[28] With no single country capable of playing the role of hegemon, as symbolized by the collapse of the Bretton Woods system, the international monetary system has evolved into a multipolar one, with the deutsche mark (now the euro) and the yen playing more important roles. The relevant question to ask when considering reform of the present international monetary regime, therefore, is not whether a hegemonic system is more preferable than a multipolar one but how the latter can be made more stable.[29] One way to achieve this is through the formation of currency blocs while at the same time promoting policy coordination among them.

The ongoing debate over whether trading blocs are likely to be building blocks or stumbling blocks on the path to free trade provides hints for analyzing the impact of currency blocs on the international monetary system.[30] The questions widely discussed concerning the global implications of trading blocs are:

28. Kindleberger (1973, p. 28).
29. There is no consensus as to whether an international system centering on a hegemon is more stable than a bipolar or multipolar system. For a survey of this debate, see Tomita (1989).
30. For a survey of the debate, see Krugman (1993); Lawrence (1995); Frankel (1997, chap. 10).

—Is the immediate effect of trading blocs to reduce world welfare or to increase it?

—Will regionalism lead to nondiscriminatory multilateral free trade for all, through continued expansion of the regional blocs until universal free trade is reached, or will it fragment the world economy?[31]

Analogously, regarding the global implications of currency blocs, the following questions arise:

—Will currency blocs reduce world welfare or enhance it?

—Will they facilitate interbloc policy coordination and contribute to a more stable international monetary system?

The Implications for Global Welfare

Regionalism has both positive and negative impacts on the rest of the world. On balance, the possibility that global welfare improves is high when trading blocs are formed among countries that belong to natural trading areas and when currency blocs are formed among countries belonging to optimum currency areas.

The welfare implications of regional trade arrangements depend on the relative magnitude of the trade creation and trade diversion effect.[32] Trade creation occurs when, as a result of a reduction in intra-union trade barriers, member countries import goods that would otherwise be produced at home. Trade diversion takes place when the preferential treatment causes a country to replace imports from the rest of the world with imports from a country within the union. The trade creation effect generates efficiency gains for member countries, as it encourages goods to be produced wherever costs are lowest within the union. Nonmember countries can also benefit, in terms of increasing demand for related intermediate and final goods. In contrast, trade diversion can be harmful to the importing country, as it now buys from a high cost producer instead of a lower cost producer. In this way, nonmember countries can also suffer a reduction in demand, with negative effects on employment and the terms of trade.

The trade creation effect is likely to exceed the trade diversion effect if member countries of a trading bloc satisfy the conditions of a natural trading area.[33] Candidates for a natural trading area are regional partners that enjoy low transportation costs, industrial countries that have much room

---

31. These two questions are posed by Bhagwati (1993).
32. Viner (1950).
33. Krugman (1991).

for intra-industry trade, and countries with complementary trade structures that can exploit a division of labor according to comparative advantage.[34] In this case, outsiders might also benefit in terms of higher demand
for their products, as trading blocs stimulate economic growth through gain
from trade, increased investment, and enhanced competition.

Likewise, the formation of a currency bloc among countries that satisfy
the criteria of an optimum currency area is also likely to improve global
welfare. The theory of optimum currency areas suggests that neither one
currency for each country nor one single currency for the whole world is
necessarily optimal. While a global currency would minimize the costs of
transactions at the microeconomic level, individual countries would be
deprived of an independent monetary policy, which may be needed to accommodate shocks specific to them at the macroeconomic level (see chapter 8). For small open countries, however, the scope for pursuing an independent monetary policy might be quite limited, with a small net benefit
from maintaining separate currencies. Thus a world consisting of currency
blocs that transcend national borders might be more desirable than either
national currencies or a single global currency. Should Asia, Europe, and
the Americas each satisfy the conditions of an optimum currency area, their
transformation into three currency blocs might actually improve global
welfare.

It is based on this logic that monetary integration in Europe has been
generally welcomed in the United States as a win-win game between the
two sides of the Atlantic. The view expressed by the Council of Economic
Advisers is representative:

> Meanwhile the United States salutes the formation of the European
> Monetary Union. The United States has much to gain from the success
> of the momentous project. Now more than ever, America is well
> served by having an integrated and prosperous trading partner on the
> other side of the Atlantic. Europe should benefit from a single cur-

34. The traditional theory of custom unions suggests that countries with complementary
trade structures are better candidates for forming trading blocs, in contrast to the theory of
optimum currency areas, which argues that only countries with competitive trade structures
should form currency blocs. Thus it is unlikely that any two countries satisfy the condition of
forming a trading bloc and a currency bloc at the same time. For example, countries at similar levels of economic development are likely to form an optimum currency area but would
benefit little by forming a custom union. By taking into consideration the possibility of intra-
industry trade among industrial countries, the theory of natural trading areas helps solve this
dilemma.

rency that supports these ends—and if Europe benefits, the United States gains as well.[35]

Specifically, "American producers will be able to export to a large, integrated European market with no cross-national restrictions on trade. U.S. firms producing in Europe will benefit from the lack of exchange rate volatility, common standards for goods and services, and a large, open market."[36] The report also dismisses the concern that a strong European economy and the emergence of the euro as an alternative international currency rivaling the dollar would harm the United States. Thus even if the euro emerges as a strong international currency, the negative effects on U.S. economic welfare are likely to be small and outweighed by the advantages of the European Monetary Union to U.S. residents.

The same logic should apply to monetary integration in Asia.[37] If optimum currency area considerations dictate that Asia's developing countries form an optimum currency area with Japan rather than the United States, their shift from a (de facto) dollar bloc to a yen bloc should benefit both Japan and the United States. Indeed, it has been the U.S. government, in the Yen-Dollar Agreement of 1984 and in subsequent negotiations, that pushes Japan to internationalize the yen.[38]

Implications for Stability of an International Monetary System

Analogous to trading blocs, which are likely to complement rather than to conflict with global trade liberalization when they follow the rules of open regionalism, currency blocs coupled with interbloc policy coordination should contribute to a more stable international monetary order.

The formation of trading blocs sets in motion forces both for and against liberalization at the global level. On the one hand, each bloc may take advantage of its size and seek to improve its terms of trade by raising tariffs.[39]

---

35. *Economic Report of the President, 1999* (p. 305).

36. *Economic Report of the President, 1999* (p. 297).

37. Alan Blinder of Princeton University, however, reminds me that the United States may be less receptive to the idea of monetary integration in Asia because, unlike Europe, Asia does not share a common heritage with the United States.

38. Frankel and Wei (1994).

39. This is based on the optimal tariff argument; see Johnson (1958). For a large country, tariffs, on the one hand, increase welfare by improving the terms of trade and, on the other hand, reduce welfare by distorting production and consumption. The optimal tariff rate, which maximizes this difference, is usually higher for a trading bloc than for individual countries composing it.

It may also become more inward looking once it has achieved a large internal market. In particular, interest groups that profit from the diversion of trade from efficient suppliers would lobby against including those suppliers as new members. On the other hand, countries are more willing to liberalize when acting as a group. Outsiders would also have incentive to join, so that membership expands over time. Furthermore, regionalism has important demonstration effects, accustoming officials, governments, and nations to the liberalization process and thus increasing the probability that they will subsequently move on to similar multilateral actions. A consensus is emerging that the positive impact on liberalization is likely to dominate if the formation of trading blocs is based on the principle of open regionalism.[40] The bottom line is that member countries should avoid raising barriers to nonmembers, as stipulated in Article XXIV of the General Agreement on Tariffs and Trade (GATT) and now the World Trade Organization. Some would go further to include open membership and granting most favored nation status to nonmembers.[41]

Likewise, as proclaimed by the Japanese government, the transition to a tripolar system centering on the dollar, the euro, and the yen is expected to supplement the United States in providing the public good of a stable international monetary system.

> The dollar, euro, and yen support the world's three major economic regions. As such, the euro representing Europe and the yen as the principal Asian currency are in a position to complement the dollar. Such complementary arrangements can contribute to the establishment of a stable international monetary system supported by the sound economic policies of the United States, euroland, and Japan. Furthermore, from the perspective of diversifying the risks inherent in floating rate systems, it is desirable to promote the international use of the yen along with the dollar and the euro. In this regard, the internationalization of the yen can be viewed to represent the provision of an international public good.[42]

---

40. Bergsten (1997b).

41. As presented in APEC (1994), open regionalism should include the following elements: the maximum possible extent of unilateral liberalization; a commitment to continue reducing barriers to nonmember countries while liberalizing internally on a most favored nation basis; a willingness to extend regional liberalization to nonmembers on a mutually reciprocal basis; and recognition that any individual member can unilaterally extend its regional liberalization to nonmembers on a conditional or unconditional basis.

42. MOF (1999, p. 8).

Specifically, currency blocs can act as building blocks of a more stable international monetary system in the following ways.

Each currency bloc can provide an island of stability to participating countries by eliminating exchange rate fluctuations among themselves. Indeed, a major motive behind monetary integration in Europe is to insulate member countries from external shocks.[43] In addition, weaker members can borrow credibility from core members by abandoning their monetary autonomy. Furthermore, monetary integration is usually accompanied by the establishment of a regional safety net, which provides prompt assistance to member countries in case of emergency. Such a framework can help build confidence and prevent unwarranted speculation.

The emergence of international currencies that compete with the dollar will impose discipline on U.S. economic policy.[44] The idea is analogous to Friedrich Hayek's proposal of abolishing the power for a central bank to monopolize seigniorage and allowing private banks to issue money on a competitive basis.[45] By rendering the international environment less forgiving of U.S. policy mistakes, U.S. policy errors could cause massive portfolio diversification out of dollar assets. The United States might have to reduce imports sharply by fiscal and monetary tightening or maintain very high interest rates to attract capital inflow.[46] If the United States allows the dollar to depreciate too far in pursuit of seigniorage, the dollar as an international currency could be displaced by competing currencies.

A tripolar monetary system would function as a safety net for the global economy in case the dollar standard collapsed. If major creditor countries

---

43. Based on the European experience, Henning (1998, p. 538) argues that "where the dominant state provides stability to the system consistent with the preferences of smaller states the latter are likely to be content with the status quo. Where the dominant state repeatedly destabilizes the system, exploiting an asymmetry in vulnerability to systemic disruption, the smaller states have strong incentives to seek monetary stability on regional terms." He provides empirical evidence to show that every time the United States disturbed the international monetary system with policy change, neglected an unstable dollar, or pressed European states for macroeconomic policy adjustments, European states responded by strengthening regional monetary integration.

44. In addition to monetary integration within Asia and Japan, the same goal can be achieved by strengthening policy coordination between Japan and Europe to stabilize the yen-euro rate. Indeed, some Japanese economists have suggested that the yen should be pegged to the euro.

45. Hayek (1978).

46. Henning (2000) notes that although the Congress, the executive branch, and the Federal Reserve would resent having their choices circumscribed, balance of payments constraints could benefit the United States as a whole to the extent that they prevented the U.S. government from pursuing and prolonging policy blunders.

and trading nations such as Japan and Germany had the bulk of their overseas assets and trade denominated in the yen and the euro instead of the dollar, the degree to which a dollar crisis would rock global capital and trade flows would lessen.

Finally, competition among the dollar, the euro, and the yen would enhance the incentive for policy coordination between the United States, Europe, and Japan.[47] Under a tripolar system, coordination gains would be larger and more evenly distributed so that all players would be more willing to cooperate in order to reap these benefits. In the case of the European Monetary Union, for example, the need for, and the benefits of, policy coordination would increase as the effects of euroland policies on the rest of the world increased. At the same time, since the number of actors would be reduced, some of the usual obstacles to coordination would be alleviated. Furthermore, a greater bargaining power for euroland might affect the distribution of gains.

On the negative side, there are concerns that policy coordination among the three major blocs would become more difficult because euroland authorities might be inclined to adopt a policy of benign neglect toward the euro's exchange rate.[48] This, however, is likely to be offset by a more cooperative U.S. stance. So far, the United States can afford to pursue a benign neglect policy because other nations have sought to stabilize their currencies against the dollar by intervening in foreign exchange markets and adapting their monetary policies. Should the dollar rate become more volatile against the euro as a result of benign neglect on the part of Europe, the United States may have more incentive to stabilize the U.S. dollar rate, through unilateral actions or multilateral policy coordination.

47. Emerson and others (1992). Major proposals to reform the international monetary system through strengthening policy coordination among the three poles include Cooper (1984); McKinnon (1988); Williamson and Miller (1987); See Corden (1994) for a survey.

48. Excluding intraregional trade, which will no longer be affected by exchange rate fluctuations, euroland's dependence on foreign trade would become as low as that of the United States, with exports representing only around 10 percent of total output in both regions. This will allow euroland to focus more on domestic goals rather than external goals and to tolerate greater volatility in the exchange rate.

References

Aghevli, Bijan B., Mohsin S. Khan, and Peter J. Montiel. 1991. "Exchange Rate Policy in Developing Countries: Some Analytical Issues." Occasional Paper 78. Washington: International Monetary Fund.

Akamatsu, Kaname. 1962. "A Historical Pattern of Economic Growth in Developing Countries." *Developing Economies* (preliminary issue): 3–25.

APEC. 1994. *Achieving the APEC Vision: Free and Open Trade in the Asia Pacific.* Second Report of the Eminent Persons Group. Singapore: Secretariat, Asia Pacific Economic Cooperation.

Argy, Victor. 1990. "Choice of Exchange Rate Regime for a Smaller Economy: A Survey of Some Key Issues." In *Choosing an Exchange Rate Regime: The Challenge for Smaller Industrial Countries,* edited by Paul De Grauwe and Victor Argy, 6–81. Washington: International Monetary Fund.

Baliño, Tomás J. T., and Charles Enoch. 1997. "Currency Board Arrangements: Issues and Experience." Occasional Paper 151. Washington: International Monetary Fund.

Bayoumi, Tamin, and Barry Eichengreen. 1994. "One Money or Many? Analyzing the Prospects for Monetary Unification in Various Parts of the World." Studies in International Finance 76. Princeton University, International Finance Section.

Bénassy-Quéré, Agnès. 1996. "Exchange Rate Regimes and Policies in Asia." Working Paper 96-07. Paris: Centre d'Études Prospectives et d'Informations Internationales (CEPII).

Bergsten, C. Fred. 1996. *The Dilemma of the Dollar: The Economics and Politics of United States International Monetary Policy,* 2d ed. Sharpe.

———. 1997a. "The Impact of the Euro on Exchange Rates and International Policy Coordination." In *EMU and the International Monetary System,* edited by Paul R.

Masson, Thomas H. Krueger, and Bart G. Turtelboom, 17–48. Washington: International Monetary Fund.

———. 1997b. "Open Regionalism." Working Paper 97-3. Washington: Institute for International Economics.

———. 1998. "Reviving the Asian Monetary Fund." International Economics Policy Briefs 98-8. Washington: Institute for International Economics.

———. 2000. "The New Asian Challenge." Working Paper 00-4. Washington: Institute for International Economics.

Bergsten, C. Fred, Olivier Davanne, and Pierre Jacquet. 1999. "The Case for Joint Management of Exchange Rate Flexibility." Working Paper 99-9. Washington: Institute for International Economics.

Bergsten, C. Fred, and C. Randall Henning. 1996. *Global Economic Leadership and the Group of Seven.* Washington: Institute for International Economics.

Bernanke, Ben S., and Alan S. Blinder. 1988. "Credit, Money, and Aggregate Demand." *American Economic Review* 78 (May): 435–39.

Bhagwati, Jagdish. 1993. "Regionalism and Multilateralism: An Overview." In *New Dimensions in Regional Integration,* edited by Jaime De Melo and Arvind Panagariya, 22–57. Cambridge University Press.

BIS. 1999. *Central Bank Survey of Foreign Exchange and Derivative Market Activity.* Basle: Bank for International Settlements.

———. 2000. *BIS Quarterly Review: International Banking and Financial Market Developments* (June).

Black, Stanley W. 1976. "Exchange Rate Policies for Less Developed Countries in a World of Floating." Essays in International Finance 119. Princeton University, International Finance Section.

———. 1990. "The International Use of Currencies." In *The Evolution of the International Monetary System,* edited by Yoshio Suzuki, Junichi Miyabe, and Mitsuaki Okabe, 175–94. University of Tokyo Press.

Branson, William H., and Louka T. Katseli-Papaefstratiou. 1980. "Income Instability, Terms of Trade, and the Choice of Exchange Rate Regime." *Journal of Development Economics* 7 (March): 49–69.

Calvo, Guillermo A., and Carmen M. Reinhart. 2000. "Fear of Floating." Working Paper 7993. Cambridge, Mass.: National Bureau of Economic Research.

Chen, Edward K. Y. 1989. "The Changing Role of the Asian NICs in the Asian-Pacific Region towards the Year 2000." In *Global Adjustment and the Future of Asian Pacific Economy,* edited by Miyohei Shinohara and Fu-chen Lo, 207–37. Tokyo: Institute of Developing Economies.

Cohen, Benjamin J. 1971. *The Future of Sterling as an International Currency.* London: Macmillan.

———. 1998. *The Geography of Money.* Cornell University Press.

Cooper, Richard N. 1984. "A Monetary System for the Future." *Foreign Affairs* 63 (Fall): 166–84.

————. 1999. "Key Currencies after the Euro." *World Economy* 22 (January): 1–24.

Corden, W. Max. 1972. "Monetary Integration." Essays in International Finance 93. Princeton University, International Finance Section.

————. 1994. *Economic Policy, Exchange Rates, and the International System.* Oxford University Press.

De Grauwe, Paul. 1992. *The Economics of Monetary Integration.* Oxford University Press.

Dornbusch, Rudiger. 1996. "Euro Fantasies." *Foreign Affairs* 75 (September– October): 110–25.

Dornbusch, Rudiger, and Yung Chul Park. 1999. "Flexibility or Nominal Anchors." In *Exchange Rate Policies in Emerging Asian Countries,* edited by Stefan Collignon, Jean Pisani-Ferry, and Yung Chul Park, 3–34. London: Routledge.

Eichengreen, Barry. 1994. *International Monetary Arrangements for the Twenty-First Century.* Brookings.

————. 1997. "Comments on Bergsten." In *EMU and the International Monetary System,* edited by Paul R. Masson, Thomas H. Krueger, and Bart G. Turtelboom, 49–57. Washington: International Monetary Fund.

————. 1999. "Solving the Currency Conundrum." Paper prepared for Council on Foreign Relations Study Group on Economic and Financial Development, New York.

————. 2000. "The Currency Composition of Foreign Exchange Reserves: Retrospect and Prospect." Paper prepared for UNU/WIDER Conference on the Future of the International Monetary and Financial System, Helsinki, November 11–12, 1999.

Eichengreen, Barry, and Ricardo Hausmann. 1999. "Exchange Rates and Financial Fragility." Working Paper 7418. Cambridge, Mass.: National Bureau of Economic Research.

Emerson, Michael, and others. 1992. *One Market, One Money.* Oxford University Press.

EPA. 1995. "Kinkyu Endaka Keizai Taisaku" (Emergency Economic Measures to Cope with the Yen's Appreciation). Tokyo: Economic Planning Agency.

————. 1999. *1998 Survey of Corporate Behaviors* (in Japanese). Tokyo: Economic Planning Agency.

Feldstein, Martin. 1997. "EMU and International Conflict." *Foreign Affairs* 76 (November–December): 63–73.

————. 1998. "Refocusing the IMF." *Foreign Affairs* 77 (March–April): 20–33.

Frankel, Jeffrey A. 1991. "Is a Yen Bloc Forming in Pacific Asia?" In *Finance and the International Economy: The Amex Bank Review Prize Essays,* edited by Richard O'Brien, 5–20. Oxford University Press.

————. 1993. "Is Japan Creating a Yen Bloc in East Asia and the Pacific?" In *Regionalism and Rivalry: Japan and the U.S. in Pacific Asia,* edited by Jeffrey A. Frankel and Miles Kahler, 53–85. University of Chicago Press.

————. 1995. "Still the Lingua Franca: The Exaggerated Death of the Dollar." *Foreign Affairs* 74 (July–August): 9–26.

————.1997. *Regional Trading Blocs in the World Economic System*. Washington: Institute for International Economics.

————. 1999. "The International Financial Architecture." Brookings Policy Brief 51.

Frankel, Jeffrey A., and Rudiger Dornbusch. 1988. "The Flexible Exchange Rate System: Experience and Alternatives." In *International Finance and Trade in a Polycentric World*, edited by Silvio Borner, 151–97. London: Macmillan.

Frankel, Jeffrey A., and Shang-Jin Wei. 1994. "Yen Bloc or Dollar Bloc? Exchange Rate Policies of the East Asian Economies." In *Macroeconomic Linkage*, edited by Takatoshi Ito and Anne O. Krueger, 295–329. University of Chicago Press.

Fukuda, Shin-ichi, and Cong Ji. 1994. "On the Choice of Invoice Currency by Japanese Exporters: The PTM Approach." *Journal of the Japanese and International Economies* 8: 511–29.

Funabashi, Yoichi. 1995. *Asia Pacific Fusion: Japan's Role in APEC*. Washington: Institute for International Economics.

Garber, Peter M. 1996. "The Use of the Yen as a Reserve Currency." *Monetary and Economic Studies* 14: 1–21. Tokyo: Bank of Japan, Institute for Monetary and Economic Studies.

Genberg, Hans. 1990. "Exchange Rate Management and Macroeconomic Policy: A National Perspective." In *The State of Macroeconomics*, edited by Seppo Honkapohja, 223–53. Oxford: Blackwell.

Ghosh, Atish R., Anne-Marie Gulde, and Holger C. Wolf. 1998. "Currency Boards: The Ultimate Fix?" Working Paper. Washington: International Monetary Fund.

Goto, Junichi, and Koichi Hamada. 1994. "Economic Preconditions for Asian Regional Integration." In *Macroeconomic Linkage*, edited by Takatoshi Ito and Anne O. Krueger, 359–87. University of Chicago Press.

Hamada, Koichi. 1985. *The Political Economy of International Monetary Interdependence*. MIT Press.

Hayek, Friedrich A. 1978. *Denationalisation of Money*. London: Institute of Economic Affairs.

Henning, C. Randall. 1998. "Systemic Conflict and Regional Monetary Integration: The Case of Europe." *International Organization* (Summer): 537–73.

————. 2000. "U.S.-EU Relations after the Inception of the Monetary Union: Cooperation or Rivalry?" In *Transatlantic Perspectives on the Euro*, edited by C. Randall Henning and Pier Carlo Padoan, 5–63. Brookings–European Community Studies Association.

Holloway, Nigel. 1990. "Building a Yen Bloc." *Far Eastern Economic Review* (October 11): 72–73.

IMF. 1997. "Exchange Rate Arrangements and Economic Performance in Developing Countries." In *World Economic Outlook* (October): 78–97.

Ito, Takatoshi. 1999. "New Financial Architecture and Its Regional Implications." Paper prepared for the First International Seminar on Financial Cooperation between China, Japan, and Korea: Issues and Prospects, Cheju Island, Korea, August 20–21.

Ito, Takatoshi, Eiji Ogawa, and Yuri Nagataki-Sasaki. 1998. "How Did the Dollar Peg Fail in Asia?" Working Paper 6729. Cambridge, Mass.: National Bureau of Economic Research.

Johnson, Harry G. 1958. "Optimum Tariffs and Retaliation." In *International Trade and Economic Growth: Studies in Pure Theory,* edited by Harry G. Johnson, 31–61. London: Allen and Unwin.

Jomo, K. S. 2001. *Malaysian Eclipse: Economic Crisis and Recovery.* London: Zed.

Katz, Richard. 1998. *Japan: The System That Soured.* Sharpe.

Kenen, Peter B. 1983. "The Role of the Dollar as an International Currency." Occasional Paper 13. Washington: Group of Thirty.

Kindleberger, Charles P. 1968. *International Economics,* 4th ed. Homewood, Ill.: Irwin.

———. 1973. *The World in Depression.* University of California Press.

Koo, Richard C. 1998. "The Weakening Yen and Japan's Credit Crunch Problem." Tokyo: Nomura Research Institute.

———. 1999. "Foreign Menace." *International Economy* (November–December) 24–27, 59.

Krugman, Paul. 1984. "The International Role of the Dollar: Theory and Prospect." In *Exchange Rate Theory and Practice,* edited by John F. O. Bilson and Richard C. Marston, 261–78. University of Chicago Press.

———. 1985. "Is the Strong Dollar Sustainable?" In *The U.S. Dollar: Recent Developments, Outlook, and Policy Options,* 103–32. Federal Reserve Bank of Kansas City.

———. 1990. "Policy Problems of a Monetary Union." In *The European Monetary System in the 1990s,* edited by Paul De Grauwe and Lucas Papademos, 48–64. London: Longman.

———. 1991. "The Move towards Free Trade Zones." In *Policy Implications of Trade and Currency Zones,* 7–42. Federal Reserve Bank of Kansas City.

———. 1993. "Regionalism versus Multilateralism: Analytical Notes." In *New Dimensions in Regional Integration,* edited by Jaime De Melo and Arvind Panagariya, 58–78. Cambridge University Press.

———. 1994. "The Myth of Asia's Miracle." *Foreign Affairs* 73 (November–December): 62–78.

———. 1998. "It's Baaack: Japan's Slump and the Return of the Liquidity Trap." *BPEA* 2: 137–205.

Kwan, Chi Hung. 1992. "Formation of a Yen Bloc: An Asian Perspective." *NRI Quarterly* 1 (Winter): 72–87.

———. 1994. *Economic Interdependence in the Asia-Pacific Region: Towards a Yen Bloc.* London: Routledge.

———. 1995a. *Enken no keizaigaku* (Economics of a Yen Bloc). Tokyo: Nihon-keizai Shimbunsha.

———. 1995b. "The Emergence of China and the Implications for the Asian Economies." Asia Club Papers. Tokyo Club Foundation for Global Studies.

———. 1996. "A Yen Bloc in Asia: An Integrative Approach." *Journal of the Asia Pacific Economy* 1:1–21.

———. 1997. "The Rise of Asia and Japan's 'Hollowing Out' Problem." *NRI Quarterly* 6 (Spring): 58–75.

———. 1998a. "A Japanese Perspective of Asia's Currency Crisis." *Journal of the Asia Pacific Economy* 3: 284–300.

———. 1998b. "The Theory of Optimum Currency Areas and the Possibility of Forming a Yen Bloc in Asia." *Journal of Asian Economics* 9 (Winter): 555–80.

Lawrence, Robert. 1995. *Regionalism, Multilateralism, and Deeper Integration.* Brookings.

Lincoln, Edward J. 1998. "Japan's Financial Mess." *Foreign Affairs* 77 (May–June): 57–66.

MacDougall, G. A. D. 1958. "The Benefits and Costs of Private Investment from Abroad: A Theoretical Approach." *Economic Record* 36:13–35.

Mahathir, Mohamad. 1997. "Asian Economies: Challenges and Opportunities." Speech prepared for IMF–World Bank Annual Meeting, Hong Kong, September 20.

Mann, Catherine L. 1999. *Is the U.S. Trade Deficit Sustainable?* Washington: Institute for International Economics.

Marris, Stephen. 1985. *"Deficits and the Dollar: The World Economy at Risk."* Policy Analyses in International Economics 14. Washington: Institute for International Economics.

MAS. 2000. "Exchange Rate Policy in East Asia after the Fall: How Much Have Things Changed?" Occasional Paper 19. Monetary Authority of Singapore.

McKinnon, Ronald I. 1979. *Money in International Exchange.* Oxford University Press.

———. 1982. "Currency Substitution and Instability in the World Dollar Standard." *American Economic Review* 72:320–33.

———. 1984. *"An International Standard for Monetary Stabilization."* Policy Analyses in International Economics 8. Washington: Institute for International Economics.

———. 1988. "Monetary and Exchange Rate Policies for International Financial Stability: A Proposal." *Journal of Economic Perspectives* 2 (Winter): 83–103.

———. 1991. *The Order of Economic Liberalization: Financial Control in the Transition to a Market Economy.* Johns Hopkins University Press.

———. 1993. "The Rules of the Game: International Money in Historical Perspective." *Journal of Economic Literature* 31 (March): 1–44.

———. 1999. "The East Asian Dollar Standard, Life after Death?" Working Paper 44. Stanford Institute for Economic Policy Research.

McKinnon, Ronald I., and Kenichi Ohno. 1997. *Dollar and Yen: Resolving Economic Conflict between the United States and Japan.* MIT Press.

MITI. 1994. *Boeki-kinyu-kawase Mondai Kenkyu-kai Hokokusho* (Report of the Study Group on Trade, Finance, and Foreign Exchange). Tokyo: Ministry of International Trade and Industry.

MOF. 1984. *Kinyu no Jiyuka oyobi Ennokokusaika ni tsuite: Genjo to Tenpo* (Current Status and Prospects for Financial Liberalization and the Internationalization of the Yen). Tokyo: Ministry of Finance.

——. 1994. *Naigai-keizai no Ittaika to Kokusai-kinyu-torihiki: Fukamaru Ajia tono Nettowaku* (Integration between Domestic and Global Economies and International Financial Transactions: Deepening Network with Asia). Tokyo: Ministry of Finance, Council on Foreign Exchange and Other Transactions.

——. 1999. *Internationalization of the Yen for the Twenty-First Century: Japan's Response to Changes in Global Economic and Financial Environments*. Tokyo: Ministry of Finance, Council on Foreign Exchange and Other Transactions.

Mundell, Robert. 1961. "A Theory of Optimum Currency Areas." *American Economic Review* 51 (September): 657–64.

——. 1999. "The Euro and the Stability of the International Monetary System." Paper prepared for Conference on the Euro as a Built-In Stabilizer in the Economic System, Luxembourg, December 3–4, 1998.

Obstfeld, Maurice, and Kenneth Rogoff. 1995. "The Mirage of Fixed Exchange Rates." *Journal of Economic Perspectives* 9 (Fall): 73–96.

Ohno, Kenichi. 1999. "Exchange Rate Management in Developing Asia: Reassessment of the Pre-Crisis Soft Dollar Zone." Working Paper 1. Tokyo: Asian Development Bank Institute.

Okina, Kunio. 1999. "Monetary Policy under Zero Inflation: A Response to Criticism and Questions Regarding Monetary Policy." Discussion Paper 99-E-20. Tokyo: Bank of Japan, Institute for Monetary and Economic Studies.

Park, Yung Chul, and Won-Am Park. 1990. "Exchange Rate Policy for the East Asian NICs." Working Paper 9010. Seoul: Korea Development Institute.

Posen, Adam S. 1998. *Restoring Japan's Economic Growth*. Washington: Institute for International Economics.

Preeg, Ernest H. 2000. *The Trade Deficit, the Dollar, and the U.S. National Interest*. Indianapolis: Hudson Institute.

Rose, Andrew K. 1999. "Is There a Case for an Asian Monetary Fund?" Economic Letter 99-37. Federal Reserve Bank of San Francisco.

Shinohara, Hajime. 1999. "On the Asian Monetary Fund." Newsletter 4. Tokyo: Institute for International Monetary Affairs.

Taguchi, Hiroo. 1994. "On the Internationalization of the Japanese Yen." In *Macroeconomic Linkage*, edited by Takatoshi Ito and Anne O. Krueger, 335–56. University of Chicago Press.

Tavlas, George S., and Yuzuru Ozeki. 1992. "The Internationalization of Currencies: An Appraisal of the Japanese Yen." Occasional Paper 90. Washington: International Monetary Fund.

Tomita, Toshiki. 1989. "International System Stability and the Role of Japan." Tokyo Club Papers 2. Tokyo Club Foundation for Global Studies.

Vernon, Raymond. 1966. "International Investment and International Trade in the Product Cycle." *Quarterly Journal of Economics* 80 (May): 190–207.

Viner, Jacob. 1950. *The Custom Union Issue.* New York: Carnegie Endowment for International Peace.

Williamson, John. 1982. "A Survey of the Literature on the Optimal Peg." *Journal of Development Economics* 11 (August): 39–61.

———. 1985. *"The Exchange Rate System."* 2d ed. Policy Analyses in International Economics 5. Washington: Institute for International Economics.

———. 1990. "What Washington Means by Policy Reform." In *Latin American Adjustment: How Much Has Happened?* edited by John Williamson, 7–17. Washington: Institute for International Economics.

———. 1995. *"What Role for Currency Boards?"* Policy Analyses in International Economics 40. Washington: Institute for International Economics.

———. 1996. *The Crawling Band as an Exchange Rate Regime: Lessons from Chile, Colombia, and Israel.* Washington: Institute for International Economics.

———.1998. "Crawling Bands: How to Manage Exchange Rates in a World of Capital Mobility." *International Finance* 1 (October): 59–80.

———. 1999. "The Case for a Common Basket Peg for East Asia." In *Exchange Rate Policies in Emerging Asian Countries,* edited by Stefan Collignon, Jean Pisani-Ferry, and Yung Chul Park, 327–43. London: Routledge.

Williamson, John, and Marcus H. Miller. 1987. *"Targets and Indicators: A Blueprint for the International Coordination of Economic Policy."* Policy Analyses in International Economics 22. Washington: Institute for International Economics.

World Bank. 1993. *The East Asian Miracle.* Oxford University Press.

———. 1997. *Private Capital Flows to Developing Countries: The Road to Financial Integration.* Oxford University Press.

Yam, Joseph. 1997. "The New Asian Drama: Monetary Co-operation in Asia." *Money and Banking in Hong Kong* 2: 41–50. Hong Kong Monetary Authority.

Yamazawa, Ippei. 1990. *Economic Development and International Trade: The Japanese Model.* Honolulu: East-West Center, Resource Systems Institute.

Index

Administrative Reform Council (Japan), 105

AFTA (ASEAN Free Trade Area). *See* Association of Southeast Asian Nations

AMF. *See* Asian Monetary Fund

APEC. *See* Asia Pacific Economic Cooperation

ASEAN. *See* Association of Southeast Asian Nations

ASEAN Free Trade Area (AFTA). *See* Association of Southeast Asian Nations

ASEM. *See* Asia-Europe Meeting

Asia: Acu (Asian currency unit), 171, 174; capital inflow, 80; debt repayment, 42; de facto dollar bloc, 129–33, 145, 154, 159, 167, 170, 182, 193; de facto yen bloc, 174, 182; development assistance to, 126; East Asian Miracle, 28; exchange rate and currency issues, 2–3, 39–45, 51–52, 61–82, 136–37, 145–46, 173–74; foreign direct investment, 18, 27, 35, 37, 38–39; inflation, 151, 169; intraregional interdependence, 15–23, 38–39; Japan and, 3, 45–56, 64, 111, 125–27, 136; monetary union and, 160, 174; need for regional monetary cooperation, 31–35; optimal peg for Asian countries, 136–50; optimum currency area, 159–66, 168; perspective on yen bloc, 4–6, 8–11; recommendations, 79–82, 136; role of the yen, 111, 117, 136, 146t; Soviet Union and, 19; trade issues, 4–5, 8, 21, 38, 42, 46–56, 63–64, 117, 136, 138, 145, 159, 165, 168–69, 170–71; United States and, 15, 38, 64–65, 145, 160, 170–71; view of yen bloc, 126, 128–50. *See also* Newly industrializing economies; Yen bloc; *individual countries*

Asia—developing countries: capital account transactions, 82; choice of currency for international use, 146; de facto dollar bloc, 2, 8, 74, 79, 149; effects on prices, 55n8; formation of monetary union, 77; floating exchange rates, 72, 156; yen bloc, 145; yen-dollar rate and, 4

Asia—economic issues: business cycles, 70; capital account transactions, 25–27; consumer price index, 160–61; domino

205

system, 98, 105; postwar economic model, 95; public finance, 98; recommendations for, 58–60; relocation of production facilities, 47, 50, 55, 57, 58, 63–64, 97, 119; shocks, 161; trade issues, 2–3, 9, 10, 20–21, 42, 45–47, 50, 51–56, 112, 119–20, 162, 168, 181; view of euro, 8. *See also* Asia; Exchange rates—yen; Yen

Japan—financial reform: banking and finance, 97–98, 109; Big Bang, 9, 83, 102, 111, 121, 122–23b, 125; cause and effects, 9, 83, 84–87, 88, 89–96, 100–06, 109, 110, 121; Comprehensive Economic Measures, 87; consumer price index, 160–61; deregulation, 103–04; economic recovery, 10–11, 83, 84, 92–94, 95, 100–01, 104–05; Emergency Economic Package, 87; fiscal policy, 92–94; Fiscal Structural Reform Act, 86, 87, 105; foreign exchange transactions, 121–22; inflation, 90, 181; interest in yen bloc, 1, 8, 109, 112; interest rates, 88, 89–90; investment and banking issues, 87–88, 105; Korea, South, and, 161–62; Large-Scale Retail Store Law, 97, 104; Large-Scale Retail Store Location Law, 104; legislative changes, 122b; manufacturing, industry, and corporate issues, 58–59, 89, 92, 96–97, 98–104; monetary policies, 88–91; optimum currency area, 169; Policy Measures for Economic Rebirth, 87; Prompt Corrective Action Plan, 87; public finance, 98; recommendations, 88–91, 93, 96–101, 104–06, 121, 125, 136; role of the yen, 9, 109–15; structural reform, 94–101; trade issues, 92, 97, 125, 136

Japan Lease Corporation, 103
Jung, Kim Dae, 127

Kobe earthquake, 86

Koo, Richard, 88–89, 91
Korea: Asian financial crisis, 26, 28; automobile industry, 138; exchange rate and currency issues, 133–35; Japan and, 127, 138; monetary policy, 5; output and prices, 140; trade issues, 42–43, 52–53

Korea, South: Asian financial crisis, 28, 29, 32, 67; Association of Southeast Asian Nations, 23; capital flows, 67; Chiang Mai Initiative (*2000*), 34; economic issues, 64, 163, 169; exchange rate and currency issues, 70, 139, 143–44; financial support scheme, 32; Japan and, 44, 55, 161–62; shocks, 161; trade issues, 44, 55. *See also* Asia

Krugman, Paul, 35, 68n3, 81b, 88–91, 180

Labor issues, 157, 158–59, 181n10
Laos, 22
Lincoln, Edward, 125n21
Long-Term Credit Bank (Japan), 88, 103

Malaysia: Asian financial crisis, 29; Association of Southeast Asian Nations, 22; currency issues, 9, 61; East Asian Economic Caucus, 11; economic issues, 163, 169; financial restructuring, 82; foreign direct investment, 45; optimum currency area, 169; shocks, 161; yen bloc and, 151. *See also* Asia

Manila Framework (*1997*), 33
Mann, Catherine, 187
Manufacturing: discovery of natural resources and, 26; foreign direct investment, 18, 19f, 45; relocation of production, 41–42, 57; trade in manufactured goods, 114. *See also* Industry and industrialization
Market of high-growth and emerging stocks (Japan; MOTHERS), 123b
McKinnon, Ronald, 74–75